ABOUT THE AUTHOR

Dick Allan qualified as a doctor in 1958. After national service in the army he joined the RAF Institute of Aviation Medicine where he developed a strong interest in thermal physiology and survival medicine. In 1990 he was appointed Director of the Army Personnel Research Establishment at Farnborough (now the Centre for Human Sciences at the Defence Evaluation and Research Agency). He is a Fellow of the Royal College of Physicians. He retired in 1995 to sail around the world.

His first experience of sailing was on the Norfolk Broads just after the war. Since then he has owned six boats and, except for the last, all were built from kits. His interest in safety and survival issues continued throughout a long association with the yachting world and and he is currently a consultant to Blue Water Rallies Ltd, who organise round-the-world rallies. He has written many articles for the yachting press, including five for Yachting Monthly on his circumnavigation in the small sailing boat *Greylag*.

To John & family
With Best Wishes

Dick Allan

SAILING MY DREAM
A Voyage Around the World
in a Small Sailing Boat

Dick Allan

Illustrations by the Author

LONGFELLOW PUBLISHERS
Farnham, UK

Published by **Longfellow Publishers**
The Spinney, Parkside, Farnham,
Surrey, UK. GU9 OJP
Tel : (44) 01252 726250

A CIP Catalogue Record for this book is available
from the British Library

ISBN 0-9533291-1-9

Printed and bound in Great Britain by
Biddles Ltd, Guildford and King's Lynn

Acknowledgements

My gratitude goes to all those who have helped me with the writing of this book and without whose encouragement and practical help the story might never have been told. Special thanks are due to my brother Michael who provided the drawings for most of the maps and whose constant interest has always encouraged me, and to Paul Gelder of Yachting Monthly for much advice and encouragement and for agreement to use my articles in Yachting Monthly as the basis for some of the chapters. My wife Janet helped with the proof reading and I will always be grateful for her forbearance during my long hours of absence at the computer. My thanks also to my crew John Anderson, David Reynolds, Rebecca South and Chee Chan and to all my intrepid colleagues on the Trade Winds Rally for their companionship on the voyage; their exploits and experiences have provided most of the stories. Last but not least my thanks to Malcolm McLaren without whose vision and energy our voyage might never have started.

To Janet

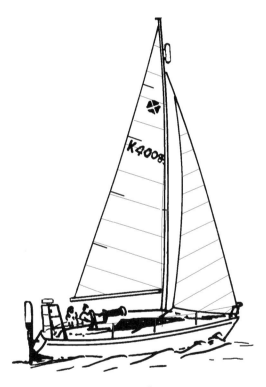

Greylag

Contents

List of Illustrations

Pen sketches

Prelude
To Begin at the Middle …

We knew bad weather was on the way, just how bad none of us could have guessed. Australia was but a few hundred miles away to the west, a safe haven snug behind the Great Barrier Reef. We had nearly crossed the vast Pacific Ocean whose waters lie across one third of the surface of the globe. And now this, a storm on the last lap!

Chris had called us earlier from *Pale Moon*, she was lying a couple of hundred miles to the north of us.

'Has it hit you yet?' He asked, his voice full of impending doom.

'No,' I replied hesitantly.

'Well it soon will, we've got 40 knots of wind up here,' he said.

'Thanks for the warning Chris,' I replied. There was now too much to be done to engage in any further conversation. *Damn it*, I thought, *and we were so nearly there.* I looked out from the cabin across a grey sea, dull in the failing evening light and already stirring itself in the strengthening easterly breeze. Occasional breaking waves gave little hint of what was to come, yet they seemed endowed with an aura of menace, such was our anticipation of the gathering storm. My crew looked anxious. John, who had been with me from the beginning, would cope; but Keith had never done any serious ocean sailing before, he was about to be severely tested.

'40 knots shouldn't be too bad,' I said, hoping to reassure them and myself also. 'It's that cold front going through. We'll put three reefs in the mainsail and set the storm jib, that should get us through the night.'

An anxious silence fell over us as we listened to the increasing wind, the tops of the waves beginning to break free in tumbles of surf against *Greylag*'s stern. At 33 feet overall length, she was a small boat to cope with storm conditions and already she felt over-pressed despite her reduced sail. For a while I felt a certain exhilaration as she sped down the fronts of the waves, but this didn't last long. The wind soon got up to gale force and the boat threatened to go head-over-heels, pitch-poling us into the raging sea and probably oblivion. We took down the remaining sails and ran on

1

downwind under bare poles, the force of the wind on the mast and rigging being sufficient to give us plenty of boat speed. We had to steer by hand as conditions were now too severe for our windvane steering to work.

It came, suddenly and relentlessly, just as darkness fell. A solid blast of wind, well over 50 knots, lay the boat over on her ear, broached sideways to the waves. We fought to get her back on a downwind course but it was hopeless, the boat was heeled so far over that the rudder was mostly out of the water. We were at the mercy of the wind and sea, 30-foot high waves crashed down upon us, filling the cockpit with water and cascading across the decks like a river in spate. We had closed our locker lids and hatches securely when the warning came, little water was actually getting inside the boat.

'This is beyond anything I've ever experienced,' I shouted to John, who was in the cockpit with me while Keith was below in the cabin, 'must be close to a hurricane now.'

'Yes,' said John, always a man of few words.

'I can't think of anything we can do to make us any safer, can you?'

'No,' he said.

We both had our safety harnesses on with strong lines attaching us firmly to the boat, strong enough we hoped to keep us on board even in those conditions. To be washed overboard would be certain death. For the first time in my life, the thought that I might die came into my head - a cold, numbing thought. I had never been frightened by the sea before and I couldn't tell whether this was fear or just the recognition of our seemingly hopeless situation. It mattered not, there was little to do except hang on. I considered streaming warps from the stern, thinking that this might do something to hold us stern to the waves rather than sideways on. But with all that solid green water tumbling over the boat, it would have been dangerous to open one of our large stern lockers to get the ropes out.

By now the sea was monstrous, huge tumbling waves fell upon us from all directions. One flattened the stanchions and guard-rail against the port side of the boat, such was the weight of water breaking against our canvas dodgers. Another burst through the spray-hood over the companionway, ripping the frame from the deck and leaving the canvas in tatters like a burst paper bag. The sail cover began to disintegrate but John managed to lash it down and save the sail from going over the side. A solar panel was torn from its fixings on the radar arch, clattering against the steelwork as it flailed in the wind - a doom-laden noise reminiscent of the

Knockdown

gale-driven clattering of a barn door at the opening of some horror movie. I watched the destruction all around me with dumb acceptance. With our lives at stake, why should I care about such damage if *Greylag*'s basic structure held together. We still had a keel, a mast and a rudder. *Greylag*'s heart remained strong even if mine was failing.

It was at this point that I learnt about the full fury of the sea. It didn't really look like a wave, not like any I had seen before. A great, grey edifice rose out of sight into the darkness of the sky, towering above us like a cliff – menacing, elemental, cold as the grave. Perhaps it was sheer terror but I don't recall any great noise beyond a vague sound of rushing water. In seeming silence, the world closing in as it does at the start of a faint, the boat was swept up into the towering wave and thrown, mast first, down the tumbling, white front as it broke into an angry boiling cascade of water. The boat rolled, I felt water all around me, involuntarily I held my breath. With a gorilla's strength my arms clung to something solid in the cockpit. Nobody shouted, nothing hurt. *Was this what death was like?* I thought, as a fleeting transcript of my life sped through my mind – *Janet a widow too soon, my children, my family ....*

It was probably only for a few seconds that time and events stood still before my senses returned and I realised that I was under water. How warm it felt after the freezing gale. Then the water was falling away as the boat came upright again, she would not give in without a fight. My neck felt stiff and immovable, it's broken I thought. My hands felt upwards only to discover that my automatic lifejacket had inflated under the water! For the first time I laughed, more from relief than anything else.

'Are you OK?' John asked.

'Yes,' I replied.

Words were in short supply, both of us were shocked at what had happened. Keith, who had been shut in below throughout all this mayhem, had begun to fear that John and I might have gone overboard in the capsize. After he had retrieved himself from under a pile of debris that had buried him as the fridge and every portside locker emptied their contents on top of him, he called through a ventilation grille to enquire after us. From his description we reckoned the boat had gone over to about 130 degrees, that is the mast had been 40 degrees below the water surface!

'Yes, I think we're OK,' I said, 'can you find us another bag of peppermints, the others have gone overboard?'

This produced a rather florid reply. 'We've all f...ing nearly drowned and all you can think about is your bloody peppermints!'

The bad part of the storm had lasted only for about 40 minutes, after that the wind moderated down to gale force and the seas became less threatening. We checked the charts to be sure there was no risk of drifting into danger downwind, happily there were miles of open sea. With a wry smile, I noticed that our position was just west of Wreck Reef.

We battened everything down as best we could, and climbed exhausted into our bunks. Sleep didn't come at once, too much adrenaline still in circulation perhaps. I lay there listening to the slowly abating storm and wondering what on earth could have persuaded me to undertake this voyage. Jumbled thoughts drifted in and out of my head. *Why does anybody do it in the face of such risks? Perhaps I should give it up right now, try to sell the boat in Australia and fly home a wiser and a safer man.* Mountaineers say they do it because it's there. Wally Herbert, the first man to cross the Arctic Sea, said of the reason why 'Those who need to ask, will never know the answer, while others who feel the answer will never need to ask.' I thought about this as drowsiness at last came over me, and I thought back to the days when I had learnt to sail, to the fun and excitements of the six boats I had owned and to how that dream of sailing round the world had become reality.

1 My Journey to the Beginning

I learnt to sail on the Norfolk Broads more than 50 years ago during several holidays with boating relatives. The Broads in 1948 were wilder and uncrowded, teeming with fish and bird-life; full of promise for water-borne adventures that would be the envy of today's young teenagers. No approved sailing schools for us, we learnt the hard way by trial and error in a splendid old wooden, clinker-built dinghy with a single, gaff-rigged sail. Soon afterwards, my father bought us a dinghy of our own and during the long holidays from school I sailed extensively around the waters of the Solent off Portsmouth, where we lived. Learned this way, sailing becomes instinctive, like riding a bicycle or driving a car. It is done automatically, without conscious thought. One acquires a feel, a sixth sense if you like, for the boat and the wind that drives it. Once learned, the skill is never lost and is surprisingly transferable from one boat to another, even to much larger boats. It is sound advice for learners to start with a dinghy, the basics are the same and the price of mistakes is much less than on some expensive yacht.

After those happy early days came medical school, marriage and a family. Sailing took a back seat for almost fourteen years. Then, in 1966, on an impulse I bought a kit for a Mirror dinghy. Even to this day the Mirror dinghy remains a popular choice as a first boat and in those days a kit which included everything, even the sails, cost only sixty-eight pounds. For two summers we sailed around the Solent, occasionally taking the boat further afield to Scotland and the Lake District. I learnt the basics of navigation and pilotage - some the hard way. I recall a buoy on Windermere which I assured my wife was a turning mark for races.

'We'll do a racing turn and leave a mere 6 inches as we go round,' I bragged.

Bang! The boat lurched violently as we hit the rock marked by the buoy! I resolved to learn more about buoys. As for tempering my over-confidence, well I am still fighting that battle. But I had caught the sailing bug well and truly by then and the dinghy's limitations began to frustrate me, I felt the urge to go further afield. Inevitably, bigger plans developed.

In 1968 we purchased the fibreglass hull and deck for a 19-foot mini-cruiser and completed her construction in our garage at home in Guildford. She was a Caprice III , a well-known little boat with a successful history and just big enough to sleep three, albeit rather snugly. We named her *Paladin*, prompted by a TV series about a wandering cowboy, of which my daughter Laurie was rather fond.

For a year we sailed her around the Solent and as far westward as Lulworth Cove. But the urge to go further was ever present. Perhaps it is instinctive, this need to travel, inherited from the earliest men who travelled outwards from Africa in search of new pastures. Whatever the explanation, wander-lust is common among sailors, an inner drive which is never really satisfied. As soon as one goal is achieved, another looms on the mental horizon demanding to be met. The next one for me was the English Channel.

A nineteen-foot boat is a very small vessel to cross the Channel but no harm came to us on the ten crossings we made over the next two years. *Paladin* had twin bilge keels; two keels that form a sort of stand for the boat and enable her, when the tide recedes, to be dried out on the beach without falling over on her side. She needed just over two feet of water to float and this shallow draft allowed us to explore every little creek and backwater. Money was short at first so we made do with an absolute minimum of equipment, just a compass and a log. And I do mean a log! Just as the old sailors used to do, we had a lump of wood on the end of a known length of string which we would toss over the side and measure the time it took to draw the string tight. From this we could calculate the speed of the boat, 10 metres of string in 5 seconds equals about 4 knots! It may have been crude but it was surprisingly accurate. We rarely went wrong navigating by dead reckoning - a simple technique by which the navigator calculates his position from the speed and course of the boat, allowing also for any effects of tide and wind. Later on we afforded a radio direction finder which was particularly helpful when it was foggy. This device enabled one to tune-in to radio beacons positioned around the channel and, with the help of a built-in compass, to get bearings of the beacons. Where the bearing lines crossed on the chart was where we were. Well, more or less - with practice one could be accurate to within 2 or 3 miles. Given the lack of accuracy, one learnt to be cautious and I always planned courses with a good margin of safety, a practice I have retained even though modern satellite navigation systems are far more accurate and reliable.

Towards the end of our third summer with *Paladin* I made a serious mistake which brought an abrupt end to the leisurely cruising I had so enjoyed until then. A friend from work, Philip Bateman, invited me to crew on his boat *April Dancer* which he had entered in a race from Portsmouth, round the Owers lightship off Selsey Bill and back to Cowes. Halfway down the first leg, Philip very generously allowed me to take the helm and I steered the boat for the rest of the race. This was an altogether different kind of sailing. I could almost feel the personality change come over me - a silent intensity, a sense of competing. My mind filled with uncharitable thoughts about the skippers of the other boats; I needed to be in front and any legal means of getting there was to be grasped. Actions were determined by the rules alone, not by any gentlemanly gestures. We achieved third place and I had been irretrievably converted to racing!

Poor old *Paladin* had to go - racing is a hard-hearted business with little room for sentiment. In no time flat I had purchased a kit to build a mean little racing machine. The new boat was called *Polypterus*, it is the Latin name for a lung-fish - I just liked the sound of it! She was a Dutch design, 24 feet in length and weighed barely one ton. A sister boat to the same design had been second in the World Championship the year before, so she had a good pedigree for racing. I built her over the winter of 1971/2, a major undertaking for a boat built in wood.

She was launched in the spring of 1972 and was second in her first race which was, coincidentally, over the same course as I had already raced with Philip Bateman the year before. We had several other good results that year but mostly it was a period of learning about racing. Racing success requires many things - a good fast boat, a good crew, tactical skills and, perhaps most important of all, an iron will to win. I seemed to have the latter in spades but the other needs were not always met.

We soon discovered that the boat was too heavy. We had made too many compromises for comfort. My crew were mostly drawn from friends and work-mates and changed too often for any serious attempt at team building. Their will to win didn't really match my own which, in their view, was beyond all understanding! I recall an occasion when one of them, Martin Allnut, fell off the boat just as we were approaching the finishing line at Cowes. We turned around to rescue him and were met not with profuse gratitude, but a look of astonishment on his face.

'I thought you would at least finish the race before coming back for me' he said.

While that may have been a comment on my character, perhaps he didn't know that the rules required one to finish a race with the same number of crew as one started with!

I had a lot to learn about racing and the lessons came thick and fast that first season. The basic rules became instinctive and soon we were developing our own little tricks of the trade. One such was employed at night when other boats were chasing us hard. We would place a piece of loo paper over the stern light, then after an interval another and another. To the chasing pack our light became progressively fainter and fainter - very demoralising to the opposition. Then, right at the end of the season, disaster struck.

In our last race that year we were representing the Ministry of Defence in a Civil Service Inter-departmental race to Cherbourg. We won the race but had to return the very next day, so as to be back in the office on Monday - a well-known recipe for bad decisions. Sunday dawned with a strong north-easterly wind, just about the worst direction for getting back to Portsmouth from Cherbourg as it involves tacking the boat for the whole 65 miles home.

We started off in favourable tide, going east from Cherbourg as far as Cap Levi before tacking onto a northerly course. Five miles out we ran into some big overfalls, large breaking waves caused by strong tide running into wind. It was very rough indeed and the boat was taking a terrific pounding. After some minutes of this, a particularly steep-faced wave came along. I turned the boat sideways to avoid plunging through the top and becoming air-borne, but we fell off the wave into a deep hollow behind. The boat dropped perhaps 4 or 5 feet before hitting the water with a terrific bang. There was a tremendous cracking sound. Nothing obvious had broken so I pressed on and we were soon out of the overfalls, although the sea was still pretty nasty. It was not until about fifteen minutes later that one of my crew, who had been below, appeared in the hatchway.

'I don't want to worry you, skip' she said, 'but there's about 4 inches of water over the floorboards down here'.

Naturally it worried me mightily and I dived below to see where it was coming from. There was quite a lot of water sloshing around but I couldn't see any obvious source. We pumped the water out until she was nearly dry and continued on our way across the Channel. At hourly intervals we had to pump again, as the water continued to come in. Eventually we got back to Portsmouth after a 16-hour crossing.

It was dark when we arrived and we were all very tired, but the boat was still leaking at a serious rate so we had to stay aboard. I set the alarm clock at intervals through the night in order to wake up and pump her out. When daylight came we were able to make a more thorough inspection and soon found evidence of cracking on several of the plywood planks on the starboard side, which had taken the brunt of the fall off the wave. I got the yard to lift her out and was astonished to find how extensive the damage had been. The planks were split across in half a dozen places and two of them had partially separated along the join between them. The damage looked too severe to be repaired satisfactorily and I went home worried and depressed.

There followed a bit of a quarrel between the insurers, who said there was a design fault (basically she wasn't strong enough) and the designers who considered the builders were at fault (the hull came ready made) and the builders who considered the damage was covered by the insurance! My solicitor, a clever man by any standards, came up with a neat solution. He said he would issue writs against all of them and they could have an expensive day in court deciding who was right, while we sat back waiting for the conclusion. This quickly brought agreement. With some money from the insurers, the builders agreed to provide me with a new boat if I would agree to transfer all the equipment and fittings from the old boat to the new. I readily agreed as this outcome gave me a second chance to put right all the little mistakes I had made with the first attempt. Thus was *Polliwog* (an American tadpole) born out of disaster.

Out went all the compromises for comfort, speed was everything. Do windows make a boat go faster? So no windows. Do we really need a forehatch? No forehatch then. And so on down to the last detail. Do three crew need three tubes of toothpaste? So we will share one between us! But we made the boat stronger in a few important places. We also made some changes to the rig and designed a new keel. All this took many months to complete so that by the time she was launched, most of the next season had gone by. But we sailed her enough to know that *Polliwog* was a fast boat and, in light winds, quite exceptionally fast. I invited my friend Peter Bruce to race her in an inshore race which he won. We put her to bed for the winter, full of high hopes for the next season.

At the start of 1975 I recruited two new, young crew. Andy and Chris had raced together in Fireball dinghies, they were keen as mustard and happy to commit themselves to a whole season of intensive racing. This was no small commitment as it involved every weekend and much of their holiday time as well. From early March we trained together so that, by the time the racing started in mid-April ,we were a good team. We made a spectacular start, winning our first two races by substantial margins. And the season went on as it had started, with many more victories which included the popular race to Dinard in Brittany and a spectacular win in the Princess Elizabeth Cup at Cowes. In the latter we beat several well-known big boats, among them Edward Heath's *Morning Cloud*. By the end of that season I had a cupboard full of silverware, victory in the Junior Offshore Group's Points Championship and a marriage in tatters.

Racing boats have a short life at the top before they are out-designed by a new generation. For that reason, and because of the inevitable turmoil over the end of my marriage, I sold *Polliwog* at the pinnacle of her achievement, exchanging her for a small house in Frimley. Divorce is a miserable experience and horribly expensive, there was no question of continuing my sailing hobby, it couldn't be afforded. For a while I tried sailing in other people's boats, but the magic had gone and I soon gave this up as well. Then, at my lowest ebb, I met and married Janet. Personal happiness returned as we rebuilt our lives over the next 8 boatless years - but finances continued to be tight. However, the lack of a boat did have some unexpected benefits. My search for a cheap hobby ended when I took up painting, first in oils and later watercolours, and this pastime has been a joy to me ever since.

By 1979 financial recovery was sufficiently on the way to allow us to charter a boat for two consecutive summer holidays in that and the following year. These were Janet's first experiences of sailing and, blessed with splendid weather on both occasions, proved enjoyable enough to let me dare hope that we would one day again have a boat of our own. That day came in 1985 when an unexpected windfall set us on the hunt for a new boat. We settled on a Hunter Horizon, a 26-footer with twin bilge keels and berths to sleep four comfortably, or 5½ like sardines! The kit for *Goosander*, arrived just after Easter that year. The fibreglass hull and deck were already bonded together so that she looked almost complete when delivered onto our drive at Farnham.

We had all the fittings and windows to fix, and the whole of the inside to build. Quite apart from it being a substantial DIY undertaking, which I have always enjoyed, there was the overwhelming excitement of having a boat again and the anticipation of all we would do in her. She was finished inside a couple of months. It was as much as Janet could do to persuade me not to work on her all night. She warned that the neighbours' friendly support might evaporate under a barrage of nocturnal hammering and drilling! *Goosander* was launched in May and in a few short weeks we were back exploring all those much-loved haunts in Normandy and Brittany, so fondly remembered from earlier years. Mind you, this was strictly cruising. Janet is not a competitive person and positively dislikes the whole idea of racing anybody for anything - with the possible exception of the January sales. An additional advantage of the twin keels was that they carried a performance penalty that made them unsuitable for serious racing. Thus they constituted a cast iron (literally) pledge that I would not again be tempted into competitive racing, with all that was involved in that.

For the next five years we cruised in *Goosander*, visiting just about every little harbour and anchorage between Fécamp in the east and Morlaix in Brittany in the west. Then in 1990, two developments led to a change of boat. First, I was promoted at work. But there was also a slight but growing frustration with the space and speed limitations of the small *Goosander*. With a bigger, faster boat we could go further afield, even within the time limitations of holidays. If one could cross the channel in ten hours instead of twelve, long weekends in France would become more attractive, and going further afield as far as Spain would be a possibility for holidays. *Further afield?* I thought..., and put the thought aside.

In the late summer of 1990, we started looking around the yards for a new boat. 1990 was about the low point of a depression in the boat business and it was very definitely a buyer's market. Most companies were offering tremendous bargains, accepting almost no profit margin just to keep themselves in business. We were spoilt for choices and unable to make up our minds. Full of indecision, we wandered down to Hamble Point marina, near Southampton. It was a Saturday morning in early September, and there she was. A spanking new Maxi 999 lay sleek and inviting on her berth in the marina.

The decision was quickly made, boats can be like that - a sort of 'love at first sight.' She was 33 feet long, substantially bigger than *Goosander*, with a sporty fractional rig and a surprisingly spacious interior. A very modern boat with considerable capability. But she had a deep fin keel and Maxi 999s had been raced successfully for several years. I sensed Janet's reservations, I think she was concerned that I might return to my old racing obsession.

'I thought you liked twin keels' she said, ' this boat has a six foot fin. Won't that limit where we can go?'

She was right of course, there would be some limitations but the boat would be fast and everything else about her was so attractive. I genuinely did not harbour any secret plans to return to racing, even though the temptation was occasionally there. Yet, perhaps deep in my unconscious mind, another thought was germinating. Here was the biggest boat we could afford (unless we bought second-hand which we were both against) and perhaps she was just big enough to sail around the world. *Around the world? Was I mad? Was this just a romantic passing thought, to be cast aside in favour of more practical things?* I couldn't deny that the thought was there. The idea, immature and premature, was truly there. I needed a boat that could do it, and no other would do. It was a day to remember.

A goosander is a small diving duck, as the Maxi was considerably larger than the Horizon, it seemed natural to name her after a rather larger waterfowl. Janet came up with *Greylag* - a large grey goose. We signed the order at the Southampton boat show, amid the usual champagne jollities that accompany those occasions.

Janet had been right about the limitations of a fin keel. The ability to dry out on twin keels greatly increases the choice of places to stop and also enables one to clean the hull or do underwater repairs, without the expense and bother of being lifted out at a yard. We came up with a neat solution. By choosing a fin keel, long enough to give stability in the fore-and-aft direction, and fitting her with legs each side, it would be possible to dry out safely. As luck would have it there was another version of the same boat that had a longer keel with winglets, and the builders could easily fit this different keel to our boat. Also a new company was marketing some cleverly designed, telescopic, aluminium alloy legs which could be broken down and stowed in a locker - a huge improvement over the old, heavy, wooden ones which had to be stowed on deck. The French have for years used legs to dry out, so there was nothing revolutionary about the idea. We went for it and thus managed to combine the better performance of a fin keel with the ability to dry out.

Greylag was launched in the spring of the following year and soon fulfilled our expectations of a much faster boat. On her maiden channel crossing she reached Cherbourg in ten hours, at times surfing down the waves at eleven knots. She was an exhilarating boat to sail and far more roomy and comfortable than *Goosander* had been. For the next four summers we cruised extensively along the southern English coast and in France, with one long voyage to Spain, which I did mainly to get my Ocean Yachtmaster Certificate - a sort of driving licence for offshore sailing.

By 1993 my plans to sail around the world had grown firm. With

Greylag on her legs

retirement coming up in 1995, when I would reach the age of sixty, that year seemed the obvious start date. Everything in my daily life became related to this goal. I read every book I could find on the subject and began to assemble a list of modifications and additions to the boat that would be needed for this voyage of a lifetime. Charts of the Atlantic and Pacific Oceans appeared on my office wall. I lived and dreamed of this adventure so intensively that I must have circumnavigated the globe a hundred times in my mind before finally setting out for real. I was doubtless a terrible bore to my friends, with a head full of this all consuming obsession, I struggled to find anything else to talk about. They put up with it bravely. I think many of those who complete a circumnavigation exhibit this same single-minded determination. Perhaps it is an essential ingredient in one's personality if one is to achieve such a goal. Many have the dream, but never actually start or give up at the first unpleasant hurdle. For myself, it was a natural ambition for a life-long sailor. But without that dogged determination that once I aimed at my competitors on the racecourse, I might have remained one of the dreamers.

My biggest disappointment at that time was my inability to persuade Janet to come with me. When it came to sailing Janet considered that arriving was better than travelling. She enjoyed the life in harbour, the socialising and exploring that are part and parcel of the cruising life, but the open ocean had few attractions for her. She is uncomfortable at sea, often on the edge of seasickness although not usually sick, and she found long periods of confinement on board such a small ship, tedious and claustrophobic. These problems she could tolerate for the relatively short journeys around the English Channel, but not for ocean voyages lasting several weeks. Nevertheless she was very supportive of my plans to go, and was keen to fly out for some of the nicer and shorter legs of the voyage.

Reluctantly I settled for this and now I am glad I did so. I have seen unhappy outcomes when husbands have put undue pressure on their wives to go on such adventures 'for loyalty's sake', even though it is anathema to them. Long distance sailing is an arduous and sometimes frightening experience and the love of it is something with which one is born. It is very different from weekends in the Solent or short hops across the English Channel and, if it doesn't come naturally, it is a foolish man who uses emotional blackmail on an unwilling partner. She may come in body but not in spirit and that can make for great unhappiness. On the other hand, it might be equally unwise for a wife to persuade her husband to abandon his plans to fulfil a lifelong dream, for he may go in spirit if not in body. Janet was right, the ocean was not for her. Thus it was decided that I would go with a crew of two other men and she would come out when we reached the exciting places.

With two years to go to the first practical start date, late summer 1995, I was already beginning to plan the route in some detail. The easy way is westabout, through the Panama and Suez canals, keeping near to the equator for most of the voyage. This keeps one in the favourable trade winds that blow with reasonable consistency from the east. Allowing for a few touristic diversions, this gives a total distance of around 28,000 miles. The time base is largely determined by natural phenomena. The hurricane season in the Atlantic and Caribbean runs from April to November with a peak risk time in September. It is a considerable risk to travel during that period, as to be caught in open water would lead to almost certain wrecking. By leaving Portsmouth in, say, July one can get across Biscay before the autumn gales and press on slowly to reach the Canary Islands by early November. Leaving there mid to late November is reasonably safe and gives one Christmas in the Caribbean to celebrate that first ocean crossing. Janet had already pencilled Antigua in her diary for a first visit.

Going through the Panama Canal in February leaves ample time to cross the Pacific and exit through Indonesia by the start of the typhoon season, normally around the end of September, and then up to Thailand for a second Christmas in the tropics (also noted in Janet's diary). From there one can cross the Bay of Bengal to Sri Lanka, and the Arabian Sea to the Red sea, and thence through the Suez Canal to the Mediterranean and home by the late summer of the second year.

On this basic plan the circumnavigation would take just over two years Portsmouth to Portsmouth; about as quick as one can do it without going non-stop. By using the two big canals, one avoids all those terrifying capes at the southern ends of the big continents, the notorious Cape Horn is for masochists and madmen! Besides that, I take the view that a genuine circumnavigation ought to be more or less around the longer, middle part of the world - at least within the tropics - rather than a quick whip around the shorter Southern Ocean, however boisterous and newsworthy that may be. This point was brought home to me by a story once told me by Dr Mike Stroud, with whom I was working at the time of his epic tramp across Antarctica with Sir Ranulph Fiennes.

'Two years to circumnavigate,' he said, 'why, I did it in minutes at the South Pole!'

It was at about this point in my planning that I found myself standing in a queue at that well-known Mecca for yachtsmen, the Maison du Vin in Cherbourg - until recently the only place in France where one could buy Australian wines! Now of course, there are Australians making French wine. To pass the time (it was a long queue) I struck up a conversation with the gentleman in front of me.

'I'm planning to sail around the world' I said, there being almost nothing else in my head at that time, as I have explained. 'Westabout, starting in 1995, I hope.'

'Oh, that's interesting' he replied, 'our club is planning a rally around the world at about that time, not a race - just cruising with plenty of stops. Would you be interested?'

'Indeed I would' I replied and he promised to get someone to send me the details.

His name was Ken Burgess and it was through him that day that I heard about the RAF Yacht Club's Trade Winds Rally. Sadly, Ken has died since then, but I will always be grateful to him for that short conversation in the wine queue.

It turned out that the Trade Winds Rally had been planned to follow almost the exact route I had planned and to start at the same time - not altogether surprising as the options are limited by the weather windows, as I have explained. The rally had come about thanks largely to the drive and energy of Dr Malcolm McLaren. It was expected that about forty boats would join and participants would enjoy the services of two rally managers. They would go on ahead to arrange berthing and smooth the way through the immigration and customs procedures, which can be quite tedious. But most of all, we would have the company of other boats and a wide range of help and advice from other skippers. It was also planned to run a daily radio net, when each boat would call in with her position and details of local weather conditions, and anyone with trouble could get help.

One hesitated a little at the thought of being too organised and tied to a rather strict timetable. However, the advantages were obvious and appealing, so we signed up to go with the Trade Winds Rally. In fact we were one of the first group of 10 boats to do so; this earned us a bottle of bubbly at the London Boat Show in January 1994. With this settled I now had to find a crew and prepare the boat to be ready by mid-summer 1995 to depart for Gibraltar from where the rally would start in October. One advantage of being on an organised rally is that there are no more options to delay the start, the whole thing gets a kind of momentum which carries one through any moments of hesitation.

Finding crew was to prove a difficult task. Wealthy owners were prepared to pay crew. Others seemed to have an endless supply of relatives willing to come. For me, it was a case of finding two people who were free to leave work and home for two years, who could afford to pay their share of the expenses, and who were prepared to commit themselves to a 28,000-mile voyage in a 33 foot boat - to say nothing of the need for basic sailing ability. Such people do not hang around on every street corner!

The problem was soon halved when John Anderson, a colleague at work who I had known and sailed with for some years, said he would like to come along. He was taking advantage of generous early retirement terms and would therefore be free at the right time. John was a psychologist and a very experienced sailor in whom I could place absolute trust. About the only problem that came with John was loss of the option to choose a married couple rather than two, independent crew. I had earlier decided that three was the right number for *Greylag*. It is always a mistake to overcrowd a small boat, however well people may think they will get on together at the start. Four was therefore not an option, except for the brief periods when Janet would be with us.

Some boats were planning to go with just a husband and wife crew and that is certainly one way of securing privacy and avoiding crew problems. But it is hard work at sea, when they would have to take alternate 4-hour watches, and I would worry if one of the pair were to become ill or injured. With three crew it is possible to have 3-hour watches at night followed by 6 hours in bed; this is a rather less exhausting routine and it is easier to cope with illness or injury.

Finding the third member of our crew was an interesting exercise and it took a good deal of effort, and forbearance beyond the call of duty. The rally organisers had started a crew list of people who wanted to go, giving details of their background and experience. The trouble is that people get carried away with the romance of it all, lured by dreams of tropical islands, blue sea and white sand, a warm breeze through the palm trees, dusky maidens. 'Live the dream' the rally advertisements said. It is easy to forget the hard work involved, the anxieties of the bad bits, the boredom of long sea passages, the difficulties of living in a space 10m x 3m with people you don't really know and may not care for when you do. Enthusiasm for the adventure is boundless, but real understanding of what is involved is rare among those who have never done it.

John and I went through the crew list, picking out a number of 'possibles', but the information was far too scanty to make firm decisions. So we took them sailing, usually for a weekend, occasionally for a week. This is an easy way to check up on basic sailing ability but that, I now know, is a very small part of the problem. First and foremost one is looking for someone with whom one can live in close quarters for a long period. In that context aspects of personality and character are more important than sailing knowledge. One can quickly teach a complete newcomer, given a modicum of aptitude, but you cannot change a person's basic personality, nor your own for that matter. People can be on their best behaviour for a weekend, or even a week. But over a longer period basic personality traits reveal themselves. Charming people at parties can be bastards when things go wrong! One can tolerate all sorts of minor irritations for short periods but in the end they will drive you mad.

We came across some strange characters during our hunt for crew, good sailors many of them but impossible to live with, or to be strictly fair, impossible for me to live with. I remember one fellow who turned up and asked if it would be OK to bring his collapsible canoe - itself almost half the length of *Greylag*! Another hoped I would understand that he drank only Lapsang Souchong tea, of which he would bring a large supply. Yet another seemed to turn every quiet moment in the cockpit into an impromptu party. He had an inexhaustible supply of slightly funny, but seriously smutty, stories. Inexhaustible only because when he got to the last one, he would start again on the first!

At times I began to feel I was on 'mission impossible', such was the patchwork quilt of human eccentricities I was trying to match up with my own that summer. In the end we chose David Reynolds, a competent sailor and a quiet fellow. Perhaps it was this latter quality which attracted me; here maybe was someone with whom I could survive the two years. As it turned out this was wrong, but we did sail together for a whole year before parting company in Bora Bora - a parting that was in no way anyone's fault. However in 1994 the crew problem was for the time being solved and I turned my attention to the boat.

Greylag already had a satellite navigation system (Global Positioning System or GPS). This was pure magic after the old RDF system - just press the buttons and it tells you where you are. I planned to take my sextant and a full set of tables in case of failure of the GPS. After some thought I decided to add a radar set to give more help with difficult landfalls. At home radar is used principally to spot ships and to help in fog. Fog does not occur in the tropics and there are fewer ships, but some of the charts of the wilder places are not very accurate and radar can be useful to resolve problems. The charted GPS position may suggest you are two miles from land, but if the radar shows something solid at one mile one takes notice!

An expensive rally requirement was for a Single Side-Band Radio or SSB. This was essential for communication between the boats when distances would be far greater than the VHF radio could manage. The SSB would also allow us to obtain weather information.

We fitted extra water and fuel tanks to cover the longer journeys. The longest of these would be between the Galapagos Islands and the Marquesas in the Pacific, a distance of some 3100 miles. Under ordinary conditions this would take about 30 days, but one has to allow for the possibility of trouble, such as dismasting, which could easily double the time. Bigger boats usually have water-makers that convert sea water into fresh. We did not have room for one of these devices and they are also rather expensive. Our large sun awning, built to provide shade in harbour (essential in the tropics), also served as a large funnel to collect water. In a downpour we once collected 16 gallons of water this way in about 20 minutes.

Electrical power is a scarce resource on a small boat and careful planning was required to be sure that we wouldn't run short. New gel batteries were fitted and two large solar panels provided additional charging when the engine was not running. However, the most important consideration was the method for auto-steering the boat - no sane person plans to steer a boat manually on a long voyage. The modern electric powered steering devices are very good but they consume vast amounts of power, especially in rough weather. The solution for us was to fit windvane steering. We chose the Hydrovane system which links a windvane directly to a small extra rudder. The vane is set so that when it is in line with the wind, the boat is on the required course. If the boat wanders, the wind pressure on one side of the vane operates the rudder and corrects the course. That's the theory, in practice it is a black art to get the thing to work well.

To deal with storm conditions I doubled up the main rigging holding up the mast and fitted an inner forestay on which we could rig a storm jib. I changed all the outside locker hinges and fastenings for bigger ones as the loss of a locker lid in bad weather can spell disaster. The main hatchway into the cabin was provided with pins to lock the washboards into place and thus prevent loss of these vital items if we were unfortunate enough to be rolled upside-down in a storm. These precautions were instrumental in saving *Greylag*, and possibly our lives, when we met just such a storm in the Coral Sea. A host of minor modifications were aimed at increasing storage space, increasing ventilation and providing shade from the sun.

I assembled a medical pack, a kit of tools and spare parts for the engine, and other important equipment to make us reasonably self-sufficient. This included sailcloth and a marvellous old Singer sewing machine, a sail-maker's machine dating from the 1930s and built like a tank. On the personal side, we were vaccinated against every possible disease (not true but it felt like it), we handed over financial management to our respective wives, we laid up our cars and we learnt to bake bread.

From various sources we obtained the absolute minimum of 140 charts to cover our journey. It would have been nice to have had more but the budget did not allow for this. Next came the pilot books, those useful sources of detailed information on how to find your way into the various ports and anchorages. One such was intriguingly entitled 'Charlie's charts of Polynesia'. On the front cover was a picture of Oponohu Bay, Moorea, the very place where they filmed 'South Pacific' and 'The Mutiny on the Bounty'. My mind wandered far away as I dreamily thumbed through the pages, full of magic little islands and coral atolls. *Was this why I wanted to go?* Probably, I thought, but it was not the whole story ...I came back to earth.

Finally I installed my electronic piano. I had struggled to regain the modest ability on the keyboard that I once had as a youth and I didn't want to lose it again. The great thing about an electronic piano is that one can play it with headphones and avoid driving everybody else crazy with the umpteenth rendering of Fur Elise!

It was amazing how this morass of practical details and planning pushed from my mind all thoughts of the risks and dangers now looming close. There was no time to dwell on the question 'why?' My life was pervaded by an all-consuming conviction that I was going to do this journey, come what may. Perhaps one has to feel something like that to summon up the energy and drive necessary to do it. As I have said, there are many who dream of such an adventure but never quite get round to doing it for real.

By early July 1995 we were ready to depart, or as ready as we would ever be. We filled the lockers with food stores and the few personal possessions that each of us would take. We bade farewell to our wives and families and early on the 18th of July, we slipped from our moorings in Portsmouth harbour and ran quietly westward down the Solent. *No turning back now*, I thought to myself. How true that was, for we would return to Portsmouth without ever turning from our westerly course.

Greylag's sail plan and accomodation

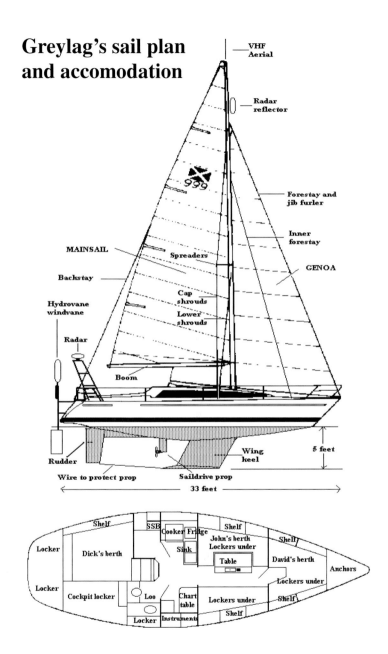

VHF Aerial

Radar reflector

Forestay and jib furler

Inner forestay

GENOA

MAINSAIL

Spreaders

Backstay

Cap shrouds

Hydrovane windvane

Lower shrouds

Radar

Boom

Rudder

Wire to protect prop

Saildrive prop

Wing keel

5 feet

33 feet

Shelf

SSB

Cooker

Fridge

Shelf

John's berth
Lockers under

Shelf

Locker

Dick's berth

Sink

Table

David's berth

Anchors

Locker

Cockpit locker

Loo

Chart table

Lockers under

Lockers under

Shelf

Locker

Instruments

Shelf

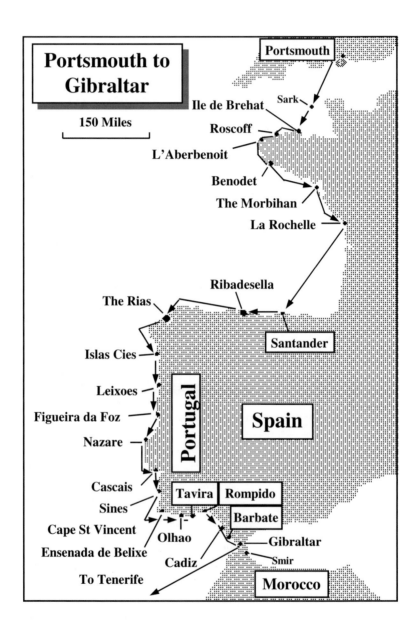

Portsmouth to Gibraltar

150 Miles

Portsmouth

Ile de Brehat

Sark

Roscoff

L'Aberbenoit

Benodet

The Morbihan

La Rochelle

Ribadesella

The Rias

Santander

Islas Cies

Leixoes

Portugal

Spain

Figueira da Foz

Nazare

Cascais

Tavira

Rompido

Sines

Barbate

Cape St Vincent

Olhao

Gibraltar

Ensenada de Belixe

Cadiz

Smir

To Tenerife

Morocco

2 Our Shakedown Cruise to Gibraltar and Tenerife

We had planned a long, slow cruise to Gibraltar. There were several reasons for this. We had to learn how to live together in a small space, to manage on a modest budget rather than the usual holiday budget, and to spend most nights at anchor and not in the comforts and conveniences of marinas. We did not have to get to Gibraltar until mid-October, so this allowed a 3-month, slow cruise which should, I reckoned, sort us out. Any problems with the boat could be put right while we were still in familiar territory. We could either learn the art of living on *Greylag* or give up inexpensively at an early stage, and we would probably have an interesting and enjoyable time, long enough to be sure that interpersonal tolerance levels could endure for two years and better by far than a non-stop long haul across the Bay of Biscay to Gibraltar.

It was a strange feeling sailing down the Solent, knowing we would not see the old familiar places and faces for two years. Preparing for the trip had been busy with little time to ponder the wisdom of such a voyage. Now we had started, a quietness descended on the boat as each of us was lost in his own thoughts. For myself, I found for the first time a few doubts creeping in and a headwind all the way to Sark did little to help. However, the dark thoughts soon vanished as the sun appeared and we made our way into La Corderie at Ile de Bréhat, where we dried out on our legs.

Sailing holidays during working life had always been a dash to the nearest marina and out to a restaurant for dinner. Now we were on a budget, the anchor would be on overtime and, armed with Delia Smith, we would have to come to grips with the realities of cooking nearly all our meals on the boat. This was not quite the chore I had expected. It soon became a challenge to upstage the others in the galley.

Our second night in La Corderie brought our first lesson in anchoring. We had set two anchors, fore and aft, to keep the boat over the nice patch of rockless sand we were parked on - rather important if you dry out every tide. This was fine while the wind was from the bow, but in the night it veered 90 degrees and got up to Force 6 while our two anchors held us broadside on. Although this certainly served to demonstrate the amazing holding power of our little Fortress anchor, it was about as comfortable as a derailed British Rail sleeper. I was regretting setting the two anchors, even though the reason was sound enough at the time, when the solution came to me. Transfer the stern anchor warp to the bow. We did this and the result was magic. She lay bows-on to the two anchors in a V, which also limited the veering about and kept us over our patch of sand.

The pattern of life was soon established; cycles of sailing, shopping, cooking and sleeping, as we made slow, steady progress westward in the beautiful summer weather. At Roscoff we spent a night up the Penze River awaiting the arrival of a visitor on the ferry. This led to a new discovery about the boat. The weather was thundery and while the sun was out we deployed our newly fitted Bimini, a canvas sunshade which fits over the cockpit, and found it also provided excellent shelter while motoring in the rain - it wasn't quite a wheelhouse but welcome, all the same.

As a kick-off point for the Four Channel,the inshore route into Biscay, we found L'Aberbenoit a quieter and prettier place than L'Aberwrac'h where we had been before, albeit with minimum facilities.

L'Aberbenoit

Our one night there was restful and we left in good spirits and thick fog. The radar was bliss - not for navigation, which the GPS did well, but as a collision avoidance system when faced with hundreds of unseen French fishing boats, and yachts returning from the Four on the last of their tide and the first of ours. Our track around Biscay was blessed with excellent weather, although the light following winds involved too much motoring. We stopped in the usual places, but also in some less well explored spots.

At Benodet we left the busy marinas alone and travelled up the River Odet. Steep wooded banks most of the way, with several suitable spots to anchor, made it a delight. You can travel about six miles upstream before there is any real risk of doing something agricultural with the keel. Salmon jump around the boat and the scenery is stunning with some impressive *chateaux*. The stream is strong (about 3 knots when we visited) so a reliable engine is needed.

Onwards to the Morbihan, where we spent a week, and then to La Rochelle. We parked in the old harbour under the famous twin towers. It was noisy there but full of interest, though one can develop an aversion to Peruvian groups with pan pipes. Thence to Santander and the northern coast of Spain. So many boats travelling south go straight to La Coruña or

The Morbihan

Bayona, that few discover the many enchanting places here. Santander is useful for supplies and the ferry, but not much else. Along the coast we found Ribadesella, a pretty little fishing port surrounded by mountain scenery. Although the entrance looked formidable, with breaking surf on the starboard side as we went in, it was not difficult. Once in, there was plenty of water against the wall. The water was so thick with mullet, you could go aground on them.

We pressed on through the Spanish Rias, which we found delightful, and then to the idyllic, sparsely populated Islas Cies, just short of Bayona. Here, when the weather broke, we hit our first real trouble. The evening forecast was Force 9 at Finisterre. The weatherfax map made your hair stand on end , it looked like a cross-section of a 100-year-old oak. We set the Fortress, a small light alloy anchor, as a second anchor to the Delta anchor at the bow and were again impressed with the success of this arrangement. It was a noisy night, but not fearsome. With two independent anchors one worries less.

Next day, we fled to Bayona with three reefs in the mainsail and the storm jib only to hear more horror stories from other boats there. The crew of one large Hallberg-Rassy (a Rolls Royce among boats) had been woken by a terrific bang and had rushed on deck to discover themselves alongside another boat. They saw that they were still attached to their buoy and informed the other boat that they must have dragged their anchor. But they hadn't. It was the Hallberg-Rassy that was wandering around Bayona still attached to her mooring which had separated from the sea bed. The collision had saved them - the next stop would have been the rocks.

After a couple of days in Bayona, the forecast was for a 20-knot south-westerly so we set out for Leixoes, our first destination in Portugal. The forecast was wrong; it was soon blowing hard on the nose, so we turned round and went back to the southern island of the Islas Cies group. The wind increased to bring our third gale in five days and we faced another hard night on the anchor. Then the real trouble began. We set the Delta in the usual way and decided to set the Fortress again too. But this time, when I drove the boat forward to drop the second anchor, I managed to get the first rode alongside the keel and saildrive. Chomp! 'You've lost your anchor!' called John. I had cut the Delta off with the efficient rope stripper on our prop. We set the Fortress and prayed it would hold while we held a conference. It did.

It is at times like this that ship's companies divide themselves into optimists and pessimists. The latter suggested we should battle our way back to Bayona and buy a new anchor. David, the ship's optimist, with what to me was almost mindless confidence, asserted we would get the anchor back if we tried. By now it was almost dark and I had cause to be glad I had listened to those who advised carrying a spare big anchor and a lot of chain. The big Delta, one size up from that recommended for our boat, was retrieved from the stern locker and deployed on 120 feet of chain. We stood anchor watches for that stormy night, taking it in turns to stay awake in case of mishap, but the boat never moved an inch.

Looking back, I suppose I can laugh at the events that followed next morning, but it didn't seem all that funny at the time. David paddled the dinghy around while I hung over the transom with my masked and snorkelled head dangling in the water.

'At least the skipper's keeping a cool head,' they teased.

It didn't work; the gale had stirred up the water and reduced visibility, I couldn't see the bottom let alone our lost anchor. Next we tried dragging the Fortress behind the dinghy. Success. We retrieved an anchor and 110 feet of warp - but it wasn't our anchor. One lost and one found at this stage. We persisted for ages, but the process was difficult. When the Fortress was not loaded with weed, it was doing its proper job anchoring the dinghy. I voted to give up, but the ship's optimist wouldn't hear of it.

'We should try again, closer to the shore,' he said.

'Just once,' I replied.

So we did, and after a short drag John declared we had caught weed again. He pulled it up to clear it and there, jammed between the blades of the Fortress, was our anchor rode, complete with chain and Delta.

We pressed on south in much improved weather from the north-east, stopping briefly at Lexoes, Figiero da Foz, Nasare, Cascais and Sines. Then around Cape St Vincent and into the spectacular anchorage at Ensenada de Belixe. The latter is reminiscent of Havre Gosselin in Sark, a favourite old haunt, but larger and devoid of other boats. We were soon in the Algarve, anchored in a quiet *lagoa* near Olhão. Here we planned to dry out on our legs to scrub and inspect the hull to decide whether she needed more anti-fouling while we had enough tidal range to do it. We picked a nice level spot on firm sand and had just gone firmly aground when a jolly Portugese fisherman came up in his dinghy to tell us that we had parked on someone's piece of real estate. We explained in broken Spanish that we were already aground and unable to move. He shrugged and went on his way. Later, we discovered that the whole of the foreshore in this part of the

CASCAIS
SEAT '95

Cascais

lagoon system is a sort of allotment scheme where the fishermen farm shellfish. We cleaned the hull as surreptitiously as we could, but anti-fouling seemed to us on the provocative side and we postponed this.

We moved east along the southern Portugese coast to Tavira and then back into Spain at Rompido. We enjoyed each of these quiet spots. Both have the basic facilities one needs, but not much else other than the scenery, which is most attractive and uncrowded. Via Cadiz we moved on to Barbate, where there was an excellent new marina.

Here I had my first confrontation with the Spanish police, and it was all the fault of a black cat. By this stage in our voyage I had discovered how to catch the mullet which were present in vast numbers in all the harbours along that coast, though heaven knows why one bothered because they are disgusting eating. I was enjoying a good deal of success when the black cat appeared on the quayside taking more than a little interest in my catch. I tossed him a mullet which was received enthusiastically and devoured rapidly.

Next morning the police arrived.

'Would you be so kind,' one said with a smile, 'as not to feed my cat.'

It was there, he explained, to chase away the seagulls who were spoiling the new pontoons, the way only seagulls know how. After its ample fish dinner the cat had, with culpable dereliction of duty, curled up and gone to sleep for the night.

We finally made Gibraltar on the 2nd of October and tied up in

Marina Bay, where most of the Trade Winds fleet were already assembled. It had been a splendid three months, during which we had logged no fewer than 1733 miles and visited forty-five ports or anchorages *en route*. We had spent three nights at sea, eight on mooring buoys, twenty-nine berthed alongside and thirty-nine at anchor.

We had learnt a lot about anchoring. We had proved that the battery management system was adequate and that the other important modifications to the rig, the fuel and water tanks and stowage provision were all effective. We had learnt to use the windvane and we had experienced long downwind legs with a double-headed rig, both untamed and with various levels of reduced sail. This arrangement consists of two headsails set like wings on each side of the boat and held out with spinnaker poles. It is a well-balanced rig and works well with the wind-vane. It is also easy to wind the sails in quickly during squalls. The mainsail is kept stowed in its cover.

We had practised our sextant work and given the SSB radio and weatherfax systems a thorough testing. But most important of all, we had learnt to live in the space. We had got on well together and, though the others needed little practice, even I had become a passable cook. We were ready to start our voyage. It was the end of the beginning.

Our time in Gibraltar was not too busy. There were only a few things to do on the boat and this left plenty of time to relax. It was fun getting to know the other Tradewinders (as we were now known), and discovering Gibraltar. It has an interesting history but I rather agreed with a friend who had described it as a grubby little town on the side of a runway.

Janet flew out on the 9th of October, it was great to see her after three months and the lads welcomed her aboard with a bosun's whistle, improvised from the one on the kettle. We all went out for dinner in Bianca's, a splendid and inexpensive restaurant on the corner of the marina.

The next day was a big one for us. We had been volunteered to do a full demonstration of a man-overboard drill, starting under full sail. We had done a little practice on the way down to Gib but this was the real thing and in front of the whole assembled fleet. David was volunteered to fall in and as the water there was not exactly warm, dressed up in a wet suit and lifejacket. He said he felt a bit panicky about it but I said he could panic for all he was worth once he had fallen in - it would add to the realism.

At the appointed time we got *Greylag* off her mooring and sailed her up and down in front of the watching crowd in the stiff Levanter breeze.

'Jump', I shouted to David, so loud that he almost fell off with fright. In no time flat John had the sails down and the engine started. We trailed our floating line and drove in a circle around poor David who by now had overcome his nerves and was acting the part beautifully - his blood-curdling cries for help made some of the audience think the whole thing had gone wrong! He caught hold of the line and we soon had him back on board.

Next came the life-raft demo for which we had borrowed a life-raft from the local chandler. 'Abandon ship' I called, and John hurled the life-raft into the water. It inflated quickly, but upside-down. John jumped into the water and soon managed to right it and we all leapt in - except Janet, who was hiding down below in case it all went horribly wrong and we became separated from *Greylag*. We invited several of our audience to try the abandonment drill for themselves and several did so. Afterwards I asked John why he had looked so worried and it was only then that I discovered for the first time that he could hardly swim a stroke!

That was the end of the work and over the next few days Janet and I went off on several tourist trips. I particularly enjoyed the one to Ronda, in Spain. The coach took us up into the spectacular mountainous country just behind the coast. We were told that many Hollywood westerns are actually filmed there and it certainly looked like Arizona in places. I liked the mountain villages, clusters of white houses arranged haphazardly on the hillsides. At Ronda we had a conducted tour of the town and visited a restored traditional house and one of the oldest bull rings in Spain.

Our coach driver ran a continuous commentary as we returned through the hills - he had a wealth of stories to keep us amused:-

'An Englishman, a Scotsman and an Irishman were trying to get into the Barcelona olympics without tickets. They saw how easily the athletes were getting in, so the Englishman picked up a telegraph pole and marched up to the gate. 'Smith, England, pole vault', he said and they let him in. The Scotsman had observed this success so he took off the nearest manhole cover and marched up to the gate with it under his arm. 'McTavish, Scotland, discus', he said and they let him in also. Ah! Thought the Irishman and rushed into the nearest hardware shop for a roll of barbed wire. Up he went with it to the gate. 'O'Reilly, Ireland, fencing', he said. They threw him out.'

At the weekend, about ten boats set out on a two-day trip to Morocco. It was a flat calm day and we motored all the way to Smir and into the new marina there. In the afternoon there was a conducted tour of Tetouan, a typical Moroccan town, complete with street markets and a Kasbah. It was a fascinating place, a rabbit warren of tiny narrow streets lined with stores that opened directly onto the pavements. It would have been easy to get lost in that place and probably never be seen again. The poverty was numbing and we saw many workshops that employed children, mostly decorating leather. Our guide had a small team of helpers who would hang around at the back of the group to fend off the pick-pockets.

The return trip was also a motoring affair, Janet's sort of weather and she was delighted to see some dolphins. Next day we were joined by our friend Keith Ellis, he was out for a visit to Gib and to see us off on the big journey. He planned to join us again in Fiji.

Over the next week we began to stock the boat up for the first leg of our voyage that would take us to Tenerife in the Canary islands. Gibraltar has a big 'Safeways' and that was a boon. They even sold butter in tins, a real help on a long trip. In between the shopping expeditions we visited the lower St Michael's caves, spectacular but some awkward climbing here and there, and we attended various parties organised for the rally. At the Royal Gibraltar Yacht Club there was a prize-giving and we were delighted to win the prize for the best prepared boat in the rally fleet.

Eventually the great day arrived, it was the 23rd of October and the official start of the rally. We said our farewells to Janet and Keith and they went off to Europa Point, the southern tip of Gibraltar, to watch the start. *Greylag* slipped away from Marina Bay on her engine, tracked west along the edge of the airport before turning south past the naval base and on down the coast to the start-line at Europa Point.

There was a stiff Levanter blowing, easterly about Force 5, as the fleet gathered for the start. I suppose it was my racing background that made me want to be somewhere near the front when the gun went off for the start. We manoevred around near the line on a reefed mainsail, with the genoa rolled up and the spinnaker pole already in place so that we could let the sail out quickly. There was an unwritten rule that one was expected to let Malmac, our Commodore Malcolm McLaren's boat, start first. I thought I would give him about a yard, so we tucked up tight under his lee quarter as the boats approached the start line. The starting gun boomed out and in no time flat we deployed our genoa and pulled up alongside *Malmac*. We were soon in front of him. The conditions were just right for *Greylag* and she sped away towards Terifa, surfing down the fronts of the waves in spite of all that extra weight we were carrying. We later heard that there had been a collision at the start between the big Hallberg-Rassy

Arabian Sands and the catamaran *Gambatte Go*.

Towards Terifa we finally relinquished the head of the fleet to *Magic Dragon*, Steven Thomas's Oyster 55. He called up on the radio to ask if any part of our hull was still in the water! *Chinatown* was also thereabouts but much further offshore. It was about then that I remembered this was not a race and it would be silly to break something important so early on. We rolled up half the genoa and proceeded at a more sensible pace.

During the evening, as we left the narrow Straits of Gibraltar, the wind moderated rapidly and by nightfall we were motoring. We remained on the engine all night and throughout the next day. Over the radio we heard that Mike Van Gent and Tracy, on their catamaran *Freeaz,* had run into some tunny nets off the coast of Africa in the night. They had a difficult time with the local fishermen but eventually managed to free themselves. I was glad we were well offshore. Later that day we were accompanied for a while by Tom Parker and his family on *Enarkay*.

Early next day a good breeze returned. It came in from the south-east which enabled us to sail fast with the spinnaker up on a broad reach. Although sometimes difficult to handle, this lovely big balloon sail always makes the boat go fast downwind. We tried our luck at fishing, trailing a gaudy lure behind the boat, and after several hours we finally had a take. It was only a small tuna but felt like a monster as we had the spinnaker up at the time and even a small fish feels big at 6 knots. Later we caught another. There were lots of Manx sheerwaters around the boat and we saw tiny storm petrels from time to time. A large turtle came paddling by, we thought it was a green turtle but couldn't be sure of the identification. It took no notice of us.

Next morning I got through to Janet on the radio, via the station at Portishead. I could hear her more clearly than on many Spanish telephones and all was well at home. The wind died again that afternoon and we were back on the motor. At least it served to charge up our batteries.

We had been at sea for just over three days when the GPS suddenly went down. This was very worrying and we immediately started a careful dead reckoning. It was quite like old times before all these new-fangled devices had appeared. I decided not to try to find the fault that night and left it for the morning. When daylight came we were still motoring but getting a little help from the sails as well. Later the breeze filled in and we were sailing again. We heard on the radio that several other boats had altered course for Lanzarote, they were running short of fuel and that island was a bit nearer than Tenerife. This was a lesson we were nearly all learning, many of us had underestimated the amount of motoring we would have to do to keep up with the rally schedule.

I set about trying to find the fault with the GPS. There was no signal at all at the set and I was suspicious that there might be a break in the cable joining the aerial to the set. Sure enough that was where it was, one of the wires had come adrift at the junction box. I re-attached it and everything was back on line. Now Malcolm McLaren, our Commodore, was rather taken with the abstruse technical details of radio systems, so John suggested that we should report our GPS failure to him at the evening radio net. He suggested we should say that ' the problem was the loss of the phase-locked loop in the active antenna!' That should get him puzzling, we thought.

That night John cooked an excellent curry from tinned beef and the wind got up from the north-east (unrelated events). *Greylag* picked up her skirts and sped along at between 6 and 7 knots all night. We saw a couple of steamers in the distance but no yachts, it was amazing how a fleet of 42 boats could disperse over the ocean - one wouldn't have known one was in a rally had it not been for the radio nets. The fast pace soon ate away the miles and by the next morning we had only 130 miles to go to Tenerife.

At dawn on the 29th of October Tenerife was within sight, and boats started appearing from left and right of us as we all homed in on the harbour at Santa Cruz. Peter Seymour and Tony Diment, the rally directors, were there to greet us and allocated us a berth in the newly constructed marina. Actually it was still under construction, but important things were in place such as the water supply.

Over the next three days we cleaned up the boat and explored the town. The Real Club Nautico de Tenerife (RCNT) hosted a terrific reception party. They had opened their doors to us and we often ate at their restaurant and enjoyed their magnificent swimming pool and showers. Santa Cruz was an interesting town with a lot of small boutiques but not much in the way of food shops. However, we heard that there was a big supermarket just out of town and the rally managers were organising some visits there to restock the boats before the big Atlantic crossing.

After we'd had our fill of the town, we left the harbour and motored up to the fishing port to refuel before moving further north to a delightful small 'harbour'. There was a beautiful white sand beach with palm trees and a stout sea wall, with only very small gaps to let small boats in and out. We managed to squeeze in and anchor. It was called Playa de Teresitas

Playa de Teresitas

and we stayed there for two days, it was such a peaceful and pretty place. On the second morning a fellow walking along the beach appeared to be gesticulating at us. The arm waving didn't look exactly friendly - he seemed to be suggesting we should go! We ignored him and eventually he went away. To my embarassment, I later discovered that yachts were not allowed in that place. It had been constructed at great expense for the swimmers and sunbathers; the sand had been brought by ship from the Sahara desert. I had wondered about that because most of the sand in that part of Tenerife is black volcanic stuff. However, I didn't feel too guilty about our trespass as we had used our holding tank while in there to avoid pumping raw sewage into such a pretty place. *Greylag* was built in Sweden and that country sensibly requires all boats to be fitted with holding tanks.

We moved next morning to a spot 3 miles further north along the coast at Ensenada de Antequera. Here the sand was indeed black, one expected to get dirty but actually it was perfectly clean. The terrain was rocky and quite steep, and an old derelict building was slowly crumbling under the onslaught of wind and sea, perhaps it had been a fishing station. There were two small houses a little way up from the beach, one looked unoccupied, and there were numerous clumps of prickly pears. Despite the grandeur of the scenery, the bay seemed a cold place - perhaps it was the black sand.

Next day we were joined by eight other rally boats that had come up for a day's outing. We were invited for drinks on *Griffyn* where John and Ruth Roberts also gave us lunch. Later the other boats all returned to the marina back at Santa Cruz. We stayed on another day, as did John and Inga on *Calidris,* before the two of us tacked back to the marina in a very light headwind. Neither of us was keen to use the engine as we were all tanked up with fuel ready for the Atlantic.

A few days later John disappeared on a 2-day hike up Mount Teide. This was a serious climb, the mountain is 10,000 feet above sea level, and John had organised a group of about a dozen like-minded masochists to go with him. They obtained permission from the authorities who provided a key to give access to the hut at the foot of the mountain, where they would spend the night before their ascent. David and I rested.

There were plans to conduct a sail past at the RCNT as a preliminary to departing across the Atlantic on the 15th of November. I wasn't too keen on this; none of us on *Greylag* enjoyed the ceremonial bits and it seemed to me there was a risk of further collisions as had happened at the mass start at Gibraltar. We decided that a better plan for us would be to start a day early. As the smallest boat in the rally this would allow us to stay in touch with the fleet for longer, as the bigger boats would take a little while to pass us.

On the day before we had planned to leave, David and John went off on the coach to the big supermarket to do the final shopping. I topped up the water tanks and jerry cans and helped John stow all the stores neatly and safely. John is a very organised fellow and kept a careful record of where everything was put. We removed the anchor from the bow and stowed it in the aft locker, it was important to keep the front of the boat as light as possible to reduce the risk of her burying her bow in heavy weather. Although *Greylag* was low in the water, she floated reasonably level. We were ready, or as ready as we would ever be.

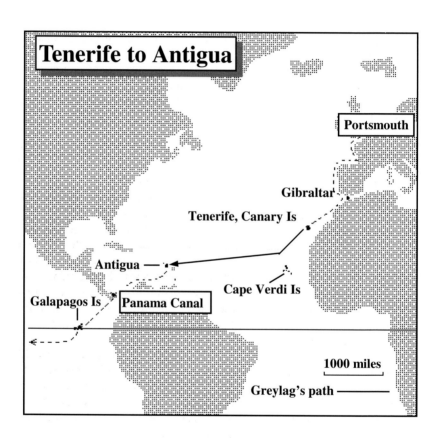

Tenerife to Antigua

Portsmouth

Gibraltar

Tenerife, Canary Is

Antigua

Cape Verdi Is

Galapagos Is

Panama Canal

1000 miles

Greylag's path

3 Crossing the Atlantic

I knew this particular departure would be a daunting experience and it was. After all the years of dreaming the moment had finally arrived to set out on our first ocean crossing. Strange how one can plan for years towards an end such as this and then, when the time comes, feel such a powerful uncertainty. As I asked John and David to let go the last of our lines, I thought to myself *am I really doing this? 2,600 miles across the Atlantic to Antigua!* Somewhere out there we would be more than a thousand miles from the nearest land. It was a numbing thought and I could easily imagine why some people give up at this stage. I fought off my last minute cold feet and concentrated on the job in hand.

On board we had food supplies to last about twice as long as the likely crossing time of three weeks. One needed ample in case some disaster, such as losing the mast, greatly extended our time at sea. Provisioning a boat for a long sea passage is no easy task even with the help of a small fridge. We relied heavily on the three staples - we would have rice with something, pasta with something or potatoes with something. The 'something' generally came out of a tin except for the first three days or so when we could keep sufficient fresh food in the fridge. After that, its main function was to keep the beer and drinks cool, with just a small corner for the butter and opened long-life milk.

70 gallons of water was spread between three storage locations, 20 gallons in the main tank, 27 in jerry cans and another 17 in two flexible tanks beneath the floorboards. The rest consisted of 2-litre bottles of assorted soft drinks. It is important to spread the water around like this so that in the event of a leak or contamination, one would not lose all the water. The minimum requirement is ½ a gallon per person per day, so we had enough to last about 46 days - more than twice our likely journey time. 40 gallons of diesel was similarly split between tanks and cans, enough to allow us to motor for about 600 miles - not a lot for a 2,600-mile journey. If we lost the mast we would have to make a jury rig out of whatever was left and sail as best we could.

There was a good breeze outside the harbour at Santa Cruz and we made good progress down the coast of Tenerife, past the small island of La Gomera way off to starboard, and out to sea. That evening the wind fell light, reducing our boat speed first to 3 knots and then to barely a knot. We ran the engine for a bit but I was not keen to use too much of our fuel at this early stage of the crossing. Our first night at sea passed quietly and each of us got some reasonable sleep. Our watch system consisted of three 4-hour watches during the day and four 3-hour watches at night, starting at eight o'clock in the morning. This plan, for a crew of three, with one on duty at a time, had the advantage that one slipped a watch each day, thus avoiding being on at the same time every night. Also, after a 3-hour night watch, each of us got 6 hours in bed. Of course one was occasionally disturbed when help was needed with sail changes, but this did not happen often as the sails could usually be adjusted by the watch-keeper on his own, without leaving the cockpit. I had made a rule that the watch-keeper would wear a safety harness at night; falling overboard is probably the easiest way to die at sea. If for any reason he had to leave the cockpit to go forward to the mast, and even though he would remain clipped on to the jackstays, safety wires that ran the full length of the boat, he would wake up one of the others to listen out until he was back in the cockpit. This was to avoid one of those ghastly mishaps when somebody falls overboard at night and no one realises he has gone until hours later.

Early on our second day at sea, a good breeze came in from the south but then slowly veered to the south-west where it remained for the next night. I tacked the boat south for the first night watch, as we needed to get further south to run into the trade winds. The saying goes *sail south until the butter melts, then turn right.* Although this sometimes takes one on a longer course, it usually pays because the trade winds provide fast downwind sailing. These considerations are of more practical significance than precisely calculating a great circle course. Although this is the shortest distance between two points on the surface of the globe, most of us are more interested in the shortest time!

For the next three days we continued to struggle on slowly, with the wind staying unhelpfully around south-west. But life was pleasant enough and at least we were slowly getting further south. We spent a lot of time fishing, trailing a lure behind the boat from a fishing rod mounted in a holder on the pushpit (the steel railing around the stern of the boat, so named to distinguish it from the pulpit at the front) I had been advised not to have a line stronger than 50-pound breaking strain. The reason given was that if one caught a fish big enough to break such a line, one probably didn't want it on the boat! After hearing of the fun and games John Cheeseman on *Saullitaire* had when he caught a 4-foot long mahi-mahi, I could well see the wisdom of this advice. Our first partial success came one evening. Suddenly the reel screamed as yards of line were stripped off. I grabbed the rod and asked John to let the sails flap to slow the boat down. It felt like a monster on the end and I wondered how we were going to get it on board. Slowly the fish came closer and we could see brilliant flashes of blue, green and red. It was a mahi-mahi or dorado, an astonishingly beautiful creature, whose anger at being caught seemed to intensify its extraordinary colours. John was poised with the gaff, but just as we nearly had him, the fish made a last desperate dive for freedom. It bore down beneath the boat and the line went slack. It was gone! I think it took the line around the rope cutter, the device mounted in front of the propeller to cut through ropes which would otherwise foul it up.

The next day brought better fortune. I caught and landed a small mahi-mahi and then, after losing another, hooked into what felt like a really big fish. When eventually it came alongside the boat, John successfully gaffed it and brought it aboard. In fact it was not a particularly big fish and weighed just on 5 pounds - a good size for eating. The fish felt so much bigger before landing was because the boat speed added considerably to the drag on the line. When the fish first came aboard it looked magnificent with those startling rainbow colours. However, after administering the last rites with a winch handle, the colours all faded to something more like one is used to seeing on the fishmonger's slab. I did the beheading and gutting on the floor of the cockpit, and washed the blood and guts down the drains with a few buckets of seawater. I'm sad to say that I found this procedure put me off eating my own fish, strange squeamishness for a doctor. Nevertheless, John cooked the thing for dinner and the others seemed to enjoy it.

In the middle of our sixth night at sea, during my watch, the wind suddenly veered from south-west to north in a matter of a minute or so. With all the noise generated by my efforts to reset the sails on the other side of the boat, John awoke and kindly came up to give me a hand. This heralded a rather unsettled patch of weather but the new wind direction was much more helpful and we made fast progress on a south-westerly course. This was most welcome, as we had travelled only 650 miles nearer to Antigua in the uncertain winds of those first six days.

There were many thundery showers, and when the big black clouds came over, we had to cope with some fierce squalls of wind. But one could see them coming and it was not too difficult to reduce sail before they arrived. Much of the time we sailed with just the two headsails at the front of the boat, keeping the big mainsail in its cover on the boom. This made it easy to roll up the genoa when the squalls arrived and proceed on just the small, number two jib. The wind eventually settled into the east and at last we were enjoying some fast sailing in the trade winds. It was easy to see why the old sailing ships came south to find these steady favourable winds for crossing to America and why they came to be known as the trades.

We were now making rapid progress and morale on board was sky high. The weather was warm and sunny most of the time and we were able to have showers in the cockpit, using our ubiquitous Hozelock garden spray device. So mean had we been with our water supply during the first week at sea, that we were now well ahead of the schedule and could afford to be generous with water for showers.

We had a visit from a tropicbird, a beautiful white, pigeon-sized bird with a long flowing tail. One wondered why they chose to be so far out in the ocean. Tiny storm petrels abounded and we had frequent visits by schools of dolphins. They are such attractive animals, we sat on the foredeck watching them criss-cross under the bow, occasionally breaking the surface for a breath, sometimes four or five at a time. They seemed to enjoy our company as much as we enjoyed theirs. No matter how close they came, sometimes within inches of the boat, they never collided with us. Their visits always caused great excitement, one of the real pleasures of ocean cruising.

Our daily mileage during that second week varied between 120 and 150 miles and during the night of our eleventh day at sea, we passed the half-way mark. This did the world for morale and we celebrated with a new 3-litre box of cabernet sauvignon, one of the twenty or so we had purchased in Safeway's back at Gibraltar. Most of the Trade Winds Rally fleet were still behind us; we knew this because each day we tuned into the radio net and plotted the positions given by the other boats. Only the big Oyster 55's had passed ahead at this stage, we had spotted one of them, *Paper Moon*, far away to the south of us one night - the only other boat we saw on the whole trip. But of course we had started a day earlier than most of them.

By now we had settled into a daily routine and, strangely, I felt less tired than I had at the end of the first week. Perhaps this was due in part to the diminishing anxiety that came as the miles went by. One felt one was getting to know the ocean, and confidence built as we coped successfully with the conditions. But mostly it was just the diminishing miles to go to Antigua. As worry lessened, so boredom became a factor for me, although the others didn't seem to have the same problem. We all read a lot and were pleased we had brought a good supply of paperbacks. John had taken to reading French paperbacks, he found this made them last longer! The boat pretty well sailed herself on the windvane for much of the time and I found the long hours with little to do rather tedious. In this mood, little events assumed great importance. One looked at one's watch and observed there were only 35 minutes to twelve o'clock when we could have our daily beer! Happy hour at six o'clock brought a glass of wine or a rum and coke; it was a time when we were all awake and in the cockpit and brought some lively conversation. The cook for the day then disappeared below to prepare our one main meal, before we settled the boat down for the night at about eight o'clock.

The nights were quite long now that we were in the tropics; it was dark by six-thirty and not light again until six or so in the morning. Very different from an English summer. Before going to bed we would generally reduce sail a little in an effort to ensure a peaceful night, without too many problems for the watch-keeper. I found being at sea a tiring experience and had no difficulty going to sleep at eight-thirty or so, and I much preferred not being on the first watch from eight until eleven. When I was, I would sometimes struggle to keep awake. However, my brain seemed to recover quickly after three hours sleep and I had little difficulty waking up to do the eleven until two watch, and even less difficulty with the two until five. John was different. He seemed to find it difficult to go to sleep early, especially when I was on watch, as I used to like to keep a light on in the cabin. I found this helped me to stay awake and one could read, always remembering to pop up and take a look around at sensible intervals (approximately at the end of each page).

On most days I would get my sextant out and do a few sun sights or the moon if it was visible. This served to keep me in practice in case the GPS failed and was also a good way to while away the time. I was encouraged by the accuracy of the old traditional method, I often found a position within three miles of that given by the GPS. John and David were also both able to use a sextant, it must have been almost unique to have three capable navigators on one small boat.

By the end of our second week at sea we passed the '1000 miles to go'. These goals assumed an importance out of all proportion to their significance. All the way across we celebrated at the slightest excuse - ¼ the way across, 1000 miles out, ½ way, 1000 miles to go! I suppose this happens with any feat of endurance. Come to think of it, I seem to remember having the same sort of thoughts at boarding school as one anticipated the holidays. Listening to the chatter on the radio one could tell that other boats were having much the same experience. All the same, it seems a strange thing in some ways - as if we were not really enjoying ourselves. I never heard anyone express regret that the fascinating journey would soon be over! It all goes to show that it is the challenge that counts, we want the achievement under our belt, to have done it is the thing, even though the doing of it is not always much fun. I often wondered what kept the old explorers going, especially the real pioneers like Columbus, who did not even know there was land at the end.

Each day at ten o'clock and six, there was the radio net. All the boats in the rally were equipped with long-range, single side-band radios (the SSBs) so we were able to keep in touch over distances of many hundreds of miles. A number of boats took it in turns to be 'net controller'. Each boat was called up in turn and asked for their position and weather, and to confirm that all was well. In this way one always knew where the nearest boat was in case of trouble, although I was surprised how rarely we ever saw anyone else. The ocean is a very big place and visibility on a good day is not much more than 6 or 7 miles. We used to amuse ourselves by plotting each boat's position and then working out the mileage each had done since the last report. It also led to occasional sneering about the boats who were clearly using their engines. Sailors can be quite silly about this, as if there were something meritorious in sailing at two knots in near calm conditions with a tank full of fuel. I would have used ours much more if I had been able to carry more fuel. Some skippers seemed embarrassed to admit to motoring and would try various ruses to explain it away. They had to run their main engines to work their watermakers, so a favourite excuse was 'we're making water'. What, for 24 hours a day? It was all good fun; indeed the radio became an important source of amusement.

During our third week at sea Antigua drew steadily nearer, 1000 miles one day, 870 the next, 740 and so on. Morale was sky high, especially as the wind remained good and favourable and the sailing was straightforward and mostly fairly fast. At dawn on our 20th day there were only another 60 miles to go to our landfall off the famous Shirley Heights. I thought with luck we might make it into harbour in the last of the daylight. Then suddenly there it was, far off and fine on the starboard bow, a thin grey line just above the horizon - Antigua. I had been looking at this spot for some time before but couldn't be sure it wasn't just a line of cloud. But now there was no doubt and a loud cheer went up from all of us. It is hard to describe the elation one feels on sighting land after three weeks at sea.

By lunchtime the distance to go was down to a mere twelve miles and as the details of the fast approaching land became ever clearer, we hoisted our courtesy ensign for Antigua. We were soon off the famous English Harbour at the southern tip of the island, but there were still a few miles to go up the western coast to our destination at Jolly Harbour. This had been chosen as English Harbour was very crowded at that time of year, full of large vessels taking part in the annual charter boat show. We made good progress using the Goathorn Passage inshore of the Cade and Middle reefs and radioed through to 'rally control' before finally arriving at Jolly Harbour at 1735. Just off the harbour entrance, we were met by the ever-helpful Peter Seymour and Tony Diment in their dinghy and guided to our berth in the marina. We were the eighth boat to arrive and I was pleased with this even though we had started a day early.

Our crossing had taken 20 days, 9 hours and 35 minutes. The logged distance was 2,505 miles, so we had averaged 5.1 knots over the whole trip. We were soon invited over for drinks on *Miss Molly*; I remember rather little about the rest of that evening!

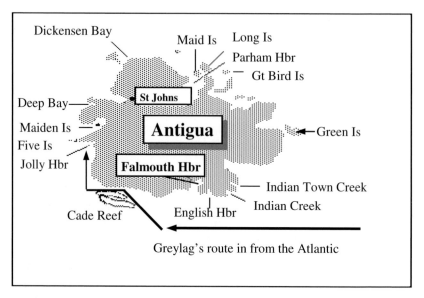

Dickensen Bay
Maid Is
Long Is
Parham Hbr
Gt Bird Is
Deep Bay
St Johns
Maiden Is
Antigua
Green Is
Five Is
Jolly Hbr
Falmouth Hbr
Indian Town Creek
Indian Creek
Cade Reef
English Hbr
Greylag's route in from the Atlantic

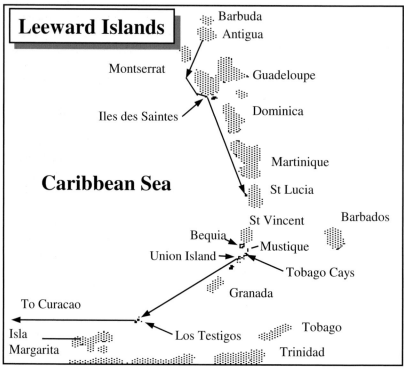

Leeward Islands

Barbuda
Antigua
Montserrat
Guadeloupe
Iles des Saintes
Dominica
Martinique
Caribbean Sea
St Lucia
St Vincent
Barbados
Bequia
Mustique
Union Island
Tobago Cays
Granada
To Curacao
Isla
Margarita
Los Testigos
Tobago
Trinidad

4 Antigua and South through the Leeward Islands

Our first few days in Antigua were almost continuous parties. The day after we had arrived other rally boats came in thick and fast. For the majority, it had been their first Atlantic crossing and so there was every reason to have a mighty celebration. As the arrivals were spread over the next three days, so indeed were the parties.

Jolly harbour had a wide range of facilities and we were able to catch up on our laundry and effect a few minor repairs to *Greylag*, and service the engine. The berthing manager, Philson Humphreys, was a most helpful fellow who could turn his hand to anything. We were having difficulty connecting up to the pontoon electricity supply, as it was a three-phase, 110-volt, American system. Phil soon had the front off the pillar and wired our cable directly into the supply wires at the back of the unit. I must confess I did a quick check with the voltmeter before switching on, but sure enough it was 240 volts all right.

The boatyard was busy with repairs to boats caught out in the recent hurricane *Luis* which had torn a path through the area, hitting a nearby island, St Martin, particularly badly. There were boats with their bows stove in and others with their topsides almost ground off as they had been driven against walls or onto the beach. It was a sobering sight. Some local boats had been lifted out and set in pits in the ground to reduce the windage. They seemed to have fared pretty well.

Alongside the marina there were shops, a bank, restaurants and a pub, the *Dogwatch,* which all of us will long remember. It was one of the cheaper places to eat and they ran a cabaret which reminded me of those seen in the old working men's clubs back home and was about as baudy! All these were within the perimeter of the marina, itself part of a larger development of holiday villas. With the possible exception of our livers, we very soon recovered from the voyage and with renewed energy we began to think about exploring Antigua. The warm sunshine and water at

28°C made everything looked most inviting.

Our first outing was a day trip up the coast to Deep Bay. John and Inga Chapman from *Calidris* came with us. It was only a few miles up the coast and there we had our first experience of snorkelling in the tropics, a pastime that was to become one of the most enjoyable experiences of the circumnavigation. Even John, who could barely swim at the start of our trip, began to make slow progress with confidence derived from a pair of flippers and a mask. As we lay at anchor in the bay, a reproduction old sailing ship came around the headland and into the bay. She flew the Jolly Roger and as she passed by, the gun hatches on our side fell open. For a moment I could have believed I was on Treasure Island. John added to the scene with his best Long John Silver imitation - 'there be no slittin' of throats 'til I gives the word lads!' Then it was all spoilt as dozens of pale skinned tourists appeared from below and gave the place the feel of a Butlin's holiday camp!

We returned to Jolly harbour via Maiden Island, in Five Islands Bay. The island was a roosting spot for hundreds of white egrets and pelicans and there were several nests with chicks. Over tea we watched the various nurseries, with their adult sentries guarding barely feathered, ugly and voracious offspring. Often at home I have watched gannets diving for fish. Pelicans do it in much the same way, but they are big birds with bills that one would hardly think helpful for a high dive. But just watch them. From about 50 feet they dive with their wings streamlined, head and neck held back and that huge bill projecting forward like the front of Concord. The success rate appeared quite high, not that one can see disappointment on the face of a pelican but it is easy to spot the lump in the throat!

Around the bay were the ruins of several old windmills, once part of the sugar plantations that thrived in so many parts of the Caribbean in the days of the slave trade. They caught the evening sunshine and stood out against the green and purple of the background hills, by now well shaded. We motored back to Jolly harbour as the descending sun grew less fierce, ever redder as it slipped behind the hills and threw a glorious claret over the western sky. *This is what I came for,* I thought.

A couple of days later we were again out by Five Islands for some snorkelling, when we heard that another small boat, *Sooty*, was due to arrive later that afternoon. She had trouble with her gearbox and would be unable to get into harbour without assistance, so we volunteered to give her a tow. Eventually she arrived with the last of the wind and we secured her alongside *Greylag*. Poor David and Jill, and their crew Roy Durrant, looked exhausted - it was now nearly a week since we had arrived in Antigua and all that time they had still been at sea. On our way into harbour we produced a round of cold beers from our fridge and I will always remember the looks of unbridled joy on their faces.

That evening there was a 'welcome to Antigua' party on the beach. It was a joyful occasion with a terrific buffet and a steel band to add local colour. The trials and tribulations of the ocean passage were now forgotten and hair was being let down with a vengeance. The evening ended with a bit of skinny-dipping. One did not know who was the guilty party nor would anyone confess to removing the random piles of clothing left on the beach. What everyone remembers is the remarkable, indeed impressive, sight of a gentleman wandering stark naked into the bar to enquire if anyone had seen his underpants! He subsequently developed a romantic attachment to a lady crewmember on one of the other boats. Perish the thought that this had anything to do with what she saw of him that night. They've been together ever since, the first of several rally romances, and now have a boat of their own.

The next few days were spent giving *Greylag* a spring clean ready for Janet's arrival on the 12th of December. I had phoned her to hear that there was snow on the ground at home and there were some worries about getting to the airport, so fingers were crossed. It may be perverse of me, but it always seems to add to the pleasure of the warm sunshine in the tropics, to hear of awful weather at home. Happily Janet's journey was straightforward and she arrived in good shape to be piped aboard by David and John (she was sometimes affectionately referred to as 'the admiral') and regaled with the many stories of our adventures so far.

Once Janet had settled in, we decided to do a trip right round Antigua. We could just about fit one in before my daughter Laurie and son-in-law Willie were due to arrive for Christmas. We set off north again from Jolly harbour, stopping briefly at Maiden Island and Deep Bay for another view of the pelicans and a snorkel, and then anchoring for the night in Dickenson Bay. It was a rather uncomfortable anchorage. The bay had a number of somewhat glitzy nightspots which held little appeal for us, but again we enjoyed watching the pelicans diving all around us for their evening meal.

Next day our objective was Maid Island, near the entrance to Parham Harbour on the north-east coast. There was a stiff trade wind blowing from the east, giving us a rough ride up past St Johns, the capital town, and across the north of the island. Up there the navigation became tricky, with narrow channels to negotiate and shallow patches, full of coral heads. This was our first experience of eyeball navigation, with a man up the mast (usually John) to spot the way through the hazards. In this territory one can move only in good sunlight, and preferably with the sun behind one, in order to see the various dangers. The charts do not record coral patches with sufficient accuracy; they grow quite rapidly sometimes. There is a rule which says '*if it's brown go round, if it's blue go through*' and this works surprisingly well in good conditions.

Our chart bore the caution *many experienced yachtsmen consider the north-east coast of Antigua, from Indian Town Creek to Horseshoe reef, is the most dangerous area in the entire Caribbean.* Maybe this once was true, but such is the accuracy of modern satellite navigation systems that I am not sure it is now quite so difficult as it was. We were quickly through the Boon Channel and the more challenging Prickly Pear Channel, and on to Parham Sound without nudging the bottom, although who knows what may have passed just under our keel. At Parham we took a little time to sort out the buoys which were not as marked on our chart. We had also to get used to the American system where the red buoys mark the starboard side of the channels going into harbour, the exact opposite to the system we were used to in Europe. *Red right returning* is the way to remember it.

Once we had sorted out the channel we were soon nudging up to Maid Island on the eastern edge of Parham Sound. Here was a perfect calm anchorage and we were soon ashore to explore. The Island consisted almost entirely of seashells and reminded me of Herm's shell beach in the Channel Islands, but without the tourists. We spent a peaceful night there, interrupted only by the occasional aircraft coming in to land at the nearby V.C.Bird airport.

Great Bird Island, a spot recommended to us by some locals, was a mere 2½ miles away. After a morning swim at Maid Island we made our way there, carefully dodging the coral reefs which abound in that corner of Antigua, and then feeling our way into a pretty little bay lying between the island to the north and a chain of islets to the south. There was a good sandy bottom for anchoring, but we had to approach carefully because the bay rapidly shallowed as we moved in. Once settled, we found ourselves in a picturesque spot and well sheltered from the north-east wind.

The edges of the bay were steep and rocky so we took the dinghy to the head of the bay where there was a good sandy beach for landing. The island was quite high and from the top we had a marvellous view over Parham Bay, with its myriad small islands and reefs. Flowering shrubs covered the island and clouds of white butterflies took flight as we made our way through the undergrowth. There were numerous lizards and in the bay to the north-west, we discovered one finishing off the contents of a tin of corned beef left there by some litterlout. Cacti that you would pay good money for at home, grew wild everywhere one looked.

But the real joy of Great Bird Island lay beneath the water. Around and between the islets to the south we found the snorkelling was superb. I had never really enjoyed this at home, the water is too cold and murky and there's not much to see anyway. Here it was riveting. It is difficult to find the words to do justice to that underwater paradise but I'll have a go. Come on; put your head in! Forests of coral stretch into the distance, so many shapes and colours. Great round domes of white brain coral, their surfaces patterned like giant golf balls. Pillar coral, finger coral, elk-horn coral, red flame-shaped coral, decorate the seabed forming elegant gardens of colour. Delicate fan corals wave gently with the movement of the water. And all this stunning scenery is alive with fish of every conceivable shape and colour - shoals of yellow striped goat-fish, brilliant blue and turquoise parrot fish, reddish squirrel fish with their big black eyes and, if you are lucky, a spectacular French angelfish, with its blue head and a black body flecked with iridescent gold. One lies on the surface enthralled with this underwater world, this natural paradise that never seems to lose its compelling interest.

That evening the wind showed signs of getting up a bit and I was a little anxious whether our anchor would hold in the rather coarse coral sand of the bay. We had on board some very long lines, in preparation for the huge locks of the Panama Canal. These now came in handy, as they were long enough to take ashore with the dinghy and tie securely to a stout palm tree. This was no place to drift away from at night and the lines ashore gave us considerable confidence, a better aid to sleep than any pill in the medical kit.

Next day we moved on south-east to visit Indian Town Creek, a narrow inlet that looked inviting on the chart. It was a blustery day and when we got there we found waves breaking over a reef, which at first sight seemed to obstruct the entrance to the creek. We lingered outside for a bit while studying the supposed entrance to see if there was a safe way in. The reef seemed to be rather more extensive than was suggested on the chart, extending three-quarters of the way across the entrance from the northern side. We crept in closer until we were able to discern a narrow channel, about 50 metres wide, unmarked and well over to the southern side of the creek. In we went, *Greylag* almost surfing over the rolling waves in the entrance.

Inside was a visual treat, a steep-sided cove with pleasant houses in spectacular gardens on the north-west shore and a dramatic rock formation, the *Devil's Bridge*, opposite. We were tempted to stay for the night but I was anxious that the difficult entrance could become impossible if the wind came in strongly from the north-east and we might find ourselves trapped. So we had a pleasant lunch and left. Getting out was less worrying than entering, it was easier to see the extent of the rocks from the inside as they were not so hidden behind the breaking surf. Nevertheless, this was no place for the timid.

Moving on south-east, we passed outside an extensive reef that prevented entry into Nonsuch Bay from the east, and then skirted round the eastern end of Green Island and along the southern coast to Rickett's Harbour. This was not really a harbour at all, but it was the most attractive bay with a back-cloth of high hills covered in green scrub which protected the bay from the prevailing wind. There were several good spots to anchor and we settled for one just off a white sand cove at the eastern corner. Green Island is undeveloped and uninhabited, in fact the island around Rickett's Harbour is covered with impenetrable scrub and cacti making it almost impossible to leave the beach - not that anyone would find that much of a hardship! We spent the day doing nothing energetic beyond Janet fashioning Coco the hedgehog from a coconut lying on the sand.

It was five days since we had left Jolly Harbour and time to move on south to English harbour - by now less crowded, as the charter boat show had finished. On our way there we visited Indian Creek, a hurricane hole running deep into the high ground just east of Shirley heights, and not to be confused with Indian Town Creek with its difficult entrance. A hurricane hole is a place of refuge where boats can hide when a warning is given. This particular one was an almost circular cove, about 200 metres across, lying inland behind high cliffs and entered via an S-shaped channel. Once in, we could not see the open sea and the degree of protection was phenomenal. There were extensive mangroves on one side, to which one could secure the boat if necessary. Of course, it was not the hurricane season when we were there and the very protection the place offered rendered it stiflingly hot and full of mosquitoes. We watched two local fishermen throwing a circular net with great skill and after a short stay we moved on.

That night we were in English Harbour. The English colonisers came to the Caribbean after the Spanish and French but were the first to establish significant naval bases to defend their interests. English Harbour is the most famous, probably because it was occupied by Lord Nelson for three years from 1784. The place is steeped in English naval history and full of Nelsonian memorabilia. If we saw one anchor said to belong to Nelson we must have seen a dozen! Nelson's Dockyard has been restored but I found it a bit too neat and commercialised, with large numbers of trading stalls and the usual collection of restaurants and shops.

Despite the ending of the boat show, the quays and anchorages were crowded and we eventually settled for a quiet spot in the upper part of the harbour. That evening we were enjoying our gins and tonic when the peace was broken by a large generator starting up on an old workboat lying close by. We tolerated it for a while but in the end patience was exhausted. We were about to take the dinghy over to remonstrate with the owner, when we noticed a neighbour from a Belgian boat beating us to it. John went over to give the fellow some moral support. He came back with the story.

'You vill turn ze generator off in ten minutes, ya?' The Belgian had said. He was a huge fellow and towered over the diminutive owner.

'But it's on to cook my dinner and watch TV', he replied defensively.

'No', said the Belgian, 'you meesunderstand me. You *vill* turn it off in ten minutes.'

John, who is also a fairly big chap, was already in the generator room in case disablement of the nuisance became necessary (the generator, that is, not the owner!) It didn't. Silence came after the stated 10 minutes. Big friends can be useful.

After a quick tour around Nelson's dockyard next day, we moved on round the headland and into Falmouth Harbour. In the marina off the Antigua Yacht Club there was a fine array of super-yachts. They made poor *Greylag* seem even smaller than she was, and made us all feel poor in comparison to the owners of those gleaming monsters. As if to rub it in, we had taken advantage of *Greylag's* shallow draught and parked inside the innermost finger pontoon. When I went to pay, the fellow in the yacht club laughed and said we were actually in the dinghy-park for which there was no charge. I got over the humiliation for sound financial reasons!

We wandered around the super-yachts with a mixture of scoffing and envy, in the way one does. One monster had a fully fitted gymnasium in the stern, complete with an array of exercise machines and a Jacuzzi. Another had its private seaplane on deck. Several had launches on davits that were pretty much the same size as *Greylag*.

Morris Bay, Antigua

On our way back to Jolly harbour a day or two later, we stopped at the Cade Reef, off the south-west corner of Antigua, for some more spectacular snorkelling. There were large shoals of black surgeon fish there, a species we hadn't seen before. Back at Jolly it was time to start thinking about Christmas. My daughter and her husband had rented one of the holiday apartments at Jolly Harbour, and there was a spare room for Janet and me. It was marvellous to have this short break from the boat and it left John and David with more room on *Greylag*.

Christmas day started on the pontoons with a little carol singing and a lot of champagne, generously provided by two of the rally boats, *Pale Moon* and *Baker Street*. It was a good party but somehow I struggled to feel that this was really Christmas. Of course, Australians must see things differently, but for we Europeans the carols, Santa Claus, roast turkey and Christmas pudding are part of a winter festival inextricably linked with snow, ice, reindeer and log fires. It may be sentimental but that's how it is. If the reality of December's weather is sometimes different, we create the imagery with spray foam and cotton wool - as the song says, 'May all your Christmases be white...'

When King Wenceslas took his young crew on their charity cruise, it was snow that lay about 'deep and crisp and even', not sand. *Why*, I thought, *are we so attached to our traditions? What would be wrong with stuffed parrot and papayas or a festival of nine calypsos accompanied by a steel band?* I suppose it just wouldn't be the same! So what do most of us do? We take our traditions with us. In among the warps and chains, the engine spares and scuba gear, people had secreted plastic Christmas trees and strings of fairy lights. *Greylag* even had a Christmas pudding. Across the harbour one American yacht sported a huge array of lights arranged tree-style between his masts; if he'd had the Salvation Army band he would not have been out of place in Trafalgar Square! One wit complained of riding turns in his tinsel as he winched up another bizarre Christmas creation.

At lunchtime the crews from the rally boats still at Jolly harbour, (some had gone to English Harbour for Christmas), gathered on the beach for a splendid Caribbean barbecue and some rather athletic party games which seemed, as they always do, hilariously funny at the time. A young lady engaged Willie in conversation.

'What do you do for a living?' She asked rather directly.

' I'm a surgeon,' Willie replied, dead pan.

' Do you have to go to Uni for that?'

But I missed the walk in December's crisp air after Christmas lunch, the Queen's speech, that warm, relaxed glow with Handel's Messiah in the evening - but not that much. A glass or two of champagne, shared with congenial friends, waist deep in the blue Caribbean Sea, soon mellowed the memory and took away the pain.

After Christmas, having seen enough of Antigua's coastline, it was a pleasure to share Laurie and Willie's hire car for an inland trip. We visited St Johns, a bustling town full of contrasts between smart shops for the tourists and the wealthy, and the rather ramshackle streets with dilapidated houses and markets for the others. We drove out to Indian Town Creek, the place where we had made that scary entrance on *Greylag* a week or so before. Now, on a brilliant calm day, we could see the entrance channel easily and it was hard to remember how difficult it had been.

My most abiding memory of inland Antigua is of our visit to Betty's Hope, a partly restored, old sugar plantation with a small museum alongside. We wandered around the old slave quarters and their work places and I was impressed with the savagery of that era and depressed that so much of it had been inspired by the British. In the museum we studied a list of the slaves, just Christian names - Joshua, Abel, Eliza…The journal recorded how they had died and detailed some of the punishments dealt out by the feudal system of justice. Many of the sugar plantations were owned by absentee landlords living in Berkeley Square, enjoying the wealth created by this slave labour, driven by the merciless, whip-hands of their plantation managers. On the walls were copies of letters written to the descendants of some of the owners, seeking contributions to the cost of restoration and maintenance of this sad memorial to the victims of a dark past. Astonishingly some of these had been refused. I left Betty's Hope in a sombre, thoughtful mood. How easy it is to forget this side of Caribbean history amid the gaiety and light-heartedness of so many of the present population.

New Year's Eve brought another splendid party, this time it was at the Catamaran Club in Falmouth bay. By now we had been in Antigua for nearly a month and the feeling that it was time to move on grew steadily - *harbours rot ships and men*! Janet returned home on the second of January. The same day we completed our exit procedures and prepared the boat for an early departure next day.

Our first destination on the voyage south through the chain of Leeward Islands was the Iles de Saintes, a small group of islands just beyond Guadeloupe. We had to leave Jolly Harbour at the atrociously early hour of 0300 in order to be sure we could cover the 82 miles before darkness made an entrance dangerous. En route we had a splendid view of Montserrat on our starboard side. Its volcano smouldered away, a long plume of smoke drifting north-westwards, but it gave little sign then of the horrors that were to follow a couple of years later when it erupted.

At Iles de Saintes we anchored in the lee of Ilet de Cabrit, and enjoyed watching the goats making their precarious way around the cliffs of that precipitous islet. Next day we met up with some other rally boats anchored close to Pain de Sucre, an accurate description of that prominent headland. *Sheet Lightning, Papa Golf, Gaviota* and *Vandal* were there, interestingly all of them from the smaller end of the fleet. Our plan was to press on south quickly to leave time to visit some of the small islands off the north coast of Venezuela, and also the San Blas reservation on the Caribbean side of Panama, before the date we were due at the entrance to the Canal.

Therefore, after less than 24 hours, we were at sea again, making our way south to St Lucia. This was a 120-mile overnight trip down the western coast of Dominica and across the Dominica Channel to the Rodney Bay Marina, at the northern end of St Lucia. There we found two old friends, *Triton,* who we had first met at La Rochelle on our way down to Gibraltar, and *Hygea,* belonging to Kiko and Mie Rutter, who had been

Marigot Bay, St Lucia

neighbours of ours at Farnham. Triton had intended to join the Atlantic
Rally for Cruisers (inevitably known as the ARC), a similar organisation to
the Trade Wind Rally but limited to crossing the Atlantic. However, they
had missed the start in the Canaries and had come over later on their own.
Hygea had done the ARC but was now deserted as Kiko, poor fellow, had
to return to the UK to go back to work.

   We stayed at Rodney Bay only long enough to restock our supplies,
and then moved on eight miles down the coast to Marigot Bay. Here was
another 'hurricane hole' but a huge contrast to the one we had visited at
Indian Creek, Antigua. Marigot Bay is stunningly attractive, with
relatively deep water and good moorings. Not surprisingly it has become
hugely popular both for visiting boats and for parties of tourists who arrive
there overland by the coach load. There is also a large charter boat base.
Our night was slightly disturbed by returning drunks.

   Next day we moved on to the Anse de Pietons, another dramatically
picturesque and famous spot further south down the coast. As we arrived,
a young man in a dinghy driven by an over-powered outboard motor met
us. He was insistent that he would find us a mooring for which service, it

was clear, he would expect a few dollars. This was rather irritating, as we didn't need help to find the obvious mooring buoys and pick one up. Just behind us another boat was arriving and they received a similar offer from yet

The Pietons, St Lucia

another boat boy. They were quicker to accept the terms and were already tying up when we arrived with our 'lad' at the same buoy. There followed a vociferous row between the two boat boys; it appeared to be a dispute over who had the rights over this particular mooring buoy! Eventually the dispute was settled, but it left an unpleasant atmosphere which contrasted greatly with the extraordinary, awe-inspiring view of the Pietons. The majestic rock pinnacles rose almost vertically, several hundred feet from the sea, creating a dramatic skyline and causing, as we soon discovered, a good deal of disturbance to the wind flow in the bay. This made the moorings uncomfortable and the night was a bit restless.

Next day we witnessed further altercations with the local 'traders'. This time it was *Gambatte Go*, a large catamaran on the rally, that got involved. A man selling fruit came by with a boatload of bananas and papayas and some slightly tired looking pineapples. He tried to persuade Taka and Kiki, our Japanese friends on *Gambatte*, to buy some. They were unimpressed with the quality and declined. Whereupon the fellow chucked a few papayas onto *Gambatte* and retreated to a safe (he thought) distance, from where he demanded payment for the unwanted fruit. He reckoned without Taka, however, who leapt into his dinghy, also with a reasonably powerful outboard, and chased the fellow round the anchorage, eventually getting close enough to return the fruit in much the same way as it had been delivered! I mention these tales because they serve to illustrate the forceful, almost hostile, selling techniques one meets occasionally in the Caribbean and which do so much to damage one's enjoyment of otherwise attractive places.

One night at the Pietons was enough and next day we set out for Bequia, 55 miles to the south. The trip was fast in a strong reaching breeze and we were soon safely anchored in Admiralty Bay. In contrast to St Lucia, we found Bequia both pretty and hospitable. The bay's perimeter is thick with trees behind which nestle a number of pleasant little cafes and restaurants where one can eat and still be in sight of the boat. This always aids the skipper's digestion.

On our way into harbour we had noticed a fast dinghy circling around, with a man with an expensive looking camera at the wheel. Early next day he came around the anchorage. He introduced himself as Tim Wright and presented us with a set of magnificent photos of *Greylag* under full sail as she had entered the harbour. His prices were pretty reasonable but I explained that we would be there only for one day which didn't seem enough time to get enlargements done, let alone framing. However, he assured us it could be done by late afternoon that day so we ordered several prints and one framed enlargement. Sure enough, he came by later with the photos and we were impressed with the quality of his work. We were also impressed with the success of his initiative as we noticed he had deliveries for a dozen other boats on the anchorage. We talked with Tim for a bit and it transpired that he had sailed himself to Bequia a few years back on one of the earlier ARC rallies. He had fallen in love with the place and decided to stay and set up the photographic business to earn an income. He had clearly made a great success of this; having arrived on an old 29-foot, 'Elizabethan' sloop; he now owned a forty footer!

Just as we were beginning to think that Bequia was free from some of the problems of the other islands, we heard that Graham and Mary Watts on *Hilda* had had their dinghy stolen during the night. Apparently the thieves had come alongside when the crew were asleep and simply cut the dinghy's painter and towed it away. After that most of us took to pulling the dinghies up on deck overnight. Another ruse, for use in the daytime, is to have an old dinghy that one can leave attached to the boat when the crew goes ashore. This encourages would be thieves to assume there is somebody aboard and they choose someone else! Techniques have become subtler than in the days of Joshua Slocum, the first yachtsman to sail alone around the world, who used to spread tintacks over the deck to warn him if the barefoot Indians of South America came aboard. *Hilda's* loss was the only small stain on Bequia's reputation and we left with a favourable impression of that pretty island. We moved south again to

Admiralty Bay, Bequia

Mustique, a mere 8 miles away.

Our night in Brittania Bay, Mustique, was spent gazing through binoculars at the sumptuous houses of the seriously rich who use the island as an escape hole. But the anchorage was not very comfortable, so despite the excellent snorkelling, we moved on next day to the famous Tobago Cays. This was an extraordinary location and it was easy to see why it was so popular. The small islands stand in the middle of a lagoon of turquoise water inside an encircling reef. There were about a hundred boats at anchor there, but we found a spot in the lee of Jamesby Island where we spent a peaceful night after an afternoon's snorkelling over the reef.

Next day we left the main lagoon and travelled outside the Horseshoe Reef to the south and on to Petit Tabac Island. This was a gem of a spot but needed calm conditions to be comfortable. We anchored south of the island and used the dinghy to travel around to the north side where there was a sandy beach for landing. We were amazed to find a New Zealand boat in the tiny lagoon there. He had gone around in the very narrow channel and was anchored with no less than four anchors to keep his boat centred over the only patch of sand among the coral heads (and I thought we were adventurous).

After a morning at Petit Tabac, we set out on the short passage to

Union Island where we planned to check out of St Vincent, the island which also controls the Grenadines and Tabago Cays. Clifton Bay at Union Island was to be our last port of call in the West Indies before moving on to the Venezuelan islands. It had been a lightning tour; we had left Antigua on the 4th of January and would leave Union Island on the 11th of January. One week in the Leeward Islands had given us time for only a few glimpses of this popular part of the world. For myself, I had been a little disappointed. Much of the Caribbean is beautiful, some of it spectacular, but its very popularity (and closeness to the US) means that it is crowded with tourists and there are numerous charter boats. The main ports seemed expensive and we did not always find a friendly welcome. I looked forward to finding some lonelier spots further along our track, and the first of these was now very close.

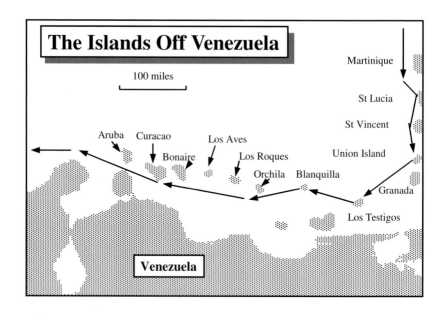

The Islands Off Venezuela

100 miles

Martinique

St Lucia

St Vincent

Aruba Curacao   Los Aves

Bonaire   Los Roques   Union Island

Orchila Blanquilla

Granada

Los Testigos

Venezuela

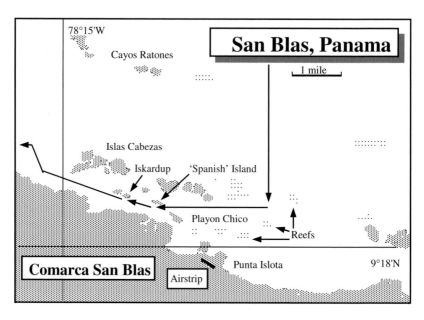

78°15'W

San Blas, Panama

Cayos Ratones

1 mile

Islas Cabezas

Iskardup   'Spanish' Island

Playon Chico

Reefs

Comarca San Blas

Airstrip

Punta Islota

9°18'N

5 Through the Venezuelan Islands to San Blas

Along the northern coast of Venezuela lie several groups of islands extending from Los Testigos in the east, to Curacao in the Netherlands Antilles in the west. They provide attractive stopping places on the way to the Panama Canal and shorten what would otherwise be a long passage. After leaving Union Island we set our course for an overnight trip of 118 miles to Los Testigos.

The first half of the trip was straightforward but further down the track we became aware of a strong westerly current tending to set us off to the west of our course. This develops under the influence of the consistent easterly trade winds in this part of the world and can be quite strong, perhaps a knot or two. As soon as we noticed it, thanks to the marvels of the GPS system which gives a read-out of the distance off course (the so-called cross-track error), we headed the boat about 10 degrees to the south to offset the effect and this kept us on our course. We had left Union Island at about 1600 hours on the 11th of January and by breakfast time the next day we caught our first glimpse of the islands. Our landfall was at Isla Norteste from where we travelled south-west, leaving Isla Conejo to starboard, and then rounding the southern tip of Isla Testigo Grande to anchor off the little village of Tamarindo.

As we approached Isla Testigo Grande the skies became filled with hundreds of frigate birds, circling in the thermals over the island. They are such graceful creatures in flight, about the size of our own gannets but black instead of white. The males have a vivid red pouch below the neck that they inflate as a form of display. The sea was pretty rough until we rounded that southern tip of the island and then suddenly we were in the lee of it and all went blissfully quiet. At Tamarindo there is a small island, L'Angoleta, joined to the main island by a reef; this provided excellent shelter for the anchorage on its north-western side. We crept in as close to the shore as the depth of water would allow and found a good sandy area to drop our anchor.

Tamarindo, Isla Testigo Grande

Officially we should have reported to the customs and immigration man at the nearby Isla Iguana village, on the other side of the bay. However, we did have Venezuelan visas so we were not all that worried about the formalities and decided to risk staying put at Tamarindo. It was the weekend and we saw no sign of officials - we believed they must go home on a Friday evening!

Tamarindo is home to a few hundred Venezuelans, mainly fishermen and their families. They send their catches by small boat to the market at Porlamar on the island of Margarita, quite a trip as it is nearly 50 miles away. We found them happy-go-lucky people, very friendly and quick to trade you fish in return for a few beers. We purchased a lobster in this way - actually it was a 'painted crayfish' and quite the most delicious crustacean I have ever eaten; better by far, I thought, than European lobsters. The houses were functional rather than pretty, but not unattractive. A communal washing and shower facility was at the eastern end of the village but we never discovered whether visitors could use it. The village had a power supply from generators and we were amazed to see street lighting along the main 'street', which was actually only an earthen pathway. A few surprises lay in wait, one was a completely hairless dog.

Behind the village the land rose steeply to 807 feet where a substantial lighthouse had been built. The light was working while we were there and could be seen from all directions around the island. Our pilot book said the view from the top was spectacular but none of us had the energy to make the climb, even though John was usually keen to do such things - perhaps he hadn't yet recovered from his ascent of Mount Teide, back in Tenerife. There was a pathway across the island leading to some spectacular sand dunes on the northern side. The weather was hot and we soon took to the water and found some of the best snorkelling we had yet come across. The water was as gin clear.

For our second day at Los Testigos we moved a mile or so up the coast to a pretty little cove where we anchored for our second night. Here again the snorkelling was excellent and I enjoyed finding a French angelfish and also my first moray eel, a spotted one. They are rather fierce looking creatures but will normally leave you alone if you do the same for them. I went ashore from this new anchorage and wandered around that end of the island. Parts of it were like the set for a western movie, with many large cacti standing, pillar-like, across the landscape. There were highly coloured lizards and an occasional iguana, prehistoric looking creatures that wouldn't look out of place in Jurassic Park. There were also snakes. I discovered this while creeping up on a lizard with my camera at the ready. There was a sudden movement, swift as lightning, and a snake grabbed the poor lizard. It gave me such a jump that my finger involuntarily pressed the camera shutter and I got a splendid photo. I wandered around for an hour and never saw another soul, just the sort of place I had hoped to find.

Returning to the cove, I found John and David in animated conversation with two local fisherman, Juan and Jose, who had beached their boat on the sandy shoreline. They explained that they had come for water and to have a shower and invited John and David to go with them. It turned out that there was a freshwater spring a little way up the hill behind the cove - a useful thing to know if one was short of water. After they had filled their cans they showered themselves using an old plastic safety hat as a scoop. John and David joined in, any opportunity for a shower was not to be missed. I mention this little encounter as typical of the friendly contact one can have with the people in these rather remote places. Talk to them, with signs if necessary and you will usually find a friendly reception and a great deal of charm and good humour.

One of the problems of being on a rally was the need to keep up with the timetable; our next deadline was the 1st of February when we had to be at Colon to prepare for our transit of the Panama Canal. For the first time

I thought how nice it would have been to have had more time to explore those islands, but one had to accept the bad with the good. For we newly retired fellows this was occasionally frustrating, but there were others on the rally who were just on a 2-year career break or between university and a job. Regrettably we had to press on or we would not have time to visit the Kuna Indian reservation at San Blas, which we were all very keen to do.

We left Los Testigos on the evening of the 13th of January for an overnight passage to Blanquilla, another small island about 75 miles to the west. Just before the island a group of islets, Los Hermanos, some little more than large rocks, lay across the track to Blanquilla. We watched them carefully on our radar screen, as it was still dark when we passed by and we needed to give them a wide berth. By seven o'clock next day, we were anchored off a small village about half way along the south coast. I visited the coastguard station and lied that we had come direct from Union Island - this was to avoid having to give explanations for not checking in at Los Testigos. I also assured them that we would check in properly when we visited the mainland in a few days; surprisingly we changed our minds about this and sailed direct to Curacao!

Shortly after our arrival a Swiss yacht, *Sarah le Noire*, came by and anchored alongside us. Pierre and Christina, with their young son Louis, came over to say hello. They were serious long-term cruisers and tremendously experienced. Pierre was a surgeon and explained his unique work escape plan. Each year he would return to Switzerland during the peak holiday period and stand locum for surgical colleagues while they had their holidays. This kept him in sufficient funds to go sailing for the rest of the year! We mentioned that we were on the Tradewinds Rally and straightaway he said he knew a Japanese surgeon, who he had met when sailing in Japan, and who he thought was also on the rally. This of course was Taka. We had seen Taka fairly recently at St Lucia so it was possible that he might not be too far away. We offered to call him up on the SSB radio at the evening net to find out where he was.

Meanwhile, both yachts moved round to an anchorage off the west of the island, at Playa Yaque. This was easy to identify as it sported a small clump of palm trees, the only ones for miles. We had to approach carefully as there were a lot of coral heads along this coast, but the water was crystal clear and they were easy to see. As at Los Testigos, the snorkelling was excellent. There were a few holidaymakers camping on the beach, apparently they had come over from the mainland by boat and were completely self-sufficient for a week or two.

That evening we called up Taka on the radio and were amazed to find that he was a mere 28 miles away to the north, en route for Curacao. What a small world it can be sometimes. Taka diverted south and arrived late that evening; we guided him into the anchorage with a mixture of flashing lights and VHF messages. There followed a splendid reunion party on *Sarah le Noire*.

We left Blanquilla early next day (that schedule again) heading for Curacao. This was a slightly longer trip with two nights at sea, but we had a good wind and made fast progress. On the second night we were just south of Isla des Aves when John and Inga on *Calidris*, who were just leaving those islands and heading for Curacao like us, called us on the radio. We watched each other's lights through the night before arriving off Spanze (Spanish) Water, on the southern coast of Curacao at first light. We had to wait for good daylight before making an entry into the harbour and wending our way up to Sarifundy's marina. This turned out to be a splendid spot so it was hardly surprising that we found several other rally yachts already there - *Griffyn, Hilda, Saullitaire, Best Respects, Ocean Gypsy, and Gaviota*. With *Calidris* and us, this made a total of eight rally boats - the most we had seen together since leaving Antigua.

Sarifundy's was a splendid institution. There was a bar/restaurant with a unique honour system of accounting. One helped oneself to beers etc from the fridge and wrote the number against one's name on the board! On trust like this, apparently nobody cheated. The owner had started up as a service agent for Yamaha outboards and gradually expanded with additional services so that now there was almost nothing one could not obtain from Sarifundy's - showers, laundry, evening meals, bread, car hire and a bus service to the local supermarket were but a few.

Curacao is part of the Netherlands Antilles and checking in required a substantial journey into the town of Willemstadt. As John and David needed the only available vehicle to do the shopping, I volunteered to ride my folding bike into town to check us in. It was nearly the death of me. Soon after leaving the marina I was passing through a small residential area when a group of three, savage-looking dogs ran out after me. They looked menacing so I tried a bit of sweet talk to no avail. Then the leader of the gang launched an attack, sinking his teeth into the toe of my sandal, stuck out to fend him off. This raised blood and panic began to set in. With three of them all threatening to join in, I decided to escape as best I could. Now a Brompton folding bike is a splendid machine but no one would claim it was the fastest pair of pedal driven wheels they had come across. So it may surprise you that mine left that location at about 40 mph, hotly pursued by the dogs, my terror-driven legs working like the pistons on the Royal Scot! Luckily the dogs gave up the chase and as soon as I had put a safe distance between us, I stopped to tie a hanky around my bleeding toe. I was thankful for having had my rabies injections before leaving home.

Willemstadt was a pleasant town and it was easy to feel oneself back in Holland, such was the influence of the colonial power on the local architecture. The harbour sported a floating market, full of fruit and veg brought over by boat from the Venezuelan mainland. I completed the formalities, did a bit of shopping and set out to return to the marina. Approaching the dog country my courage failed me and I sat by the roadside until someone came by in a car and kindly agreed to give me a lift. I was mighty grateful.

That evening we all met in Sarifundy's to discuss arrangements for the next leg. There were a few problems, as we now had to skirt around the coast of Columbia before crossing the south-west Caribbean to Panama. Columbia, with its drug runners and pirates, posed a threat to yachtsmen and all of us planned to give the country a wide berth of at least 100 miles. We were concerned that the daily net, in which we all reported our positions, was a bit of a give-away as many modern pirates tune into the radio to find out where likely victims might be found. Some have even been known to send out Maydays to lure unsuspecting yachtsmen into false rescue missions and enable the pirates to rob them. A solution to this latter problem emerged at Sarifundy's that evening. We would give our positions in a coded form by adding 10 degrees to the latitude and longitude. Thus a boat at, say, 12°N, 72°W, would report her position as 22°N, 82°W. Henceforth, we all agreed, this would be known as the Spanish position! We opened a competition for the best, illustrated description.

We left Spanze Water early next morning and headed west in a good sailing breeze. South of Curacao there were massive shoals of flying fish, so many in fact that I was able to get some good video of them. Usually by the time one had got the camera out they had disappeared but here they were all over the place, emerging from the water in shoals, flying for perhaps 50 yards before splashing back into the sea. They seemed a bigger species than those we had seen in the Atlantic.

We planned our route with a wide berth around Columbia and kept our fingers crossed that we wouldn't meet any trouble. On the second day out from Curacao, we were visited by the US Coastguard. They flew around us and called up on the radio, asking our name and where we were headed. We responded with the details, and after exchanging greetings, they disappeared. It was comforting to know that the US patrols this bit of coast so thoroughly.

On the evening of the next day the wind started to increase and we had to shorten sail considerably. 'David', on the yacht *Mistine,* an amateur forecaster who gave an excellent daily forecast over the radio, had suggested things would improve but the forecast on the rally radio net had been less encouraging. The latter was right. That night the wind increased up to a full gale - our first since leaving home. Luckily it came from the east and we were able to keep sailing downwind before it, with only a tiny slip of headsail held firmly with a spinnaker pole. The sea became big and several times we took waves in over the stern. But the water soon drained out of the cockpit drains and things remained manageable if uncomfortable. Our Hydrovane windvane coped well with the conditions; this made life easier for the helmsman. By morning the wind began to ease and the improvement continued as we sailed south past 11°N and on towards our destination on the northern coast of Panama. We now expected to arrive there early the next day, the 23rd of January, after 4 days at sea. John and Ruth Roberts in *Griffyn* were close behind us and heading for the same spot.

The San Blas reservation stretches for a hundred miles along the northern coast of Panama. Yachts normally enter at Porvenir at the western end where there is a customs and immigration office but that would involve back-tracking east if one wanted to see more of the reservation than just the touristy, western end. We had heard that it was possible in moderate weather to enter further east and with the help of a rather poor photocopied chart, we had planned what looked like a reasonable entrance through the reefs. There is a small island called Iskardup, we had been told, with an airstrip on it and lying a mile north-east of a headland called Islote Point. The headland was marked on our chart but not Iskardup, which could have been any one of several small islands in the vicinity. We set our landfall waypoint at a safe distance to seaward of the outer reefs and another inside them where there was a wide channel to enter. Once there, we decided, we should be able to eyeball our way in, as we would be within a mile of Islote point.

We arrived off the reef in the early afternoon with good sunlight to help us in. *Griffyn* was with us and it was decided that we should go first as we had considerably less draft than the big Fisher 46. We pressed on towards our inshore waypoint and reached it without difficulty. There had been no shallow water on the way, so we radioed *Griffyn* and she followed us in. At the inner waypoint we hesitated, confused by the plethora of small islands, none of which coincided with the co-ordinates we had been given for Iskardup. We were surrounded by white water breaking on the reefs east and west of us. We were reviewing our position while we still had the option to return safely to sea, when a small plane came over and landed on Islote point. 'That must be it', someone said, remembering that we had been told there was an airstrip on Iskardup. But it wasn't. The airstrip was clearly on the mainland and there was no way through the reefs in that direction. Navigational confidence was now beginning to wane so I fell back on basics. North of the airstrip I could see an island covered with the palm-thatched huts of a Kuna village. Between the village and another island to the north-west, we spotted two yachts at anchor.

'That must be safe water', I said, 'we'll try to get there, drop the hook and leave finding Iskardup until tomorrow.'

The reef-hopping experience we had gained back in Antigua now paid dividends as we slowly picked our way between the various patches of white water lying between us and the Kuna village. I was pleased we hadn't spent all the time there in Jolly harbour. The lumpy sea was helpful as the waves broke over the shallow bits and made them easier to spot. What followed was pure magic. The sea quietened down as we approached the village and slowly the shores became lined with Kuna Indians, ones and twos at first, then dozens - men, women, and children galore. It seemed that the whole village had turned out to welcome us, happy smiling faces, children waving, all a riot of colourful clothing against the background of primitive wooden huts with palm-thatched roofs, crowded so close together that some of them edged over the sea on stilts. It was a joyful sight and all of us were moved by it, the more so as it came with a huge sense of relief, following our exciting passage through the reefs.

Ahead lay a small island, all white sand and palm trees, with the two, anchored yachts in the lee to the south-west. I approached the first, *Borromeo;* she was flying a Spanish flag.

'Excuse me', I said to the gentleman in the cockpit, 'but could you tell me which of these islands is Iskardup.'

'It's that one over there, the way is clear from here,' he replied in perfect English.

His name was Juan de las Barcenas and his quiet reassurance was much appreciated. Mind you, he volunteered that he had never seen anyone come in there from the east. I believed him.

I cast an eye back to *Griffyn* just as John came through on the VHF to say he had gone aground. There he was just off the village and surrounded by dozens of canoes whose occupants appeared to be thoroughly enjoying the fun. Luckily John had a neat little hand-held echo sounder, and one of his crew was driving around in the dinghy to try to locate the deeper water. With the help of a large anchor, *Griffyn* hauled herself off the sandbank and followed us up to the anchorage off Iskardup Island. We settled ourselves down in the last of the daylight. Everyone was dog-tired and we slept like logs.

Next morning I peeked out of my cabin to see what kind of place it was that had been so hard won the previous day. I caught my breath, standing there in the still light of dawn, amidst the most picturesque surroundings imaginable. I recall thinking *'Why go round the world if one could stay here forever.'* Romantic nonsense of course, but it was that sort of place.

Iskardup is a very small island, barely 150 x 100 metres, covered with coconut palms and surrounded by coral reefs, extending from east to west around the northern side of the island. The anchorage on the southern shore is thus well protected, and we found we could get quite close to the Island, as there was deep water almost to the sandy beach. Astonishingly there was a 'hotel'. It consisted of about a dozen small round huts with thatched roofs, two beds and a loo. Clearly it was a place for one of those unusual holidays out in the wild. It had all been constructed in sympathy with the surroundings, so that it somehow added to the attraction of the place. On the southern side was a small restaurant and outside this, a large banner was stretched across some bushes, it read 'Welcome to the Trade Winds Rally'. One of our managers must have told them some of us might visit.

A number of Cayocos, I would have called them dug-out canoes, were drawn up on the beach - one large one had an outboard motor and was probably the supply vessel. It would also have been used to convey guests from the airstrip at Islote point to the Island. All around the bay we saw other canoes sailed by the diminutive Kuna Indians, scarcely bigger than the African pygmies. They sported a variety of sails made from just about anything handy - old bedspreads, flour bags, pieces of polythene sheeting. Yet the ever-smiling Kuna handled them with consummate skill.

Iskardup

To the west lay another island, barely half a mile away, uninhabited and green with palm. A mile or so to the east was 'Spanish Island', as we had named it after the two Spanish boats anchored there, and the more substantial Cabezas further offshore to the north. They provided an effective barrier against the vigorous western Caribbean Sea so that once inside this outer barrier the whole area was relatively tranquil, astonishingly beautiful against the blue and green backdrop formed by the high Panamanian hills separating San Blas from the Pacific Ocean beyond. I thought of the Spanish pioneer Balboa who had once stood on those hills and been the first man to see the Pacific Ocean. South-east of Iskardup, about a mile away was the Kuna village of Playon Chico where we had first arrived after our hair-raising journey through the reefs.

In the two days after our arrival we knew that another 5 yachts were planning to come in, more or less on the same route we had used. This caused ourselves and the *Griffyn* crew some concern, as there was plenty of potential for an accident in those dangerous waters. We decided to go back by dinghy to our entry point and guide them in through the coral reefs. Luckily they arrived in two groups so we organised a couple of convoys with us at the head, and John's daughter Judy using the portable echo sounder to map out a channel. They all got in without mishap so that by the evening of our second day there, *Greylag* and *Griffyn* had for company

Papa Golf, Ocean Gypsy, Hilda, Gambatte Go and Luck of Argent.
On one day we visited the village. After paying our respects (and giving a present) to the headman or Saila, we were free to wander around the many displays of local crafts. The most traditional of these were the colourful molas, intricately sewn from layers of cloth cut to create patterns as the colour of each successive layer is revealed. It seemed the whole village turned out for this occasion, many to trade with us but others just joining in the welcome. There was a warm feel to the place that changed the otherwise grim aspect of the evidently poverty-stricken dwellings. At the end of the main street stood an ugly brick-built church, sorry testimony to the intrusion of missionary zeal into the admirable Kuna culture.

Most nights we ate in the restaurant where good, cheap fare was served in idyllic surroundings. The waitresses all wore their traditional molas with colourful, bead decoration around their arms and ankles. Towards the end of our stay we were treated to a display of dancing by a group of Kuna who came over from the village. It was staged among the palm trees under a nearly full moon that lent added spookiness to the haunting sound of their pipes.

We left Iskardup on the 26th of January going west to Tiger Island, a rather larger island than Iskardup with a substantial village and an airstrip. We anchored there with Gambatte Go who invited us to dinner. Kiki is a marvellous cook and we thoroughly enjoyed her chicken dish, served with rice and seaweed. We were unable to go ashore at Tiger Island because the red flags were flying. Our pilot book warned that these flags indicated that some sort of exorcism process to remove evil spirits was taking place and visitors were not welcome. Nevertheless it was a pretty anchorage and we enjoyed watching the comings and goings of the tiny aircraft as they wended their way from airstrip to airstrip along the coast. A ramshackle building served as the airport lounge and control tower combined, on the approach of an aircraft a head would appear at the window, I think he was the air traffic controller.

From Tiger Island we moved north-west next day, stopping briefly at a tiny island, which we called Kwadale, the name someone had pencilled in on our chart. I think they had meant to identify Kwadule, an island a little further to the east. Kwadale was a minute little desert island, about 75 x 50 metres with white sand and palm trees and absolutely nothing else. As at Iskardup, the northern edge was shielded by reefs, leaving a calm anchorage, over sand, to the south. It looked so inviting, like everyone's dream of a deserted tropical island of the sort shown on holiday postcards, but without the blonde in the bikini. Anchoring was interesting because the deep water ran almost to the beach and one could have anchored very close in, had it not been for the steep slope of the sand falling away from the island. Dropping the anchor on this simply led to it sliding down the hill.

After a long lunchtime we moved on again north-westwards to Hollande Cays which form part of the outermost, seaward chain of islands. We found a good anchorage just south of Caobos Cay, sandwiched between the Cay and a reef to the south of it. In the middle of happy hour a fellow came along in a dugout canoe. He said he was the harbourmaster and could he have $5 for the community - there was a village on a nearby island. He seemed genuine enough so as well as the $5, we gave him a postcard showing a London bus and an old British Airways magazine. It may seem surprising but such things are always welcome and he went away with a big smile on his face.

After Hollande Cays, we made a short visit, accompanied by *Hilda*, south to the Ciedrus River, which we found totally obstructed with mangrove. We anchored just outside, in what appeared at first to be a totally deserted spot. But no sooner had we settled there, than canoe loads of Kuna ladies emerged from nowhere to come alongside with their bundles of molas. They were more persistent sales ladies than we had met at Playon Chico and we had difficulty getting them to leave us in peace, even after we had made a purchase. We had the same difficulty at Porvenir, where we went next day. The western end of San Blas is more accessible and gets visits from cruise ships from time to time. The local communities have become more commercialised and expert at separating dollars from the tourists.

At Porvenir we finally made our official entry into Panama, paid the $25 entry fee and left after two hours. In truth that was all the time it merited, with its busy airstrip, modern buildings and even a tourist shop by the pier. To the south and west of Porvenir lie several village islands with many anchorages in more interesting surroundings than Porvenir itself. We found one close to the mainland peninsular, to the west of Porvenir and anchored for the night. A local canoe came by, loaded with old plastic bottles and cans. He asked us if we wanted to buy any fish and explained that he was on his way to the spring to collect water. He disappeared up a small creek on the mainland. We went ashore to see the place and found a substantial spring with fresh water flowing freely towards the sea. While there, we sat and watched a pair of sea eagles who had a nest in a nearby tree. However, it was not long before we were smothered with swarms of the dreaded 'no-see-ums', midge-like insects that settled down on our ankles and arms in such numbers as to turn them grey. We were grateful they stayed onshore for the night. By now our deadline for the Panama Canal was drawing close and it was time to leave San Blas. It had been a glorious cruising experience, quite the most enchanting, unspoilt area we had come across so far. We left on January the 30th and sailed westward along the coast for a day before stopping off for the night at Isla Grande. Just as we arrived there, an American yacht, in trouble with a broken transmission coupling called us up.

'British yacht to seaward of us, this is *The Naked Lady* on your port side!'

With a message like that we quickly offered to stand by her as the two of us sailed into the anchorage at Isla Linton, just beyond Isla Grande. In the event she managed without a tow. At Isla Linton we met a friendly American, Tom Ziegler, who had extensive knowledge of Panama and was able to give us helpful advice about Colon. He has subsequently published an excellent pilot book on Panama which I am sure will soon find a place on every visiting boat. From Isla Linton it was a longish day's sailing to Colon, a bustling crime-ridden city at the entrance to the Panama Canal. We moored ourselves among the other Trade Wind Rally boats at the yacht club - about the only secure spot for a foreign yacht. Over a cool rum and coke, I thought back over our journey so far. We had crossed our first big ocean and the Caribbean Sea, and it was barely three months since we had left Tenerife. Our log showed we had covered nearly 5,000 miles. That left only another 23,000 miles to go. It was a sobering perspective.

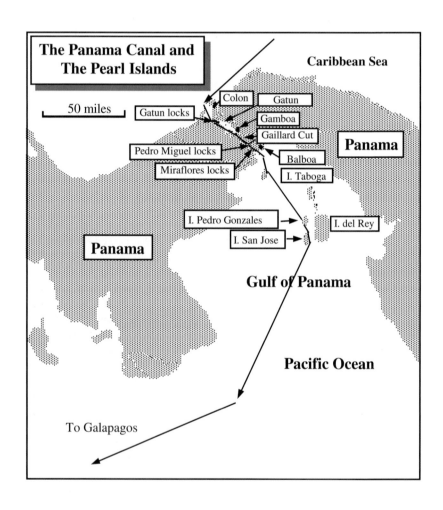

The Panama Canal and The Pearl Islands

Caribbean Sea

50 miles

Colon

Gatun

Gatun locks

Gamboa

Gaillard Cut

Panama

Pedro Miguel locks

Balboa

Miraflores locks

I. Taboga

I. Pedro Gonzales

I. del Rey

I. San Jose

Panama

Gulf of Panama

Pacific Ocean

To Galapagos

6 Through the Panama Canal to the Pearl Islands

Colon is a dangerous town to wander around alone or at night. The yacht club is fenced in and guarded and one spends most of the time within its confines. A park, full of iguanas and their burrows, provided a little interest inside the fence and meals in the club were passable. Outside the club, one goes everywhere by taxi and the standard fare of $1 takes you anywhere in town. Downtown there is a tax-free area, the *zona libra*, with restricted entry and well guarded. I went there to obtain a few spares for the engine and outboard and experienced no difficulties. The *zona* is reasonably safe to walk around, there are banks and it is the best place to go shopping, although the armed guards standing by the tills of the supermarkets made one feel a little nervous.

Our main task at Colon was to get the boat ready for the canal and this involved getting her measured by the Panama Canal Commission for the assessment of charges. Peter and Tony made all the essential arrangements with the Commission. Yachts are measured with almost the same thoroughness as big vessels, but the officials were courteous and efficient and it was all quickly completed.

The Caribbean end of the Panama Canal, just around the corner from Colon, has a flight of three locks at Gatun. These take the boats up 85 feet to the man-made Gatun Lake - created by damming the Chagres River. It stretches for twenty-three miles to Gamboa, where there is an anchorage and a pilot station. Yachts go to this point on their first day and then stay overnight before moving on, through the famous Gaillard Cut, to the Pedro Miguel lock. This is the first step down to the Pacific and is closely followed by the Miraflores flight of two locks that lower the boats to sea level.

The plan was for the boats to gather near the entrance and lash themselves together in pre-arranged groups of three. There were one or two firm rules for the canal transit. Each boat had to have a pilot on board and we were required to have four long warps of 20mm minimum diameter and 120 feet in length. We were supposed to have four line handlers in addition to the skipper - no small requirement for a boat as small as *Greylag*! We knew about this before starting and we already had the necessary warps on board. Luckily, the canal authorities did not insist on the four line handlers. As the boats were going through in groups of three, the centre boat did not need lines and there was sufficient manpower in the group to manage the four lines required.

Our group consisted of Roy Newey's *Gaviota* in the middle, Chris and Fiona Tonge's *Sheet Lightning* on the starboard side and *Greylag* on the port side. With this arrangement, the centre boat was in control, but all had their engines on so that the raft could be turned one way or the other by getting the outside boats to go into forward or reverse gear - like a twin-engined motorboat. The two outside boats were responsible for the lines used to secure the three-boat raft in the centre of the lock.

Early on the morning of the appointed day we all departed from the yacht club and went to a waiting area where, in due course, a launch came along with the pilots. Ours was a pleasant fellow with a keen sense of humour, and he had a trainee with him. We soon joined up with *Gaviota* and *Sheet Lightning* to form the group and moved off towards the massive Gatun lock. A flight of brown pelicans passed overhead as we approached.

'Ah,' said our pilot, 'the Panamanian Air Force!'

Just before we got to the entrance we were bombarded with missiles, hurled across the raft of boats by some burly fellows peering down at us from the top of the lock. The 'missiles' were weighted, leather-bound objects known as monkeys, a bit like cricket balls, attached to a thin cord. They were thrown with remarkable accuracy and we were required to attach our heavy lines to them so that the fellow on the edge could pull them back to the large bollards on the edges of the lock. Once we were tied on, we winched the lines tight to hold the group securely in the centre of the lock. Just as well we did so because once the massive gates closed behind us, the water was let in from underwater tunnels and caused a good deal of turbulence. Because of the large number of rally boats going through, we did not have to share the lock with commercial vessels which was a considerable relief. Our group was the third of five secured down the centre of the lock. This gives some idea of the size of the chambers - they are 110 feet wide and 1000 feet long.

With the gates shut and everything secure, the water level rose steadily until we were at the top of the first chamber. Then the front gates opened and we proceeded, still tied together as a group, into the next

Balboa Yacht Club

chamber where the procedure was repeated, and then again for a third time to reach the top level. The Gatun locks are arranged in two parallel flights so that as we were going up, we had a fine view of an enormous container vessel on its way down, on the other side. The big boats are manoevred from one lock to the next by diesel locomotives on tracks at the side.

After emerging from the top lock, the rafts separated and we were invited by the pilot to set sail and motor-sail the twenty-three miles to Gamboa. I was surprised at the beauty of this part of the canal. The lake has tree-lined shores and many small islands, some of which had private houses, and one a holiday complex. I felt as though it could have been the River Dart, had it not been so hot and humid. This illusion, however, was quickly shattered when we came round a bend to be confronted with another enormous, flat-sided container vessel coming the other way. These are known as 'panamax' vessels, as they are built to the maximum dimensions capable of getting through the locks.

At Gamboa we anchored in pleasant surroundings and slowly recovered from the day's excitements. Our pilot was collected by a launch and went ashore after warning us not to try to swim as there were many alligators. We never saw one, but no one swam! The night was peaceful and, surprisingly, there were not many mosquitoes.

At eight o'clock next morning our pilot returned and we were soon on our way down the Gaillard Cut. This part of the canal was carved out of solid rock when the canal was built, over the period 1903 to 1914, at the cost of some 20,000 lives among the workers who were stricken down with malaria or the dreaded yellow fever. At one point there was a large plaque erected in memory of those who died. On our way down the cut we passed several other big vessels en route for the Caribbean. We tried to avoid meeting them at the bends, because at those points they needed the whole width of the canal to turn. Most had tugs in attendance at the bow and stern to assist them round the corners. After our experience at the Gatun locks, we had no difficulty negotiating the three water-steps down to the Pacific Ocean, at San Miguel and Miraflores.

Above the Miraflores locks there is a small yacht broker's yard. We were told that this is the cheapest place in the world to buy second-hand yachts. Entry into the Pacific is like a one-way valve, once you've set off it is quite difficult to turn around and fight your way back against the trade winds. It is not uncommon for yachtsmen to get fed up with the whole thing at this point, or marital breakdowns develop with one or both spouses wishing to go home. Yachts caught up in this are often left at Miraflores because it is cheap and, being inland of the lock, very secure from theft. A smart cruiser can often be obtained there for half its real value!

After leaving the last lock we motored on down the estuary and under the impressive 'Bridge of the Americas' to find an excellent mooring at the Balboa Yacht Club. This is something of a Mecca for circumnavigators, nearly all of them stop there for a while whether going westwards or back to the Caribbean. It is a lively place and the beer and food are cheap. A short bus ride takes one into Panama City where there are supermarkets and banks.

It was at this point that we fell victim to a disgraceful fraud. It was put about the fleet that we needed a 'fumigation certificate' for entry into Galapagos - our next destination. For $90 dollars, we were told, this fellow would come round and fumigate the boat and give us a certificate. He turned up and spent all of 5 minutes walking round the boat with a small, hand-held, insecticide spray anointing the guard-rail. What a racket! There was no possibility of such a procedure having any beneficial effect and the fellow more or less admitted that it was just to satisfy the bureaucrats. But that hardly justified his exorbitant $90 charge which could be described only as daylight robbery. (When we got to Galapagos no one ever asked to see a fumigation certificate).

Meanwhile there was great excitement aboard *Ocean Gypsy*. In the middle of the night one of them, I think it was Laura, had been woken by something slithering across the berth. She had sat up smartly to see a snake disappearing behind the woodwork. Hunt for it as they might, it could not be found and they all had to go and spend the rest of the night on *Griffyn*. Next day they called in a snake expert but he also failed to find it. He thought it had probably been brought aboard in the packaging of a new loo delivered a day or two before. The story had a happy ending, except perhaps for the snake. The next night Doug's son-in-law spotted it on the navigation table and, book in hand, came down upon it with such an almighty blow that both the snake and the table suffered a rapid demise! I could well imagine what a worry this must have been for them and their relief was palpable.

On our first day at Balboa we studied the beach at low tide to identify an area of hard, level sand, where we could dry the boat out on her legs to redo the antifouling. In the Caribbean there had been only a few inches of tide, so there had been no opportunity to do this job until now. At Balboa the tide was over 3 metres and there was a good beach just alongside the yacht club. We took *Greylag* into shallow water at dawn next day and put her aground about an hour and a half after high water. In no time the club boatman came over in his launch and offered us a tow! Try as we might, we could not persuade him that we had gone aground deliberately and didn't need rescuing. I don't think he had ever seen a yacht on legs before.

As soon as the tide had gone out we cleaned off the hull and started to repaint it, but just as we completed one side, the heavens opened and an almighty downpour developed. It was bad enough that it threatened to prevent us finishing the job, but what was much more worrying was that I had failed to notice a large storm drain opening out onto the beach, just above where we had dried out. In the downpour this started to spew out a veritable torrent of water which ran down the beach close to *Greylag*, threatening to wash the sand away from under her legs and tip her over. No one digs as fast as a man in a panic and we soon built up a veritable sea wall of sand and rocks to keep the water away. Luckily it worked. As soon as the shower was over the hull dried off quickly in the warm sunshine that followed and we were able to resume our painting. When the tide returned we refloated without trouble and returned to our mooring with a nice clean bottom ready for the Pacific crossing.

Next day we completed our refuelling and re-victualling and I bought a cruising guide to the Ilas Perlas, the 'Pearl Islands' that lie in the Gulf of Panama, just a few miles offshore. We intended to visit them before pressing on to Galapagos. In the same shop as I bought the guide, I found a large-scale chart of San Blas, showing clearly the area around Iskardup. At last I could see in detail how dangerous our eastern approach route had been and that an easier way in had been available, barely a couple of miles to the west! We were now ready to depart for the Pearl Islands next day.

Our first stop was at Taboga, a populated island just 8 miles from Balboa. We got there with *Miss Molly* and *Sheet Lightning* but when the wind got up in the afternoon, the anchorage became lumpy and we spent an uncomfortable night. We left early next day and moved to Isla Pedro Gonzales, a short day's sailing to the south. On the way we saw a pod of whales far off on our starboard side, unfortunately too distant to identify them with certainty. Approaching Pedro Gonzales we ran into a patch of sea alive with leaping rays. I had never seen anything like this before, the rays were perhaps around 10 pounds in weight and would emerge at a rate of knots from the sea, like newly launched Polaris missiles. We tried to think of an explanation for this extraordinary behaviour and decided that either they were attacking prey on the surface and overshooting, or it was a method for getting rid of parasites. It was certainly spectacular.

At Pedro Gonzales we ran into Ensenada Honda, the bay at the northern end of the island and joined several other rally boats at anchor. As with Taboga, the bay was not very calm and we rolled uncomfortably. However, this was made up for by the spectacular bird-life we found. There were huge flocks of pelican, egrets and shags, together with a few sea eagles and the usual gulls and terns. At low tide next day we watched a spectacular avian feast, as shoals of small fish came into the bay and started a feeding frenzy among the birds. This was the most enjoyable event at Ensenada Honda but we soon decided to move to the western side of the island in hope of finding calmer conditions. Before moving we purchased a stick of bananas from a fellow in a canoe. We suspended these from a halyard and lowered them into the sea for a few minutes - a technique we'd discovered for getting rid of cockroaches and the occasional tarantula.

On the western side of the island we found a good anchorage at Ensenada Playa Brava. This was like chalk from cheese compared with Ensenada Honda, calm and surrounded by high tree-clad cliffs. The snorkelling was excellent even though the water was not quite as clear as in the Venezuelan islands. After drinks on *Sheet Lightning*, we had a restful night at last.

The next morning was warm and sparkling, we were definitely going to stay for at least another day. Tom Smith from *Best Respects* reported that there was a small lake just around the headland to the south and what at first he had thought to be floating logs, had moved. We went round by dinghy and, sure enough, the 'logs' moved - they were alligators! The first I had ever seen in the wild. That afternoon several other rally boats arrived and a beach party was planned - we decided to stay yet another day.

We left soon after daybreak on the 13th if February, heading south again to Isla San José. We settled at the southern end, in an anchorage known as 'Robinson's'. There we found an old, rusty, steel boat on a mooring and read in our guide that it belonged to a German couple, Dieter and Gerda, who had sailed here, settled and never left. They lived in a house close to the bay and grew a good supply of fresh vegetables for sale. Mind you, one had to spend some time listening to Dieter's tales about the island and its visitors - a few moments' companionship that were part of the price of the vegetables. We stayed for a couple of days in that peaceful spot, gathering our energies for the 675-mile voyage to San Cristobal in the Galapagos Islands.

On St Valentine's day we set sail for Galapagos. A good breeze got us on our way but in the evening of that first day it died on us and we had to use the motor. We were now in the Inter-Tropical Convergence Zone or Doldrums and approaching the equator which we expected to cross just before San Cristobal. We kept slightly south of our course in search of more wind and passed close around the northern side of Isla Marpelo. The island belongs to Equador; it was a forbidding place with high cliffs rising sheer from the sea. What looked like a naval vessel was standing off the island and there was an oil rig. We decided to give it a wide berth.

Soon after leaving Marpelo the wind returned and once again we were able to sail. It was at this stage of our journey that I began to worry about my compatibility with my crew David. There were various reasons but one thing that was beginning to get me down was my inability to hear what he was saying in his very quiet voice. I found myself asking him to repeat almost everything and this was getting on my nerves. Perhaps I was going deaf, I thought, but I didn't really believe it. It was one of those things that you don't notice on a short trip but can become very irritating over a longer period. I hoped things would improve but I recorded my doubts in my diary.

The remainder of our journey to Galapagos was uneventful save for some medical advice to the crew of Nefertiti. She had suffered a nasty fire aboard (believed due to the starter motor jamming), and although they had managed to put the fire out, two of them had inhaled large amounts of smoke. Happily they recovered well but the boat was in a terrible state with much of her wiring burnt out, several batteries destroyed and a lot of smoke damage to the interior. I wondered how they would get all this fixed in Galapagos - not the best place to seek major repairs.

At night we often noticed that we were surrounded with boobies, one could catch glimpses of these large gull-like birds silhouetted against the moonlit sky. They appeared to be attracted by the numerous small squid that came to the surface in our wake at night. Occasionally we would find them on the deck in the morning and we were not sure whether they had been washed there by the odd wave or, more likely, dropped by the boobies. It was something to take an interest in during the night watches, but a big disadvantage of those night visitors was discovered in the morning, splatted all over our canvas work and decks!

On the 20th of February we crossed the equator at 0951 hours GMT, in longitude 88° 04.81' West. It was early in the morning by ship's time. By noon that day we sighted San Cristobal Island and in the gathering sunset, we enjoyed a blissfully calm approach to the harbour at the southern end of the island. As we passed between the island and a large off-lying rock, Sleeping Lion Rock, silhouetted against the setting sun in the west, we were surrounded by schools of dolphin and patrolled by flocks of frigate birds overhead. It was almost dark as we entered the harbour at Wreck Bay, helped into the anchorage by John Roberts on *Griffyn,* who shone his bright spotlight to show us the way. All around us were moored fishing boats covered with sleeping sea lions, whose mournful 'barking' was a continuous background noise. Truly we had arrived in Galapagos.

Several other rally boats were already in the harbour and they invited us to join them in the local Hotel Orca for a few drinks. Tired though we were, we agreed to go ashore. At the entrance to the hotel there was no sign of our friends, just a rather official looking gentleman looking at us as if we should not have been there.

'I want to see your fumigation certificate,' he said, holding out his hand. Perhaps that 90$ piece of paper was going to serve some purpose, I thought.

'I'm afraid it's on our boat,' I replied awkwardly.

'This is no good,' he replied, 'I will have to fumigate you here.'

Whereupon he produced a small aerosol fly spray and commenced an unnecessarily thorough job on us - armpits, down the neck, up the shorts! At this point our friends appeared from nowhere, all creasing themselves in laughter. The 'Official' was actually the hotel proprietor, Pepe, and he had been put up to this trick by our friends. We had a pleasant evening ashore and returned to *Greylag* happy, still with the slight smell of fly spray, and more than ready for a good night's sleep.

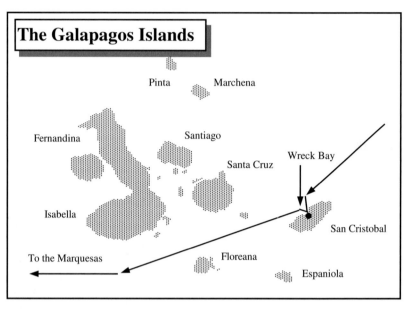

The Galapagos Islands

Pinta Marchena

Fernandina Santiago

Santa Cruz Wreck Bay

Isabella

San Cristobal

To the Marquesas Floreana

Espaniola

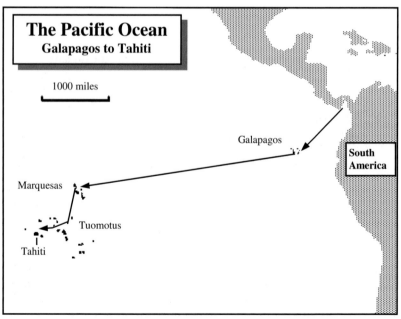

The Pacific Ocean
Galapagos to Tahiti

1000 miles

Galapagos

South
America

Marquesas

Tuomotus

Tahiti

7 Galapagos and the Long Pacific Crossing

Next day we awoke to the call of the sea lions. There were literally hundreds of them in the harbour, some in the water, many more lolling about on the fishing boats. So many had managed to board that some of the boats were on the point of capsizing under the weight. One had actually been capsized, and not content with that, the sea lions were sunning themselves on the upturned hull. We sat and watched them for hours; they were a constant amusement during our stay at San Cristobal.

That first morning we made a start by cleaning the bird droppings from the deck and sails, followed by showers in the cockpit using the river water which we had brought with us from San José. I then went ashore to organise some fuel and to deal with the formalities. John and David agreed to stay aboard to refuel *Greylag*. The fuel arrived in cans on a boat and was siphoned into our tanks.

The sea lions at St Cristobal

At the bank I had my first experience with their funny money. The local currency is the sucre and there are 2,900 sucres to the US dollar! Even a modest withdrawal meant asking for sucres by the half million. In the shops we got used to this by adopting a rough and ready rule - expressing the sucres in thousands and dividing by three to give dollars. Thus 6000 sucres became 2 dollars.

In order not to overload local facilities, the rally had been split into two groups for the visit to Galapagos - the other half were at Isla Santa Cruz. On San Cristobal, two establishments became regular meeting places for our half of the Trade Winds fleet, the Orca hotel and Rosita's restaurant. We soon discovered that Pepe, the Italian proprietor of the hotel, had a handle on most things that one might need. He offered to organise a coach trip around the island and assured us that we would be able to see most of the wild life for which the Galapagos Islands are famous. Some of our colleagues had booked rather expensive boat trips around other islands but John and David showed no enthusiasm for these. As David rather characteristically put it 'I want to see what I'm getting for my money first.' I was becoming convinced that I would not be able to tolerate him much longer! However, we decided to rely on Pepe and his coach trip. Later we heard that those who went on the boat trips had been pretty uncomfortable and had not seen much more of the wildlife than was available on the coach tour of San Cristobal.

Within walking distance of the harbour one could find much of interest. We walked eastward through a large area of scrub containing a variety of impressive cacti. The going was quite rough as the whole island consists largely of volcanic pumice; in places it looked like the surface of the moon with numerous craters dotted across the landscape.

We saw some of the small finches that had so fascinated Charles Darwin when he came here in the *Beagle*. About a mile and a half to the east was a cliff overlooking the sea from where one could observe the sea lions and an occasional shark. This vantagepoint also gave us a magnificent view of the frigate birds that flew close by at eye level; they nested in this area of San Cristobal. There were also a few of the famous blue-footed boobies.

Pepe's coach trip, at twenty dollars each, turned out to be good value. We started off at a small bay in the north of the island, where there were more blue-footed boobies and tracks in the sand where turtles had come ashore to lay their eggs, but no turtles. The snorkelling was interesting, the fish being rather larger than those we had seen so far. After lunch at a fruit farm (several of us stocked up with fresh pineapples and vegetables), we visited a large volcanic crater, inactive and full of fresh water. There were many frigate birds circling and our guide explained how they would fly low over the water and scoop up a drink. If ever they had the misfortune to ditch, they were unable to get themselves airborne again and would die.

To end the day we were taken to the extreme southern tip of the island. There we found a large colony of sea lions. Among them were some huge, fully mature males bearing the scars of old battles fought for dominance. This was a breeding colony and there were many baby seals.

They were remarkably unconcerned with our presence and we found we could get very close with our cameras and videos. Also there were large numbers of marine Iguanas. These lizard-like creatures, mostly 2-3 feet long, are common in the Galapagos Islands. They basked on the rocks, sometimes as many as six in a group, but their colouring provided such good camouflage against the rocky background that one didn't always spot them even when looking right at them. If one got too close they would turn and spit at you, but mostly we were ignored. In the sea they are remarkably good swimmers. We returned to the boat feeling it had been a very good day out for a very reasonable price - an unusual experience in the Galapagos Islands that have the reputation for being expensive.

On our last day we busied ourselves restocking the boat and topping up the fuel and water. Shopping was difficult, as there was little choice in the way of tinned foods; we yearned for a Tescos or Safeways. John did a good job under difficult circumstances but we would continue to rely heavily on the staples of rice or pasta and the dreaded tins of tuna.

Marine Iguana

That evening, Commandant Hugo invited the whole fleet to a barbecue in the officer's mess at the naval establishment alongside the harbour. They were most hospitable and came with their wives and older children to make a most enjoyable occasion. After we had eaten, a local musician played his guitar and sang for us and then, much to our surprise, Hugo also volunteered a few songs - he had a very good voice. At this stage we all felt we ought to contribute to the entertainment. Mike Van Gent from *Freeaz* quickly organised and led a group of us to sing a few sea shanties. 'I'll go no more a'roving', 'what shall we do with the drunken sailor' (appropriate at that stage of the evening) and 'Cwm by Ar' wafted over the harbour, the language problems of our hosts helping to disguise some uncertainties over the words! Our efforts seemed to be appreciated and Hugo produced several bottles of malt whiskey to round the party off. This proved to be the first of several such cabarets in subsequent ports of call and the group became known as the 'Shantymen'.

Next day we left on the long trip to Nuku Hiva in the Marquesas, 3,038 miles away to the west - by far the longest sea voyage of the circumnavigation. Few sailors, let alone other mortals, have ever made this journey although many dream of doing so. What is it like to cross so vast an ocean? Is it difficult, or frightening, or boring? What does one do all day? In an effort to convey some of the answers here are some day-to-day extracts from my journal.

Wednesday 28 February 1996. Departed Wreck Bay, San Cristobal, at 1340 hours. Very slow going in a WSW headwind. I opted to go south on starboard tack to try to escape from the Inter-Tropical Convergence Zone (ITCZ). By midnight we had made just 36 miles and were struggling to get past Isla Espaniola.

Thursday 29 February. Remained quiet all day, we have run the engine for 5 hrs so far. As darkness fell the wind improved but was still from the WNW, we were making around 5 knots on a course between 220 and 230° magnetic. At midnight we had 2,961 miles to go, so we've made only 77 miles towards Nuku Hiva in a day and a half. Rather discouraging.

Friday 1 March. Wind continues to be NW and we've now come south to latitude 3°S. Nuku Hiva is at nearly 9°S so we have plenty of southing yet to make. The weather is cloudy with patches of rain - feels like the Solent in summer. Overnight the wind backed into the south and we were able to get onto port tack and make 240° at last.

Saturday 2 March. A good day. The wind is now firmly in the south and we seem to have picked up the South Equatorial Current which is giving us about a knot over boat speed. I am suffering a bit of a tummy bug, uncomfortable but bearable. Despite this I feel happier now we're making better progress.

Sunday 3 March. Good sailing all day and night. 2,570 miles to go at midnight so we've nearly done the first 500. No troubles with the boat but I still have the tummy bug.

Monday 4 March. Still going well, we covered 147 miles in the 24 hours to 1000 hrs. I got the sextant out for a set of star sights at 0600 hrs - good to keep in practice and working out the position using the conventional tables gives me something to do during the day. David does this with his Psion computer and I argued with him that the same catastrophe that might destroy the GPS, a lightning strike for example, might also damage the computer. It was a magic moonlit night with occasional showers that produced a moonbow. I've never seen one before. It was just a white bow, not coloured like a rainbow in the sun. Tummy has improved.

Tuesday 5 March. Still going fast. Distance to go is now down to 2,360 miles. We all read a lot but most of our off-watch time is spent sleeping. The constant rolling of the boat is quite tiring.

Wednesday 6 March. We had the spinnaker up for most of the night and today. We've been at sea for a week, distance to go 2,215 miles (145 miles done yesterday). We celebrated the end of our first week with garden spray showers in the cockpit.

Thursday 7 March. Wind increased to 15-18 knots from the SSE and miles to go now down to 2,060 (155 miles done yesterday). I saw a pair of shark alongside the boat. My turn to be chef tonight - it'll be fried rice with tinned prawns and the last of our fresh green peppers. *Calidris* say they've found weevils in a pack of pasta from Colon. They are quite close to us now and kindly offered us water, but our own is lasting well.

Friday 8 March. Still fast sailing, 1,925 miles to go. I did some moon sights and got an accurate position crossing them with sun sights. It is comforting to know that we wouldn't be lost if the GPS packed up.

Saturday 9 March. Disaster! At 1600 hours, John called from his bunk 'we've got trouble'. And we had. The port lower shroud had started 'stranding' at the T-terminal at the top end. Several of the 19 individual wires that are twisted together to make up the shroud had broken and there was a serious risk of loosing the mast, as this was the windward shroud. We rapidly deployed halyards down to the rail to support the mast and took all the sails off quicker than we've ever done before. I went up the mast and found that 8 of the 19 wires had already broken. As the wind was likely to stay in the SE, we decided to swap the lower shrouds over so that the good one would be on the windward side. This was easier said than done as the boat was rolling and life up the mast was a bit precarious. With this sort of breakage in mind I had fitted two U-bolts below the spreaders to which we could attach a spinnaker pole to replace a broken shroud, the bottom end being clipped to the deck rail. We did this but it was a disaster, the fittings very quickly broke free from the mast. It impressed me just how big a strain the lower shrouds take in rolling conditions.

Although we had spare wire and Stalock fittings (these can be used to join up rigging wire using simple tools), none of these could replace the T-bar fitting that attached the shroud to the mast. I cursed myself for not having thought of this. We fell back on a simple solution which was to put a rope strop around the mast, above the spreaders, and bowse it down to the deck fittings using a four-part tackle. By taking the strop around the front of the mast, round the opposite spreader and back around the front of the mast, we were able to keep the mainsail track unobstructed. This allowed us to continue to use the mainsail. It took a while to fix this in place but afterwards it seemed to work quite well and we were soon sailing again, albeit with the sails well reefed in. We called up *Calidris* on the radio and they kindly agreed to check in with us at regular intervals in case we were in further trouble. (In fact they remained within VHF range for the rest of the voyage to Nuku Hiva).

Sunday 10 March. The night passed without difficulty, our temporary repairs to the rig remaining effective. We made some measurements of the lower shroud and radioed them through to Malcolm McLaren on *Malmac* who had kindly agreed to fax the details home using his satellite communication system (Satcom C). I hoped Janet would be able to cope with getting some replacements sent out to Nuku Hiva. In spite of our problems, we were still able to carry a good amount of sail and progress was satisfactory. At midday we had only 1,600 miles to go - very nearly half way!

Monday 11 March. In the night the wind got up to 20 knots plus and I was again concerned about our rig. Happily it all stayed secure. *Miss Molly* came up from astern and passed close by us during the morning. She was rolling and surfing down one or two of the waves; it was a spectacular sight to see that big 55-foot yacht sailing like a dinghy. Heaven knows what we must have looked like to them. We got some splendid video of her as she went by - Linda offered us a cup of tea; she was only joking, it would have been a bit dicey to go alongside in the rolling conditions. By mid-afternoon the wind dropped again and I heaved a sigh of relief.

Tuesday 12 March. I am 61 today. I opened cards from Janet, Ann and John. John had also written a little poem for me in the log, here it is:

IF (With apologies to Rudyard K)

If you can deal offhand with viral colic
(And weevil infestations,just in fun)
And redesign your rig in mid-Pacific
With gaffer tape and pulleys by the ton,
If you can hear the calls of other yachtsmen
When all around are stricken deaf and dumb,
And sail your boat through calms where others motor,
And navigate the world by rule of thumb,
If you can drain the unforgiving tumbler
Of sixty mils (or more) of coke and rum
Despite the greying beard and failing eyesight
You can't complain of being sixty-one!

It was a happy day and another good day's progress with the spinnaker up.

Wednesday 13 March. Wind stayed light all day and we made barely 3 knots through the water although the westerly current is still giving us another knot. We mostly sailed with the genoa and drifter poled out each side at the front and the mainsail back in its cover. The main is very uncomfortable in the quieter weather as the rolling makes it flap from side to side, even with the boom held firmly with a fore-guy.

Thursday 14 March. It is John's birthday today. Progress still slow, only 100 miles in the 24 hrs to 1000 this morning. 1,106 miles to go. We've been at sea for more than two weeks now. How I enjoy the cool rum and coke each happy hour!

Friday 15 March. A good breeze set in during the morning and we saw a ship pass two miles astern of us - only the second ship we've seen on this trip. I was startled by a yell from John in the middle of the night. A flying fish, attempting to go over the boat, had entered cleanly through the open hatch in the cabin roof and got straight into bed with him! They smell disgusting, the fish that is. At midday we passed the '1000 miles to go' mark - great celebrations.

Saturday 16 March. It's David's birthday today. What a strange coincidence that all three of us should have birthdays within a four day period. Still slow but steady progress, we've 900 miles to go.

Sunday 17 March. Today we changed the clocks back 1½ hours to GMT -9½. The rally boats have been doing this at regular intervals so as to keep ship's time in line with the day-night cycle. We'll soon be at the opposite side of the world. I have never read so many paperbacks in my life! I do find life out here a bit boring for much of the time. Apart from boat talk, we don't seem to have much to say to each other. It may be just that everyone is feeling a bit tired but I think there is a bit more to it than that. We're very different people and apart from our interest in sailing we seem to have little else in common. How nice it must be to sail with a bosom pal.

Monday 18 March. *Calidris* caught us up today and settled about 3½ miles away on our starboard beam. We were able to hoist the spinnaker, this boosted the day's run to 134 miles.

Tuesday 19 March. I finally traced a fault in our hand-held VHF to a corroded contact in the external power supply plug. I soldered in a bypass. While in this DIY mode, I built a computer fan into the ventilation duct providing cooling to the fridge compressor. It has been struggling for a bit. At least these little jobs gave me something to do - I still find life a bit boring most of the time. Malcolm McLaren forwarded a nice message from Janet and confirmed that our new rigging should be waiting for us at Nuku Hiva. We are down to 500 miles to go.

Wednesday 20 March. It rained for most of the morning, and was still quite windy. *Calidris* is in sight, a great comfort to us. At teatime the wind moderated and the weather improved. There are now only 353 miles to go and we reckon we will arrive at Nuku Hiva on Saturday the 23rd.

Thursday 21 March. A really horrible day, it rained for hours and we never saw the sun. *Ocean Venture*, who was three miles behind us, called through in the evening to say they had a squall with 42 knots of wind over the deck. We heeded the warning and removed all sail except for about one foot of genoa at the front. When the squall arrived, the boat behaved very well but we took a big wave in over the stern. I was pleased I had closed everything down and put the washboards in the companionway. By midnight all went quiet again, the skies cleared and we were able to see the dramatic comet just alongside Arcturus. John had spotted it when it had first appeared several days ago; it was easy to see with the naked eye, its tail stretching for several fingers width at arms length.

Friday 22 March. We are getting really close now - 100 miles to go. *Calidris* has gone ahead by about ten miles. I arranged with John Chapman to call him at 2300 hours to discuss whether we should go north or south of Ua Huka, the island before Nuku Hiva. It is nice of them to keep such a good eye on us.

Saturday 23 March. Dawn found us a few miles north of Ua Huka with just a few miles left to get to Nuku Hiva. We arrived in Taiohae Bay at 1030 hours, just behind *Ocean Venture*. It was lumpy at the entrance to the bay but once in we found ourselves in a calm anchorage with spectacular green covered, steep hills all round. After 23 days at sea, the feeling of elation on our safe arrival was tremendous, heightened by our relief that the dodgy rig had survived that 1500-mile journey from mid-Pacific. Before finding a spot to drop the hook, we called in at the big ship quay to refuel. The problem was there were large swells coming into the bay and these made it dangerous to go alongside the quay. Peter had devised a way round this difficulty which involved us dropping the anchor well away from the quay and then backing in towards it. When we were about 5 yards away we threw a line and he attached the fuel gun for us to pull back to the boat and fill up. I found it necessary to keep the engine running so that I could use it each time a surge threatened to drive us into the quay. It was all a bit too exciting but we got away with it.

After that, we were pleased to find a quiet spot on the other side of the bay.

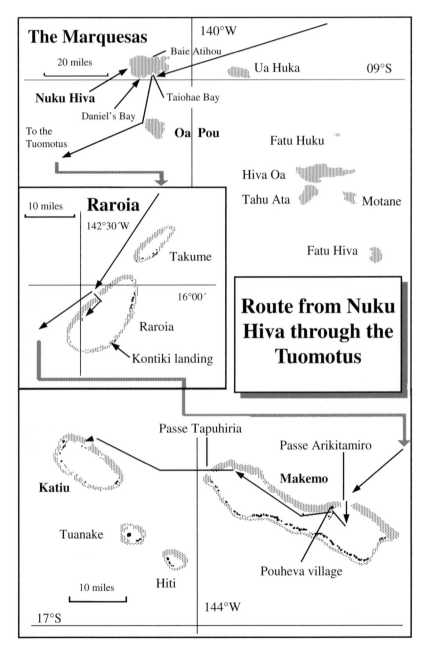

The Marquesas

140°W

20 miles

Baie Atihou

Ua Huka

09°S

Nuku Hiva

Taiohae Bay

Daniel's Bay

To the
Tuomotus

Oa Pou

Fatu Huku

Hiva Oa

Tahu Ata

Motane

10 miles

Raroia

142°30´W

Takume

16°00´

Raroia

Kontiki landing

Fatu Hiva

Route from Nuku Hiva through the Tuomotus

Passe Tapuhiria

Passe Arikitamiro

Makemo

Katiu

Tuanake

Pouheva village

10 miles

Hiti

144°W

17°S

8 Polynesia - The Marquesas and the Tuamotus

We had arrived at Taiohae Bay early in the morning and after settling on our anchor, we were soon ashore. The bay was in striking contrast to the Galapagos. There the landscape was brown and the vegetation sparse. Here the coastal fringe was vivid green with lush tropical trees and plants extending up the tall hills to the north of the bay, until finally giving way to the grey and purple of the high rock escarpments. These in turn rose into the low clouds. After weeks of the ocean, here indeed was somewhere close to Paradise.

Around the bay there were a few shops and a bank and one or two small restaurants. But the centre of activity for the rally boats was at the Keckanui Inn, a small hotel run by an American lady, Rose Corton. She had come to Nuku Hiva with her husband many years before and decided to stay. Her husband died a few years ago but Rose carried on with the business and she is now something of an institution in the bay. The hotel was home to Peter and Tony and we went there first to make our number with them.

The first to greet me was the ever-cheerful Tony holding out two coils of rigging - our new lower shrouds. It was a great relief to see them, now all we needed was for them to fit. We booked a place for dinner that evening and then proceeded with our formal clearance procedures at the immigration offices further round the bay. At Nuku Hiva one makes a temporary entrance into Polynesia, to be confirmed when one later checks in with the authorities in Tahiti.

On the boat next day we set about replacing our tattered lower shroud. In fact we replaced both lower shrouds, keeping the old one that was still intact as a spare. I was pleased to find that the new shrouds were precisely the right length and fitted perfectly. That job done, we all got our swimming gear on and made a start cleaning off the goose barnacles from *Greylag*'s waterline. It amazed me to see the extent to which these large barnacles had colonised the hull, the larvae must be able to grab hold and settle, even with the boat doing about five knots. They were all around the waterline but especially at the stern. It took a determined scraper to remove them.

Two large canoes raced by, each of them driven by eight incredibly strong fellows with a paddle. We had heard that canoe racing is an important event around the islands and this lot certainly looked competitive. Ashore I managed to get through to Janet who was getting excited about her visit to Tahiti, little more than a month away now. I used up a 5000 Central Pacific Franc phone-card (about £30)! Janet was pleased to hear that the rigging fitted, apparently there had been a little confusion because the first fax had referred to cap shrouds (the ones that go to the top of the mast) rather than lowers and they couldn't understand why they were so short. Luckily they guessed right.

After another day's leisurely recovery, we booked ourselves on a tour of the island in a 4x4 vehicle - the only sort suitable for the local terrain. Setting off in the early morning we climbed up a winding road towards the north of the island. The views were truly astonishing; we could look down from several hundred feet to the fleet anchored in the bay. We passed a few banana plantations but I was surprised that there was so little agricultural development. Given the wet and warm environment one would have expected to find much more in the way of fruit growing. Horses abound on Nuku Hiva, we saw them all over the island; there are said to be wild ones off the beaten track.

Once over the first set of hills we looked down into the next big valley, Taipivai valley. A spectacular waterfall fell from the cliffs opposite us, spectacular for its 300-metre height rather than its width, which was narrow. Our guide explained that the famous American author Herman Melville had climbed down that waterfall and settled in the valley with a local girl, Fayaway. His life with her in the valley is described in his book 'Typee'. It was much later that he wrote his more famous 'Moby Dick'. There is a memorial to Herman Melville on the seafront at Taiohae Bay. Another famous visitor was the painter Gauguin. He lived with a succession of young girls, mostly in Tahiti, and died in Hiva Oa a few miles away.

In the valley we visited a Tiki site. These places, they are called maraes, were once the taboo sites of human sacrifices. Fierce battles went on between the tribes in the various valleys on the island and the unfortunate prisoners were brought to these places to be sacrificed. The bodies were then eaten, it being believed that somehow the strength, skills and bravery of the victims could be acquired in this way. Human flesh was known as 'long pig' and it is said that human sacrifices continued until the early part of the present century. The sacrificial platforms were surrounded by stone Tikis - carved figures with fierce faces and magnificent evidence of manhood. Many of their erect organs had been broken off on the instructions of the early missionaries who regarded them as ungodly. The whole place felt a bit spooky, as if haunted by the spirits of the fallen warriors - this was probably only the power of suggestion.

North from Taipivai valley we reached the coast at Atihou Bay. Robert Louis Stevenson had once visited this place; it was certainly easy to see from where his ideas for Treasure Island may have come. There were more Tiki sites in this valley and these were all the more striking for the extraordinary backdrop of rocky pinnacles rising steeply from the green forests around their bases. In all my travels I never came across a more exotic landscape than we found in Nuku Hiva, though perhaps Moorea and the islands off the west coast of Thailand were comparably striking. The Mayoress owned the local village restaurant at Atihou and she served up a splendid lunch. After that it was time to return over the hills and back to Taiohae Bay and the boat.

Two days later, our energies renewed, we took *Greylag* westward along the coast to Anse Hakatea, or Daniel's Bay as it is popularly known. Daniel has lived there with his family for a number of years and is always pleased to greet visitors. His wife suffers from arthritis and was delighted when we gave her some painkillers from our medical pack. However, our main reason for visiting Daniel's bay was to see the waterfall that we had heard was within a good day's walking distance from the bay. We asked Daniel how to get there and he volunteered the services of his grandson to guide us. Young Francois was eleven years old and quite a small lad, but he could out-walk any of us twice over. He set off inland at a cracking pace as we old fellows struggled to keep up. There were times on that trek that I began to wonder whether it had been such a good idea as all the way up the valley we crossed and re-crossed a fast flowing stream, often up to our middles in water. I wondered if we might get covered with leaches, Humphrey Bogart style, but this did not happen. There were shoals of vividly coloured tropical fish of the sort seen only in aquaria at home.

After two and a half hours we reached the magnificent waterfall and the hard work seemed worthwhile. It fell, in two or three stages, 340 metres from the top of the high cliffs to a large pool at the base. We cooled off in the chilly water there and then sat for a while, admiring the attractive

Atihou Bay, Nuku Hiva

scenery and the butterflies, as we regained our energy for the long walk back to Daniel's Bay.

Back at the bay, we found Daniel hard at work fishing. He had a long net that he was slowly pulling out into the bay, the water up to his neck at times, but still just within his depth. He pulled the net in a large semicircle out and back again to the shore. He then started to retrieve it, hand over hand, onto the sandy shore. We were more than a little surprised to see how successful he had been, as the net came in loaded with perhaps twenty sizeable fish. They looked remarkably similar to the grey mullet we are so familiar with at home. Some of our colleagues bought a few. That evening we returned to Taiohae Bay feeling exhausted but happy with our day out. We felt we had seen a bit of the wilder side of Nuku Hiva.

Next day, our last at Nuku Hiva, we spent topping up the water and fuel and getting some fresh fruit and veg aboard. Just to make things more difficult, it poured with rain all day. This is the price one pays for the beautiful lush vegetation - and well worth it, I think. In the evening there was a dinner at the Keckanui Inn followed by Polynesian dancing by a local group. When I look back on the many dancing groups we enjoyed in Polynesia, I think the group at Nuku Hiva was the most impressive. The girls may have been prettier in the Cook Islands, the setting more romantic in Tahiti, but for sheer impact the dancers in Nuku Hiva were best. The girls did their bottom-wobbling as always, and I wouldn't deny I enjoyed that! However, it was the men who were more impressive than other groups. There was a hint of threat and confrontation in their steps and they were magnificently muscled and athletic. 'I like that one', was heard from a lady in the back row! One could easily imagine this dancing preceding the eating of the captives from battle.

Next day we set off south to Oa Pou, a short trip of 28 miles. Approaching the island we had a splendid view of one of the most dramatic skylines in the Marquesas. Huge pinnacles of rock rose hundreds of feet out of the dark green of the wooded hills. The humid air, flowing from the south-east, condensed around these pinnacles to form clouds trailing downwind, a strip for each pinnacle. It reminded me of the cloud that forms downwind of Gibraltar when the Levanter is blowing from the east. We anchored on the north-west side of the island, in Hakahetau Bay, where the anchorage was secure enough, although we rolled a bit. Next morning it was raining but after it had cleared up we made our first attempt to get ashore. This was no easy task as the swell broke against the small quayside in a way that made landing extremely difficult. The only way we managed in the end was to get John all ready to leap off and then, picking a space between waves, making a run for the quay. As soon as we were just close enough, off he leapt and I retreated quickly before the next swell arrived. David went next and only just made it. I returned to the boat and made a few sketches of that incredible skyline (one of which appears here).

When the time came to collect them the swells were if anything a bit worse than before, so I just ran the dinghy along the quay at speed, shouting 'jump!' at the appropriate moment. It was an exciting exercise and perhaps we were lucky not to get wetter than we did. *Magic Dragon* arrived later and I went ashore with them, their bigger dinghy was a bit easier to handle than our small one, but it was still necessary for their crew to pick a moment to drop us off between the swells. The village was neat and clean and bedecked with flowers everywhere. There were two churches, white-walled with red corrugated iron roofs - one was used as a leading mark for entering the bay. One old codger invited us into his house where he had a few items for sale, including oranges and papayas. He produced a complete turtle carapace, but I explained that my wife was

The extraordinary pinnacles at Oa Pou, Marquesas

a member of Greenpeace and would not approve.

From Oa Pou we headed for Tahiti where Janet and our friend Eileen were due to arrive on the 21st of April. Between the Marquesas and Tahiti a vast spread of coral atolls lay across our track, stretching for 700 miles from Rangiroa in the north-west to Mururoa in the south-east. These are the Tuamotus, gloriously dangerous places where the careless can die but the prudent can discover natural riches beyond the dreams of most.

Yachts travelling westward usually call in at Manihi or Rangiroa, atolls on the direct tourist route to Tahiti, with hotels (there are ten on Rangiroa) and other facilities. They lie at the north-west end of the group. Further south and east the atolls are rarely visited. Serene and unspoilt, they await the more adventurous. We planned a route through the middle from Raroia to Makemo to Katiu.

There was no doubting the hazards in the Tuamotus and many yachtsmen have come to grief there; our pilot book referred to them as the 'dangerous archipelago'. The atolls are low and difficult to see until close. Many are bereft of navigational aids and the passes into the central lagoons are narrow, fringed with coral hazards and have tidal streams that run at up to 6 knots. With a little care, though, trouble can be avoided and the rewards are great.

Daylight navigation (generally between 1000 and 1600 hours) is essential, as is a reliable engine. Although one can plan to arrive at a *passe* at slack water, it is almost impossible to avoid some serious tide plugging. The problem is that the streams of water are only partly generated by the rise and fall of the tide, only a few inches in this area. Much of the flow comes from the big Pacific swells breaking over the reef on the windward side of the atoll. Huge volumes of water cascade over the reef into the lagoon, from which the only escape is through the *passe* on the leeward side.

In strong winds, this effect can be powerful enough to generate a permanent outflow in the *passe*, with no period of inflow or even any slack water - just a short spell of less adverse tide around Low Water. We discovered this the hard way right at the start of our visit, when we arrived at Raroia after a four-day, 388-mile trip from Oa Pou.

Raroia is a large atoll some 25 miles along and 10 miles across the lagoon. Thor Heyerdahl drifted ashore there in the raft *Kon Tiki* in 1947. We arrived off the *passe* on the north-west side in the middle of the night and reached up and down between waypoints set five miles off until daylight came, when we approached the *passe* at 'slack water'. It had been blowing quite hard from the east and we soon discovered a strong 4-knot tide in the *passe*. We pressed on slowly and for a short while, in the narrowest part, the adverse tide reached just over 5 knots. Here we made another disconcerting discovery. The chart showed a minimum depth of 4m on our track, but suddenly the echo sounder flashed 2m ... then 1.6m... panic! A few revs off the engine soon dropped us backwards. We checked the chart. Yes, there should have been 4m. We pressed forward again. Several times we saw 1.6m on the echo sounder, but we never touched the bottom.

I have since discovered that these were false readings, due possibly to echoes off the interfaces between layers of water at different temperatures. In these swirling waters layer effects are common as the water reaches the *passe* from all directions in the lagoon. We saw it several times after that, but we always found it very worrying. One yachtsman I spoke to about it said 'Oh yes, I turn the bloody thing off!' Brave man.

We got into the lagoon eventually and proceeded cautiously to the village where 'Charlie's Charts', an indispensable pilot book in the Tuamotus, showed an anchorage. It all looked very attractive; turquoise water, white sand beaches and the motus, (the small islands on the perimeter of the atoll), decked with palm, vividly green in the morning sunshine. But there was a serious snag. The strong wind was blowing across the lagoon and causing very uncomfortable conditions on the lee side by the village, Garumoa. Given also that the anchorage was surrounded by coral heads, I felt this was not a safe place to stay overnight.

Disappointed, but resolute, we pulled up the anchor and put to sea again. This was a hard decision to make but staying when conditions were wrong was a sure way to disaster. Our outward passage with the current through the *passe* had all the hallmarks of white-water rafting. We were out in just a few minutes. Mind you, I found this 'shooting of the rapids' more worrying than plugging against the flow. If you make a mistake you cannot really stop, and hitting coral at 10 knots is likely to spoil your day. Outside the atoll we were on the lee side of the reef and the sea was much quieter.

We had time to kill, as we didn't want to arrive at the next atoll, Makemo, in the middle of the night again. Also we had some trouble with the jib furling gear which I wanted to investigate. So we approached the reef looking for somewhere to anchor but it was impossibly deep right up to the reef which falls away like an underwater cliff-face. As the wind was offshore we just stopped and drifted while I took a look at the furling gear. The trouble was due to the rotating halyard slider; it had unwound enough to let several of the ball bearings drop out. There was nothing we could do about that until Tahiti, but it was not a serious problem as we had our No2 genoa and the spinnaker. I radioed Malcolm McLaren on Malmac to ask him to send a fax to Janet to ask her to bring the spare ball bearings with her to Tahiti. This call led to a certain amount of ribaldry.

'The trouble is, Malcolm, we've lost our balls...'

'Tell me news, not history' he replied!

That evening we set sail for Makemo, a large atoll less than 50 miles away, where we thought we might find more shelter from the strong east wind. We arrived off the *passe* at daybreak and mooched around while the sun came up, when we went in. Again it was hard work against a 4-knot tide, but passe Arikitamiro was unusually well marked, and we felt more confident than we had at Raroia. We anchored in the lee of a patch of coral with a pearl farmer's hut on it. There we had some protection from the seas that were still too big for comfort. Not long afterwards we were joined by a Canadian boat '*Lootas'*, with Greg and Florence Barbour. They came from Vancouver. Florence spoke good French and this was going to be most useful ashore.

Happily, the weather soon improved but not before we had

The lagoon at Makemo with the pearl farmers huts

experienced one of the most spectacular thunderstorms I have ever seen. The lightning was continuous, nasty, streaky stuff. It's an ill wind though...; we filled our water tanks with ease.

Ashore next day, we met up with Galileo (yes, that really was his name), who showed us around the little village. He had spent six years in Canada and spoke good English. Nothing was too much trouble for him and he soon organised a trip for us in the school bus to the end of the motu.

As with most of the atolls, copra production is the mainstay of the local economy and we passed numerous coconut plantations. Halfway up the motu, we came across the small airstrip. It had a large wooden hut on it, which Galileo described as Terminal One.

At a fisherman's house we learnt about the black pearl farming, another important activity in several of the Tuamotu atolls. The oysters are seeded by introducing a small shell (they come from the Mississipi River) into the internal organs of the oyster. This acts as an irritant and causes the oyster to lay down the layers of pearl over the 'seed'. Getting the seed in the right place is a highly skilled exercise and even an expert seeder, (they mostly come from Japan), gets a success rate of only 60% or so. An easier technique is to stick a plastic shape to the inside of the oyster shell with Araldite. This in time becomes a blister pearl and is then carefully cut from the shell and machined into an attractive pendant. I bought some of these for a few hundred PCFs.

At the fisherman's home we saw a turtle waiting to become dinner. Although strictly controlled, the capture of turtles is still a legal activity. On our way back to the boat we saw a chicken farm and a young lad trying to entice a moray eel from its lair in one of the lagoon backwaters. Pigs wandered around freely. Everywhere people smiled and said hello (in French) and we felt very welcome.

Back at the village there was excitement on the newly built wharf. A shark was mooching around. I thought of the wonderful snorkelling I had enjoyed on the reef that morning; one knows sharks are around, but seeing one still makes the heart beat a little faster. Hordes of youngsters crowded round our dinghy, full of questions. We took two boatloads of them out to *Greylag*. The children were thrilled - we were exhausted.

A day or two later it was time to move on. We planned a daylight trip down the whole length of the lagoon (20 miles or so) to stop near the Tapuhiria Passe, at the western end, before parting for Katiu next day. The lagoon was full of coral heads and reefs, but in the strong sunlight these were easy enough to see and avoid. Several had the pearl farmer's huts on them and we anchored in the lee of one for lunch and a snorkel. The coral there was alive with fish and the water so clear that you hardly knew it was there. Spectacular clams with brilliantly coloured mantles, blue, turquoise, green and red lay among the coral, glued on immovably. I met a black-tipped shark. It seemed more frightened than I was; I got out all the same.

Ashore, the white beach and the coconut plantations were alive with small red hermit crabs. We heard later at Katiu that these are used to treat the poisonous sting from the stonefish. We saw signs of the ravages of the coconut crab, which bores into the nut, devouring the contents, and leaving a small round hole about an inch across. The shells are left lying around like so many discarded tit boxes.

This end of the atoll was once the site of the main village but this was destroyed by a hurricane in 1906 and they had rebuilt it in its present, slightly higher site at the other end of the motu. Hurricanes - they are called typhoons in the Pacific - are a real threat to life in the low-lying atolls. The slightest storm surge and the sea is all over them.

Next day we left early for Katiu, a short trip of 24 miles. Charlie's Charts suggested that the *Passe* Pakaka into the lagoon might be difficult so we approached with due caution. In the *passe* we noticed a newly built wharf over on the starboard side and soon a fellow appeared, waving us over. We had been about to enter one of the narrow and shallow entrances into the lagoon itself, but the man on the shore seemed determined that we should go over to the wharf, so we did. It was a narrow escape, as we discovered when Léopole, the gendarme, explained that the coral in the entrance had grown a lot and it was now impossible to enter the lagoon. Alongside the wharf we were surprisingly comfortable. Although situated right in the main *passe,* the outflowing stream produced an eddy alongside the wharf of about half a knot. The fast-flowing water further out killed the waves so that all was calm, and trouble free. By the time we were tied on we were surrounded by children, bubbling with enthusiasm, full of questions and eager to get on board.

With an average of three visiting yachts a year, our presence was clearly quite an event. The kids were tremendous fun and we got to know them well. Such romantic names they had - Toimota, Maruia, Florentina. Philipe, the schoolmaster, gave us a tour of the village, Pouheva. This took little time as only eighty-four people live on Katiu. The families have names that bear witness to the past indiscretions of British sailors - Winchester, Williams, and Harris! Everywhere was simple, neat and tidy; there were two small stores and a Catholic Church. Philipe introduced us to Teiki, the school director, who invited us to dinner next day.

We spent the rest of the day playing with the children, swimming and sketching. There were many picturesque spots to inspire the would-be painter. Some older boys were fishing off the wharf in water so clear that you could see the fish take the bait, and could not fail to catch one. There was great excitement at one stage when two huge Napoleon groupers turned up, giant carp-like fish of about 100 lbs.

Next day *Lootas* arrived from Makemo, encouraged by our enthusiastic messages over the radio. Our dinner with Teiki was a surprise. He apologised that he had not had time to prepare a turtle (sighs of relief) and said we would have to put up with lobsters. This turned out to be about five for each of us and accompanied by barbecued mahi-mahi and marinaded fish. It was all delicious. I soon understood when Teiki explained that a family could live on $50 a month, $25 each for rice and sugar and the rest came from the sea. I wondered whether the simple life would lose its attraction after a few months, it certainly seemed enviable on a short visit.

But the real surprise came when Teiki explained that he had learnt to seed oysters and had an interest in the black pearl farming on Katiu. He showed us the instruments used to introduce the seeds - they looked good enough for brain surgery! A good seeder can earn as much as $2.50 an oyster - $20,000 a month in the season. Teiki modestly claimed a 30% success rate, which was good locally.

Teiki didn't drink alcohol so we were unsure what to take him as a present for all his hospitality. In the end I gave him one of my watercolours; he had seen me painting earlier in the day and shown a lot of interest. He seemed really pleased with this. Next day he came to the boat and said again how much he had appreciated the gift and would I accept a small present in return. He took my hand and filled my palm with black pearls - generosity which so overwhelmed me that I could hardly thank him for the lump in my throat.

Next evening the beautiful Florentina, a teenage girl who had been most helpful in getting us bread and papayas, asked if she could bring her guitar and sing for us.

'Yes please', we chorused.

She came with her young brother and they sat in the cockpit, under a full moon, and sang local songs in their own Polynesian language. It was an enchanting moment in an enchanting place. At Katiu we had found a corner of paradise that all the travel brochures talk about, but few visitors

The entrance pass at Katiu

ever really find.

On the 15th of April we said a sad farewell and set sail for Tahiti, travelling around the northern end of Katiu before turning west and picking a careful route at night between two atolls, Fakarava and Faaite. Our progress was then fast and uneventful until we were close to Tahiti on the evening of the third day at sea. It was then that we heard on the radio that *Jonathan*, a rally boat from Italy, had engine trouble and might need a tow into harbour. We arrived off Papeete Harbour as darkness fell but Jonathan was still several miles away in a wind that was dying fast, so we went back for them and took them in tow for the last few miles into harbour. *Jonathan* was a biggish boat, 42 feet overall, so it was quite a struggle for the diminutive *Greylag* to tow her in through the *passe* against a knot and a half of tide. She managed it all right and Tom Smith and Chris Ewins soon met us in a dinghy with a powerful outboard. They took *Jonathan* off us and settled her in a berth against the Quay.

Finally we were in Tahiti, that famed island so inseparable from most people's dreams of the South Pacific, that conjures up visions of the Bounty and her infamous mutiny and the wayward Paul Gauguin, whose dusky maidens we have all seen in the art galleries of the world. In my berth that first night I wondered whether Tahiti could live up to her reputation.

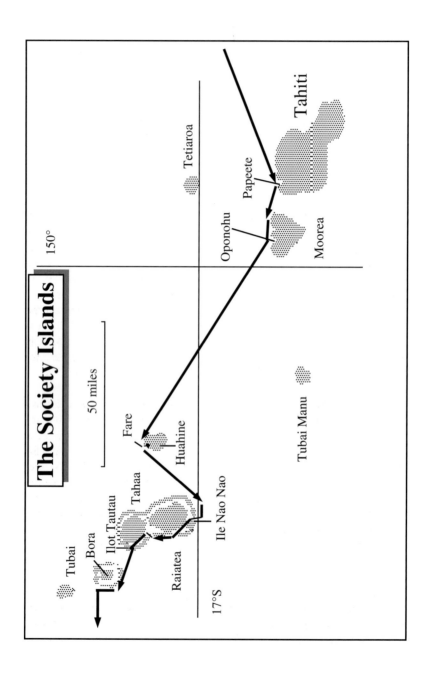

The Society Islands

50 miles

150°

17°S

Tubai

Bora

Ilot Tautau

Tahaa

Raiatea

Ile Nao Nao

Fare

Huahine

Tubai Manu

Tetiaroa

Oponohu

Papeete

Moorea

Tahiti

9 Tahiti, Island of Dreams -But the Best of the Society Islands Lie to the West

We awoke next day to the hustle and bustle of the Papeete waterfront. It was colourful but far from peaceful, with a busy main road running alongside the quay. Looking out from the harbour one could see the silhouette of Moorea just a few miles away, we looked forward to going there as it has the reputation for being a most beautiful place. The harbour itself was substantial, with an oil terminal and several commercial wharves. The yachts were all moored sterns to a brand new quay, right alongside the centre of the town. We wandered around and soon discovered that this was a very expensive place, it would be easy to spend fifty pounds a head on an evening meal, a bottle of ordinary plonk cost £12 and spare parts for boats were astronomical. There was however a good market where things were relatively cheap.

We had a few repairs to get done. The adjustable spinnaker poles had broken the nylon stops that fixed the length of the pole; I fashioned some new ones from a block of nylon. Next came the VHF aerial. We had been having some difficulty with VHF communications and I suspected the aerial was the cause so I went up the mast and retrieved it. A brief examination revealed serious corrosion; it was a wonder it had worked at all. Luckily I had been sufficiently certain the aerial was the cause of our problems to ask Janet to bring a new one with her, this would save the prohibitive cost of buying one in Papeete. John went through our stores and sorted out the lockers with his customary efficiency. He and David did an excellent job cleaning up the cooker - I would not have liked Janet to see it as it was.

We soon discovered the only cheap place to eat out - half the rally fleet seemed to be there! There was a car park behind the customs house where, of an evening, a large number of travelling food trailers would set up for business. They were known as the 'roach coaches' - probably unfair, as the standards of hygiene looked passable. They were like large caravans; the sides opened to form a canopy and a bar along which one sat, side by side as in a pub. The menus varied but there was a preponderance of Chinese style food, and all was reasonably priced. At night the place had a jolly atmosphere and we enjoyed the cosmopolitan mixture of itinerant sailors who homed in on this place from all corners of the globe.

At last it was the 21st of April, the day of Janet's arrival. Actually her plane was due to arrive at two in the morning, not the most convenient time to get to and from the airport. Malcolm McLaren offered to drive me out in his hire car. This would have been a generous offer at any time, but to sit up into the small hours to do it was very kind of him. At the airport I purchased a couple of leis. It is a local tradition to place these garlands of local flowers around the necks of newly arrived visitors as a welcoming gift. Janet and Eileen arrived on time and emerged from the customs looking radiant, despite the long journey they had just completed. It was 4 months since I had last seen Janet at Antigua and it was so good to see her again. They were both delighted with the leis. Malcolm drove us back to the boat where, despite the ungodly time of night, a small welcoming party developed on the quay.

Next day, after a quick walk around the town with Janet, I set about replacing the VHF aerial with the new one she had brought out with her. She had packed it meticulously in a long cardboard tube - no mean feat for such an awkward object, three feet long and delicate with it. We soon had it installed at the top of the mast, using the old cable to pull the new one down the mast and into the cabin. Next came those nylon balls for the furler that had caused me so much embarrassment with Malcolm. At least these had been easy luggage for Janet. Our repairs were now complete.

After a further day in the noise and hullabaloo of Papeete, we were all agreed that we should go on a short trip around the west and south of the island. We motored west inside the reef, refuelled at a small marina just beyond the airport, and then out through the *Passe* Taapuna. We watched some spectacular surf riding there on the big waves breaking over the reef. Outside the sea was lumpy and as our course around the north-west corner of the island was to windward, we motor-sailed to make better progress; things got easier once we were round the corner. We reached down the west coast before turning east along the south of Tahiti Nui, the larger of the two lobes of the island.

We entered inside the reef again through *Passe* Rautirare. Here again, the breaking waves each side were enormous, but the *passe* itself was wide and deep so we got in without difficulty. Inside, all was calm and blissful and we found a picturesque anchorage in the lee of Ile Pururu. This was a really nice spot with stunning views of Tahiti Iti, the smaller south-east peninsular of the island, and the tall green-clad hills of Tahiti Nui. Just along the shore from the anchorage was the small village of Mataiea where Paul Gauguin had lived during his time on Tahiti. Ile Pururu was deserted except for some chickens, we supposed it was used as a sort of natural chicken pen.

The next morning we moved south again, still inside the reef, to a perfectly beautiful anchorage alongside the botanic gardens - Tahiti's answer to Kew. This was also the site of a Gauguin Museum so we were able to go ashore by dinghy and do both. This did cause us a little difficulty as we realised that coming by dinghy, we had by-passed the ticket office at the gate. However, we explained to the officer why we had appeared to come from the inside and paid our dues.

The gardens were very well kept, with many interesting trees and flowers. The museum though was slightly disappointing. Although it had a lot of information and artifacts from Gauguin's life, both on Tahiti and the other islands of Polynesia, there were only three rather poor examples of his painting. It seemed a pity that here, where he lived, one could not see more of his work. It would have more impact in this setting than displayed among a host of other impressionist paintings, in some grey-walled gallery in Paris or Washington. But then, I suppose fewer would see them.

We returned to Papeete next day to be there for the President of Polynesia who was paying a visit to the Trade Winds fleet the next morning. There was quite a celebration on the quay with dancing and a free breakfast. The President arrived with Malcolm McLaren, both sporting leis around their necks. They visited a few of the boats, but not *Greylag* - not grand enough for such an occasion. The dancing was pretty, almost sentimental but without the impact of the Marquesans on Nuku Hiva.

That evening we went out with the crew of *Calidris* to an Italian restaurant about which they had heard good things. We found Lou Pescado's about four blocks back from the waterfront - always a good place to look for a cheaper meal. It was a riot. The chef, Mario, combined his cooking skills with an almost continuous cabaret act. Non-stop repartee was delivered with theatrical abandon, along with the pizzas. 'Watcha your backsas!' The incorrigible Mario would yell, as he delivered them on long handled pans, like bed warmers, into a traditional clay oven. 'Thees one a no gooda' he sang as another was hurled across the kitchen into a waiting bin. The price of the pizzas was worth paying for the cabaret.

An evening later, John returned together with two locals, Marilyn and Georges, who he had met on his long walk inland. They spoke only French but we followed enough to get a good insight into life on present day Tahiti - very different from the romantic image in the travel books. There is clearly a lot of politicking between factions who favour greater independence and those who recognise the economic advantages they enjoy through their close association with France. David sat in the cockpit and never said a word. '*Est-ce que vous êtes ennui?'* Marilyn enquired of him. She had sussed him out quickly, I thought, pleased that it was not just me who noticed. *I am going to have to do something about it soon,* I thought to myself.

Next morning we cleared out at Tahiti customs and sailed the short journey across to Moorea. As we left through the *passe*, Janet and Eileen cast their leis on the water, as is traditional when leaving Tahiti. We passed by the famous Cook's Bay, having already decided to go the extra mile to the next bay, Oponohu. This decision was prompted by a conversation on the VHF on which we eavesdropped. It was a discussion of the relative merits of the two bays. 'Not Oponohu' said the female voice, 'there's nothing there. The best pubs are at Cook's Bay, the Bali Hai Hotel is there!' It all goes to show that different people like different things. To us, Oponohu sounded most attractive. We entered the bay and settled on our anchor. The lady on the radio had been right, there was nothing there in the way of pubs or hotels. But there was everything I had dreamed about back in England.

The perimeter of the bay was fringed with palm, intensely green on the shady side to the west, viridian in the evening sunlight on the eastern side, nearest to us. At the head of the bay the hills rose from the palms in soft green waves. These in turn gave way to tall, grey-green rock edifices. Rising high into the sky, they caught the sun on their western sides, accentuating the deep purple shadows of the eastern faces. On the left the flat-topped Mont Tohivea gave way to a low col as the eye moved westward, and then rose dramatically to the high pointed peak of Mont Muaroa before falling away again as a ridge of lesser, tooth-shaped outcrops. But the main glory was that massive central peak of Muaroa. On the three sides we could see it was buttressed by solid rock supports, looking for all the world like a rough-hewn version of the upstream end of

Oponohu Bay, Moorea

Notre-Dame Cathedral. The buttresses cast long dark shadows over several miles of the surrounding hills. So calm was the bay that all this magnificent structure was reflected in the sea. Truly this was the finest scenery we had seen, small wonder they chose this very bay to film 'South Pacific' and 'The Mutiny on the Bounty'.

Inland next day, we walked in the countryside around the tall hills. Everywhere was green and lush, in places park-like where the land had been grazed by cattle. There were several flowering trees, decked in a deep orange-red blossom that shone out from the green background. We saw a few houses but no shops and only a handful of people. This island warmed the soul; it had a spiritual dimension that so imprinted itself as never to be forgotten.

We departed from Moorea next day, I wished we had been able to stay far longer but the rally schedule beckoned. Our next destination was the island of Huahine, 80 miles to the north-west of Moorea. We planned an overnight passage so that we would arrive with the sun in the morning. It was a good fast sail in the steady trade wind from the east and we arrived off the airport at the northern end of the island before turning west and

The hotel among the trees, Huahine

through the *Passe* Avamoa to anchor off the main village of Fare. There we got bread and stores and filled up our water tanks before moving south inside the reef to Baie Baurayne. The water there was fairly deep and we had to anchor in about 9m. It was a pretty spot and nestling among the trees was an 'environmental' hotel. Each suite was a separate building with a bedroom, veranda and jacuzzi. Janet looked at the creature comforts longingly but I had heard that the rooms cost £200 a night. Even a coffee on the beach was £3. We settled for the free view and the snorkelling, which was good.

We spent a peaceful night in that place but when we came to leave next day, we found we were unable to retrieve our anchor. The chain had wrapped itself around some coral heads and although we could see what had happened clearly from the surface, the water was too deep for me to dive down and release it. Luckily young Clive, crewing on *Vandal* nearby, was a confident diver and had no difficulty getting down the nine metres and releasing us.

Further south, but still inside the encircling reef, we anchored *Greylag* on the outer edge of the channel so that we could take the dinghy out to the reef for a snorkel. The water here was wonderfully clear and there was a huge variety of marine life to see. For the first time we saw an octopus and also another moray eel. Janet was interested but cautious. For

114

Parea village, Huahine

the night we moved down as far south as it was possible to go without going outside the reef, to the small village of Parea. The evening was calm and we enjoyed a magnificent sunset along with our happy hour drinks. Inga and John on *Calidris* were anchored nearby, how often we had been close to them ,both at anchor and at sea.

Next morning we returned to Fare to restock our stores, only to find that the supermarket was closed that day, it was a Saturday. We went back down the lagoon to Baie Haavai where we had heard there was a Chinese supermarket. Sure enough there was and we got most things we needed except beer. Just as we got back on board we were hit by a fierce squall that caused us to swing so violently on our anchor that we hit some nobbly bits of coral towards the shore. It sounded horrible and though nothing obvious had been broken I resolved to have a good look back at Fare. On diving under the boat I found that the wire running between the keel and the rudder (to keep fishing nets away from the prop) was broken at the keel end and was dangling from the rudder. I removed the remaining bits for repair. This exercise took about four dives, as I had to hold my breath while undoing the shackles, but the job was not too difficult in the clear warm water - I wouldn't attempt it in the Solent! Back on board I discovered that it was the spring, there to absorb shocks, that had broken. I was able to repair and replace the wire, although it took four more dives.

Janet and I went ashore for dinner, which was nice but expensive - a bottle of Beaujolais cost £22. I was pleased to have a short break from *Greylag* which was proving rather overcrowded with five of us on board and this was placing further strains on my already difficult relationship with David. I knew I was going to have to do something about that situation soon.

Next morning we left early for our next island destination, Raiatea. This was a short journey of 26 miles. We headed for the southern end of the island, intending to go inside the outer reef at *Passe* Nao Nao. When we arrived we found it quite difficult to identify the *passe* with certainty. Even though our chart gave a bearing to one of the mountain peaks inland, we found it impossible to identify with confidence which of the several peaks was the one to put the compass on. In our, by now, much practised technique, we slowly edged towards what we thought was the *passe* and luckily it was. We took some bearings on a more obvious landmark and recorded them in the log so that we could pass the information to others.

Inside the reef we first sailed over to the western side of Ile Haaio, but we found the water impossibly deep to anchor. Approaching close to the shore, the echo sounder was still showing 20 metres when John, who was in his usual position at the front of the boat, yelled out 'stop!' The reef, barely a foot under the water, had suddenly appeared. We had often found this problem, the depth of water being either 20 metres or one. We returned to Nao Nao, an island just inside the *passe* where we had entered, and there we found a nice anchorage on sand at the western end of the island. It was a most attractive spot with a splendid view of Ile Haaio against a background of the high mountains of Raiatea rising to 13,000 feet. I got my paints out.

That night we discovered that a strong SE wind at high tide drove a lot of sea over the outer reef and this caused a current of about a knot to run through the anchorage in a north-westerly direction. It caused us to nudge a sandbank, but a second anchor soon solved the problem.

Next day Janet and I went ashore to explore. To our surprise we found an old WW2 airstrip running the length of the island. It is easy to forget how close some of these islands were to hostilities during the war with Japan; many such airstrips were constructed as part of the defensive measures. Raiatea is so mountainous at its southern end that this flat island must have been an obvious choice. We also came across two cats. They appeared to be living wild and were more than a little enthusiastic when Janet returned later with some food for them.

Bora bora from Ilot Tautau, Tahaa

The following day we made our way northward inside the reef as far as *Passe* Toamaro. There we returned to the open sea because the passage inside the reef became too shallow. Further north we were able to return inside at *Passe* Rautoanui from where we made our way to a neat little marina near the western end of the airport. The marina was run by the well-known 'Moorings' Charter Company. Here we met up with four other rally boats, *Best Respects, Ocean Gypsy, Lucky Seven* and *Sooty. Pale moon* and *Baker Street* were at anchor just outside.

Once we were settled I got out the ubiquitous Brompton folding bicycle and rode into the town of Uturoa, on the north-east side of the island. There I found a lot of useful shops and the prices were much cheaper than buying stores at the marina.

Next day we moved north again to Tahaa, an island separate from Raiatea but within the same encircling outer reef. We had heard from our friends on *Papa Golf* that there was a tiny motu, Ilot Tautau, on the reef opposite Baie Tapuamau on the western side. We soon found it but the water around was full of coral heads and quite shallow, so we approached rather gingerly and anchored a good 150 metres from the motu.

Ashore we found a good spot for a barbecue and agreed with Pat, Jim and Joan from *Papa Golf* to return in the evening. This turned out to be one of those idyllic places that one will never forget. Over towards the setting sun lay the famed island of Bora Bora, its twin peaks instantly

117

recognisable from the hundreds of picture postcards one had seen. The palm-covered motu had a white sand beach and there was plenty of brushwood and flotsam lying around to make up a good fire. Some local fishermen came by and sold us a few of their catch to bolster up the dinner. We watched the sun set behind Bora Bora. At first a bright red ball descending to those twin peaks, then a dull claret sphere, sinking beyond the purple silhouette of the island. It was all very romantic, our sentimentality aided greatly by Jim's powerful rum cocktail which he had brought in lavish quantities.

As darkness fell we found numerous land crabs emerging onto the foreshore from the palm forest behind. My crew were unable to resist placing a few of them in the *Papa Golf* dinghy. The shouts and screams of the PG crew soon disturbed the still of the night, as they discovered the occupants of their dinghy. There would, I was sure, be reprisals!

Next day we left for Bora Bora. *Nefertiti*, a large rally boat that had arrived late the previous evening, turned this short trip into a bit of a race. Dave Buckpitt, her skipper, liked to show what she could do and the strong easterly wind was just what he needed to get her going. He piled on the sail and fast though *Greylag* was, we were unable to catch him before we followed him into the lagoon at Bora Bora, through the *Passe* Teavanui.

Bora Bora is an attractive island but much more organised for tourists than the other islands we had visited. Nevertheless, it was pleasant to be a bit closer to civilization for a spell and we enjoyed the hospitality of the yacht club close by the anchorage. Actually we were not anchored, as John on *Griffyn* kindly allowed us to moor alongside her. The water was very deep so I was delighted to accept the offer, anyway *Griffyn* was a big boat and being alongside her was not that different from being alongside a quay!

Ashore I fell into conversation with Chris and Fiona, the owners of *Sheet Lightning*, who said they were desperate to find a replacement crew for the longish legs ahead. I explained that things had become fraught between David and me and I thought it would be a very good idea if we had a spell apart. It would also ease the overcrowding on *Greylag*. They agreed to talk to David and later, to my very great relief, they said they would take him on for a trial. I felt obliged to say to David that I wasn't going to insist that he go but he agreed to give it a try.

Ashore we found a few cheap little places to eat out and chose one for dinner. It consisted of a caravan/café reminiscent of the 'roach coaches' back in Tahiti. We enjoyed a steak and chips for the princely sum of 900 PCF - about £6 each.

Next day, a beach party was organised by David Hughes from *Miss Molly* on the near-by Motu Tapu. It was a little way off, so we decided to take *Greylag* over rather than go all that way by dinghy. We soon collected quite a convoy of dinghies behind *Greylag* as first Wendy and Edwin, the crew from *Griffyn*, and then David Macmillan from *Arabian Sands* and finally the crew from *Calidris* all tied onto our stern. The Motu was ideal for a party and the snorkelling out there was very good.

That evening we visited the local Sofitel hotel for a buffet dinner and another display of Polynesian dancing. The buffet was a disaster, as when we arrived most of the food had gone down the throats of the hotel residents. Several of our colleagues refused to pay and there was a certain amount of unpleasantness. However, the dancing was most enjoyable. After they had completed the formal part the girls and boys went among the audience and picked people out to go on the floor and try for themselves. A handsome hunk picked out Janet to have a go at the bottom wobbling - she did very well.

Next day we moved the boat south to an anchorage just west of Ile Toopua. This was a pleasant spot and conveniently close to the quay at Vaitape, the main town. There we could refuel and top up our stores and water ready for our departure next day on the long leg to the Cook Islands. In the evening a flotilla of charter boats turned up and anchored close by, and in the sunset a small boat turned up with a colourful group of locals who played and sang, as their boat wove in and out of the moored charter boats. This had clearly been organised by the Charter Company and we enjoyed the free entertainment.

In the morning we took the boat over to the quay. While John, Janet and Eileen went off to do the shopping, David and I did the refuelling. He then went off with his gear to join *Sheet lightning*. Though I knew this was necessary, I still felt a bit sad that it had come to this. Afterall, I had picked him from many others and we had been together for a whole year through many adventures. It just goes to show how difficult the crewing problem can be. We soon departed Bora Bora for the Cook Islands.

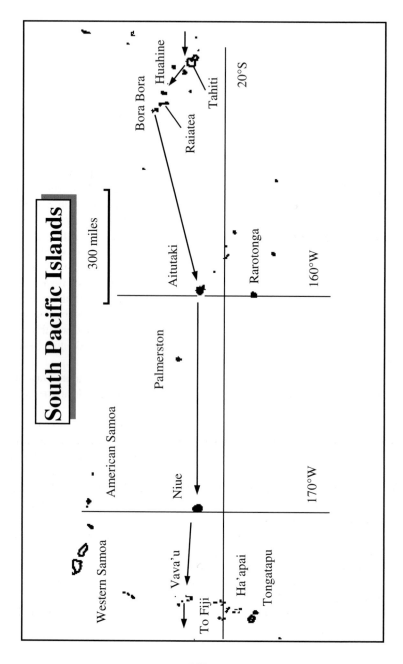

South Pacific Islands

300 miles

Bora Bora

Huahine

Raiatea

Tahiti

20°S

Aitutaki

Rarotonga

160°W

Palmerston

American Samoa

Niue

170°W

Western Samoa

Vava'u

To Fiji

Ha'apai

Tongatapu

120

10 Two Island
Gems in the South Pacific

We left Bora Bora in high spirits. It was a beautiful day, the sea sparkled and the wind blew warm and gentle from the east. We looked back at that twin-peaked skyline, so instantly recognisable, and watched it slowly fade into the distance, turning blue-grey before the last tip sank below the horizon. Ahead lay Aitutaki, a small atoll in the southern Cook Islands, some 420 miles to the south-west. Once again we studied the ubiquitous 'Charlie's Charts'. It was clear that the entrance into the lagoon would be difficult, the channel being both tortuous and shallow. But there were encouraging notes in 'Charlie's Charts' saying that the New Zealand Navy had used explosives to remove a few coral heads and improve the channel. By now we had accumulated a lot of experience at finding our way through coral reefs, so we didn't worry too much about this new challenge. In any case, it was four days sailing away.

The wind dropped down to a bare Force 2 during the morning and the day became hot and stifling as the temperatures climbed to the high nineties. With the boat doing a bare two knots, we decided it would be safe to swim off the stern, provided someone kept a good lookout for sharks! We had seen a few in the lagoons in the Tuomotus, but they had been fairly small reef sharks and not dangerous. However, this was the open ocean and we had occasionally seen some really big ones around the boat. We took turns to climb down the ladder at the stern and drift behind the boat, hanging on to the bottom rung. After hours sweltering in the cockpit, this was bliss. We saw no sharks.

For the next two days we made slow progress in quiet conditions before things got lively on the third day out. Some big shower clouds came up from the east and the wind freshened to a Force 6. It was uncomfortable but at least we were making fast progress. We calculated that we would arrive off Aitutaki in the small hours of Day 5 and would probably have to wait for the sun to come up before tackling the difficult entrance. With the better wind we made 131 miles on our third day and by four o'clock in the morning of the fifth day we were off the entrance to Arutanga Harbour, on the west side of Aitutaki. Alongside the diagram of the entrance in 'Charlie's Charts', there was a note saying *Very narrow channel (50 ft), shallow depths, many heads. Not evident until close, so it is dangerous.'* We exercised due caution and waited for the sun before nosing our way towards the entrance. Several of our friends on other boats had arrived by now, but as we needed less water than most of them it fell to us to attempt the entrance first. It looked rather daunting with a strong tidal current flowing across the channel. This made it necessary to head off and sidle in crab-like in order to stay in the channel. Visibility was good though and we could easily see the coral reef each side of us. We were soon through the first part of the channel and things then became easier as the strong cross current disappeared, allowing us to feel our way into the tiny anchorage. It was so small that we had to anchor fore and aft to stop the boat swinging around and leave room for the others. Eventually nine arrived and we tied the boats together in groups of three to make best use of the limited space.

Soon after we had settled a powerful hail came across the water and I looked up to see a large lady summoning us ashore. We inflated the dinghy and off I went to complete the entrance formalities. Actually they were informalities; I had never met a more friendly and welcoming group of officials. Cindy, who was in charge of health matters and customs, was a large, cheerful lady for whom nothing seemed too much trouble. I asked her about a party in the local Rapai Hotel, which we had heard took place on a Friday evening.

'Oh yes,' she said, 'but you'll have to book. I'll take you there.'

She led the way to the back of the customs building where she had parked her scooter. I looked at it, then at Cindy and back again to the scooter. I didn't really believe it was capable of supporting both of us! Unperturbed, she got astride and pointed to the small ledge of seat behind her. I struggled on, not wishing to offend someone so willing to help. The rear wheel sank to the limit of its springs and we sped off down the road to the Rapai. Though my arms reached only half way round my generously proportioned chauffeuse, I regained my confidence as I discovered that our combined weight gave a certain stability to the arrangements.

The lady at the Rapai looked at me with a slight air of distrust.

' Yes,' I repeated, 'I would like to reserve 28 places for me and my friends, we've heard it's a splendid party!'

She still looked doubtful, they are not used to that many visitors all at once and she wanted to be sure I wasn't pulling her leg. Cindy came to the rescue, confirming that there were indeed nine yachts in the harbour, and the lady from the Rapai booked us in against the security of my Mastercard.

Back at the harbour, a huge cruise liner, the 'World Discoverer', had anchored off the reef and the crew were busy ferrying passengers ashore in a large inflatable dinghy. Theirs was a lightning visit and by lunchtime they had gone on their way. How, I wondered, could anyone learn anything about the place in so short a time. Whistle-stop tourism must be very frustrating for any but the 'been there, got the tee-shirt' brigade.

Our introduction to Arutanga was made all the more pleasurable by meeting up with Father Don, the local Roman Catholic priest. Actually we had already met him on the airwaves; it was he who had replied to our VHF radio calls when we arrived. Amusingly, and appropriately for that matter, he answered to the name 'Sky Pilot'! He was a mine of information and very amusing company. He described his presence in Aitutaki as a sort of punishment posting which followed some altercation with the bishop back in New Zealand. As a fellow reactionary, I warmed to him immediately, though I could easily see how he might not have been flavour of the month with the church hierarchy. Unconventional he may have been, but he entered into everything on Aitutaki with bubbling enthusiasm and fought hard for the interests of the islanders. No sooner had we shaken his hand than he was taking our orders for bread and muffins, which he himself baked as a profitable sideline. The profits, I hasten to add, were donated to the Church or other good causes.

'Father Don stories' were legion and before we had departed our colleagues had added another. He had told them that the local hospital's ambulance was *caput* because although they had acquired a new engine for it, unhappily nobody on the island knew how to install it. Unbeknown to Don, David Forsyth and Eddie Scougall were experts on diesel engines and later they generously donated a day's work to fit the new engine. They have made friends for life on Aitutaki!

Our evening in the Rapai Hotel was one to remember. After a splendid buffet supper, we were entertained by a troupe of local dancers. The show started with a welcome challenge from the Chief, resplendent in his raffia 'grass' skirt and spear in hand. It reminded me of the Haka performed by the All Blacks before their rugby matches and probably has similar origins. Then on came the dancers, four men and eight girls, to give us a brilliant display of Polynesian dancing. As a medical man, I took a professional interest in the extraordinary hip movements; their lower lumbar intervertebral joints must be of the ball-and-socket variety! We heard that this group was highly regarded and had won many competitions in Tahiti.

Next day we travelled to the north-east of the atoll for a boat trip to Tapuaetai or One-foot Island. Our guide for the day was Nane. She was also the Mayor's wife so we felt privileged. Nane drove us to the northern end of Aitutaki where the island curves round to the east before breaking up into a chain of smaller islands, or motus, along the eastern edge of the central lagoon. Nane was full of stories. She told us how her ancestors had come by boat from other islands to the north. On one occasion a canoe had got stuck on the reef and in an effort to get it off, one of the men had broken his back when the canoe fell on him. It happened on the next island to Aitutaki, which was consequently named Akitua or Broken-back Island.

A wooden bridge links Aitutaki to Akitua and there we found a substantial resort hotel. One could well understand the choice of this place. It was idyllic, with white sand all round and palms to give shade. Here was our first view of the lagoon, and a more inviting place one could not imagine. The atoll is roughly triangular with sides about eight miles long. The lagoon is shallow and so encumbered with coral heads as to be unnavigable by anything other than the small, outboard-powered open boats used for tours. We were soon on our way to One Foot Island, speeding across the turquoise blue water, trusting that the boatman knew the water well as we passed innumerable sandbanks and coral patches. He explained that New Zealand had used the lagoon as a flying boat base during WW2, the old Sunderland flying boats had come in here to refuel.

There are two stories as to how One Foot Island got its name. The more romantic has it that a father and son were escaping across the lagoon from warriors on Aitutaki Island. The father carefully trod in the son's footsteps in the sand to give the impression that only one fugitive went that way. He was caught and killed and the warriors left, assuming there was only one. The more mundane story is that the island was named for no better reason than its footprint shape. On One Foot we enjoyed a barbecue. One young fellow got things going by splitting up coconuts for firewood. This he did by impaling them on a sharp wooden spike set in the ground - the coconuts were unripe and did not yet contain hard shells. Inevitably the fare was tuna, but it was nice enough cooked in soya sauce over the fire and accompanied by oodles of fresh fruit.

Afterwards came more dancing, this time by some young girls, perhaps eight or nine years old. They were absolutely charming. Apparently all young girls learn the basic dancing skills as tiny tots. The music and singing were provided by the cook and the boatman, no job demarcation disputes here! I admired their versatility, 'Mr Wonderful is my name' one of them replied.

Back at Arutanga that evening we all enjoyed fish and chips in the little café by the harbour. Not unlike home except that the fish was Wahoo and delicious. Next day was Sunday and the crews divided their support between Father Don's Catholic Church and the Presbyterian rival down the road. We are not churchgoers but after all the help we had received from Father Don, we were happy to go and support him. Besides, it was a joy to listen to the singing.

Halfway through the service one of our colleagues fell to the floor in a dead faint. We carried him out and he slowly recovered on the front porch. But I was concerned that there might be something more serious behind the incident, so we summoned the ambulance and in due course an open-backed truck arrived to take us to the hospital. This was how we first learned of the broken down ambulance, which our friends subsequently repaired. Happily the local Thai doctor and a New Zealand medical student under training declared the patient fit after an ECG and a thorough check.

That evening the heavens opened as a tropical low-pressure system developed just west of Aitutaki. I was glad we were not at sea, the weather forecasts were dreadful, with winds up to 50 knots expected. Despite the rain we all went off to the Crusher's Bar for a meal. This establishment is a well-known Aitutaki attraction and we looked forward to a good evening. Getting there was a problem as there were no local taxis. One or two of us were lucky enough to get a lift in a tourist's car, but most travelled on the back of a truck with only a rough tarpaulin to protect them from the torrential rain.

We had an enjoyable meal but got drenched on the return journey to the boat. Some of our friends who stayed late, got involved in an altercation with the drunken restaurant owner, during which Pat from *Papa Golf* was beaten around the head with an iron bar and required a number of stitches at the hospital. The story spread around the island like wildfire and next day everyone had a slightly different account of what had happened. The islanders were very unhappy that such a thing had occurred on their normally peaceful island and, given the importance they attach to hospitality, were clearly embarrassed. To set their minds at rest we put up a notice at the local post office; we were advised that this was the usual way to convey a general message. It said how much we had all enjoyed our stay at Aitutaki and that after all the fun and pleasure of our visit, one small bump on the head would very soon be forgotten! And so it was, except possibly by Pat Gordon who owned the head!

The day after the Crusher's bar incident, it was still raining cats and dogs and a fierce wind blew across the harbour. We were anxious that the boats might drag their anchors and several put strong lines ashore. Mostly these were secured to palm trees but *Sheet Lightning* secured hers to a large steel barge moored at the edge of the harbour. They didn't know at the time that the barge was itself moored only to some big rocks on the edge of the harbour. In the very fierce gusts, these began to move and for a short while, we feared the barge would come adrift and sweep across the harbour, taking all of us with it. Luckily, this did not happen.

The bad weather was caused by a nasty tropical low sweeping past just north of us. Conditions at sea must have been very bad indeed and we were glad to be in harbour. We heard on the radio that *Miss Molly* had an outboard motor swept from her stern rail during a knockdown. *Gambatte Go*, had her dinghy swept off the back of the boat, taking the davits with it. We heard the full story later when they arrived in Aitutaki for a rest.

We had decided to stay another day to give the weather a chance to settle, it had already improved quite a bit. On *Papa Golf*, a catamaran owned by Pat Gordon (him with the bumped head), they decided to leave early. Unfortunately, Pat misjudged the cross-tide and went aground at the side of the channel. Luckily the improving weather saved him from any serious damage; he would have been in a difficult position if it had turned nasty again. He was stuck there for 24-hours before a local boat pulled him off.

On leaving Aitutaki we had planned to go to Nuku Alofa at the southern end of Tonga and then cruise north through the Ha'pai Islands to Vava'u. This was a rather ambitious plan for the time we had available, so we changed our minds and decided to go to Vava'u via a tiny isolated island called Niue. This plan had the advantage of providing a break in an otherwise long journey. Even so, Niue was 640 miles away and this would be Janet's longest ever sea voyage.

We set out in a lumpy sea but by the evening the wind had disappeared and we had to motor. And so it went on for the next 5 days, the longest spell of calm weather we had yet experienced. We set the engine revs at the most economical rate, as we had barely enough fuel to get to Niue and none of us fancied drifting around for days waiting for a breeze.

In the afternoon of our sixth day at sea it was time for a shower. Although *Greylag* did not have any built in shower facilities, we did have our Hozelock garden spray device which one could pump up and use very effectively in calm conditions such as we were enjoying that day. With the girls on board, the procedure was for the boys to busy themselves down below when it was the girls' turn. Before disappearing below I rather foolishly failed to cast a weather eye astern, and so did not see the large bank of cloud creeping up on us. Eileen was in mid-ablutions when a stiff breeze came in ahead of the shower cloud. The mainsail was up at the time so I called out to Eileen that we would have to come up soon and take it down. The squall then got worse and poor Eileen had to grab a towel as John and I came up on deck in a big hurry. We were too late! In a fierce gust of wind the mainsail split in two with a horrible tearing sound. We let the halyard go and got the sail down on deck, but it was badly damaged and unusable without repairs. Happily we were quite close to Nuie and had just enough fuel to make it on the engine, but we would not get there until after dark and I was worried about a night-time landfall. I radioed through to John on *Saullitaire* who had already arrived. He soon set my mind at rest when he told me there were several large mooring buoys in deep water off the small town of Alofi on the west coast. He said he would shine a torch when we arrived. At nine o'clock we were there and, with the help of John's torch, we soon tied up to a buoy and settled down to a good meal and a long sleep.

Niue is a small island about 12 miles by 10 miles, with thirteen small villages spread around the coast. It was formerly administered by New Zealand, but is now semi-autonomous, although still dependant on New Zealand for financial aid and defence. The population was small and getting smaller as many of the locals disappeared to Aukland to find work or a more sophisticated way of life. One or two of the villages have been more or less abandoned by this emigration. Alofi is the main town and the seat of local government. It also has the only harbour, a simple concrete quay running out over the coral fringe with a narrow channel dredged along its southern side. The supply ships (about one a week) back into this channel and tie up alongside the quay. There is no breakwater so the swell from the Pacific arrives unhindered, making for very exciting dinghy landings.

Avatele Bay, Niue

We soon met up with Wally and Mary Saunders, two delightful New Zealanders, who ran a local garage - one of only two on the island. Wally went out of his way to help us and the other four boats, which had come to Niue. He was full of information about the island; he and Mary seemed pleased to have the opportunity to talk to other westerners. Niue is very isolated and has very few of the facilities one would enjoy in New Zealand, they must have felt rather lonely at times. Such places are fascinating and beautiful for a short visit, but I cannot imagine living there on a permanent basis, yet it was their choice.

Our entry formalities were speedily dealt with and we turned to the next priority, which was fuel. All the boats had arrived with nearly empty tanks. There were no fuel pumps on the quayside but a local garage owner (the other one), agreed to deliver 200-litre barrels and provide a hand-pump to fill our cans. This was quite a task as most boats needed about two hundred litres and this all had to be transported to the boats in 10 or 20 litre cans! It would not have been so bad if it had not been for the wave surges, making it very difficult indeed to get the heavy cans into the dinghies. In the end everyone managed to refuel and we all repaired to the only hotel on the island, about a mile and a half up the road. We soon found out that one only has to start walking and someone offers a lift, I don't think we were ever passed by a vehicle without it stopping and offering a lift.

At the Niue Hotel we met the manager Kevin, another native New Zealander. We were amused to discover that he was also Commodore of the Niue Yacht Club! Needless to say, we were soon all signed up as members, for a lifetime subscription of 10 dollars. For this we received a club burgee, consisting of a map of the island with its latitude and longitude - just the thing for a bit of one-upmanship back home. At 19°05'S, 169°55'W this was a long way from home!

We enjoyed a good lunch and stayed on for an even better dinner with some splendid, if expensive, New Zealand wine. Kevin kindly offered us the use of his veranda to mend our sail. This was going to be a big and difficult job and we needed somewhere to lay the whole sail out flat. Also it was going to help a lot to have an electricity supply for our sewing machine - I didn't fancy sewing about 20 metres of seam by hand. Kevin drove us back to the boats after dinner.

Next day was sail mending day. We were soon ashore after a bit of a struggle getting the heavy sail into the dinghy. We carried it in turns up the steep hill from the quay and soon met up with a friendly fellow who offered us a lift to the hotel.

'It's round the back', he said. We went there but couldn't see a car.

'Hop on the back and hold on well', he said, indicating a huge flatbed transporter of the kind one sees moving bulldozers around. Up we hopped; there was plenty of room even if the seating was makeshift. We soon arrived safely at the hotel.

A badly torn sail is not an easy thing to repair, even with the help of a sewing machine. Luckily I had a roll of sticky sail material which we stuck over the tear after carefully lining up the torn edges. This is not strong enough for a final repair, but it holds the sail in shape while one stitches a patch on the other side using thicker sailcloth. It took us all day but the result was reasonably satisfactory. That evening we enjoyed a good meal at Ciao's, a local Italian restaurant; we certainly felt we had earned it.

Next day was more restful; Janet and I went down to the delightful little beach alongside the harbour. There we found a huge variety of fish and coral in the rock pools on the foreshore. By now we had discovered another common species at Niue - sea snakes! There were lots of them around the harbour area, black with bright yellow bands and about 2 feet long. They were all over the place. Some lingered menacingly near the iron ladder where the dinghies unloaded passengers; others would appear around the boat moorings. Sea snakes are deadlier than land snakes but it is said to be rare for them to bite. They have small mouths making it difficult for them to attack large animals like us. I made such reassuring remarks to Janet but she remained wary of them. One boat, *Aditi,* had a snake come up the cockpit drains!

Next day, our fourth at Niue, Wally organised a trip round the island. Our guide for the day was 'Honey Lady', as she is universally known on the island - when she is not guiding, she runs her honey farm. She took us first to Limu pools, spectacular inlets from the sea with gin-clear water and lots of exotic fish. And (you've guessed it) sea snakes! I swam off to enjoy this marine wonderland and was just studying a small octopus lurking beneath a coral head, when I noticed three sea snakes advancing on me from three different directions. They are curious creatures and will often come to see what you are doing. *Don't panic,* I thought to myself, *remember they don't bite, as you're always telling everybody else!* But then I recalled Janet's comment during a sugar shortage back in the seventies - 'Never mind don't panic' she had said, 'panic first!' So I did. Unfortunately the only way out of the corner I was in took me across a shallow patch of coral and I emerged from the water with blood streaming down my front from some nasty coral grazes. It looked worse than it was. One of my colleagues remarked that it was the first time he'd seen someone with flippers go up on the plane! After that, I became more reticent with advice about the non-biting sea snakes.

Our next stop was at Teluva arches, near the northern end of the island. Getting there involved a walk through a 'coral forest'. Presumably some volcanic eruption had once driven Niue up from the sea, carrying the coral with it. The fossil coral was indeed tree-like. The arches were magnificent, huge flying buttresses of rock stood out from the cliffs, made all the more spectacular by their reflections in the calm water below. It reminded me of Étrétat in Normandy, where Claude Monet did a series of paintings, except for the complete absence of tourists or development. Anywhere in Europe or America such magnificent scenery would be a huge tourist attraction. There it was almost deserted, its grandeur unknown in a corner of the world which would be well described as the back of beyond.

Before returning to Alofi we visited some of the small villages. Just a few tens of families surviving on a meagre agriculture - coconuts, goats, chickens and fishing. We saw one village that appeared completely deserted. *All gone to Aukland,* I thought, but Wally said there had been some nasty bug in the local water and it had been decided to evacuate the village.

That evening, we returned to Ciao's for a great pizza feast with

Sicilian white wine.

We were due to leave next day for the Vava'u Islands at the northern end of Tonga. At 220 miles, this was a shorter journey than the last one and would see us across the international dateline, thus losing a day altogether. By the time the 3rd of June was over, we would be across the line and it would be the 5th. One fellow on the rally was very upset by this, the 4th of June was his birthday! For us on *Greylag* we would reach 180° West and that would be halfway around the world.

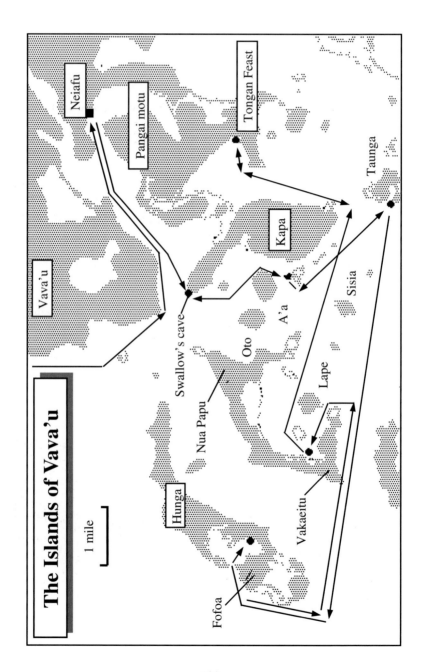

The Islands of Vava'u

1 mile

Vava'u

Neiafu

Pangai motu

Tongan Feast

Swallow's cave

Kapa

Taunga

Oto

A'a

Sisia

Nua Papu

Lape

Hunga

Vakaeitu

Fofoa

11 Tonga - the Deserted Islands of Vava'u

The voyage to Tonga from Niue was 220 miles. We left Niue early on the 3rd of June and soon ran into some strong 25-knot winds, but we sailed the boat conservatively and happily the girls' stomachs seemed to be thoroughly seaworthy. John and I were now doing alternate watches but Janet and Eileen also got up to keep us company. By the second night the weather had improved and by dawn we were within sight of the Vava'u group of islands at the northern end of the huge Tongan Archipelago. We skirted round the northern edge of Vava'u Island then south past Port Refuge and Tuungasika Island and up the 'fiord' to the town of Neiafu.

At Neiafu we tied up at the customs quay and were visited by a succession of officials from immigration, health and customs. There were tight rules prohibiting the importing of fresh vegetables and a few other commodities, the officials took all of these off us. John, our resident curry

Neiafu Harbour, Vava'u

133

expert, complained bitterly at the loss of a large bunch of garlic cloves.

'Suppose,' he said to the official, 'that I can't get any more.'

'If you can't,' said the official, 'come and see me and I will give them back to you.'

So much for the rules. We were highly suspicious that the officials used the confiscated vegetables in their own households!

After we were cleared in, we took a mooring buoy further up the harbour and were soon ashore. The town was a ramshackle place with an assortment of small stores and a bank. There were pigs wandering around all over the place, apparently this was commonplace throughout Tonga. An American, Don Coleman, ran a small boat yard on the shore and provided water and fuel. He had a small, thatched 'entertainments' lounge where we all repaired for a party that first evening. It was a merry affair and two of our colleagues managed to fall into the harbour. They were swiftly rescued. Eileen seemed to be getting on like a house on fire with Pat, the skipper of *Papa Golf*.

Next morning I decided to have another go at repairing an engine injector seating which was leaking a little, as it had been on and off ever since we left France. Just as I had the injector out, a terrific squall came whistling through the harbour. The gusts were over 40 knots and several boats around us dragged their anchors. We had a few anxious moments hoping that we wouldn't break our moorings. This would have been serious without an engine, as anchoring in the very deep water would have been problematical. Despite all this, I managed to fix the injector with a new copper washer and some Hermatite gunge.

Later that day I met up with Geoff Pack, the Editor of Yachting Monthly, who gave me the good news that my article on San Blas (that seemed a long time ago) would be published in the August edition. Geoff gave me some useful tips on writing for the magazine and we arranged a rendezvous for the next morning so that he could get some shots of *Greylag* under sail. Little did we know at that time that Geoff was already a bit under the weather with a form of cancer from which, sadly, he later died.

After the photo session with Geoff next day, we set off to explore Vava'u. We were never ones to stay in harbour for long, there were almost always more interesting things to do in the surrounding area. This was certainly true of Neiafu. We retraced our tracks down the 'fiord' and stopped for a while off the famous Swallow's Cave at the northern end of Kapa Island. I say 'stopped', but there was no question of anchoring in the impossibly deep water. John and I took it in turns to keep the boat on station while the others took the dinghy into the cave. There were many stalactites inside and it was possible to land on a small beach and walk through to an inner cave, which was open to the sky overhead. We never saw any swallows!

After the cave we went south again to an idyllic anchorage at the southern end of Kapa. The snorkelling there was spectacular with an extraordinary range of sea slugs, large and highly coloured creatures like cucumbers on the seabed. The big ones were perhaps two feet long. This spot was much loved by Prince Charles when he was brought here during a visit to Tonga. That evening we enjoyed happy hour watching some brightly coloured kingfishers fishing off the island; they were half as big again as the native British variety. As darkness gathered, some enormous fruit bats emerged from the trees on the island.

The morning broke sunny and sparkling and two ladies in a canoe selling their basketwork visited us. It was very high quality work and they were excellent 'salesmen' - Janet and Eileen purchased a few items to take home. Later we moved south to Taunga Island which our pilotage notes said had the most beautiful beach in Tonga. We had great difficulty getting *Greylag* in close as the water was shallow and there were many coral heads. We anchored well off and went in by dinghy, peace of mind being greatly aided by John volunteering to stay aboard. We walked across the island and came across a cemetery in among the trees; it was a cared-for place and several of the graves were beautifully adorned with flowers. Taunga was certainly a pretty spot; the beaches were pure white sand and the lee side was flat calm, so that the curve of the bay allowed one to see reflections of the palms across the water. We met two young boys from the village, with their dog Mex.

The anchorage at Taunga was too exposed to stay overnight, so we moved to the lagoon at Hunga Island. This island was comparatively large and together with the small island of Fofoa, surrounded a substantial lagoon with only a very narrow entrance. This was barely 50 metres wide and there was a large rock in the middle and a shallow patch just inside. Its other difficulty was a strong tide running out on the ebb but happily this was minimal when we arrived and we got in without trouble.

Once inside we made our way across the lagoon, lured to the bay on the other side by the presence of three New Zealand boats at anchor. We presumed, rightly, that they knew a good spot. We got talking to the New Zealanders who had come over with a group of yachts for the season.

Dick Allan
1996. Vavu'a

Hunga Island from the lagoon, Vava'u

From the bay at Hunga I walked along the ridge that ran the length of the island and enjoyed the many tropical flowers and butterflies. Near the southern tip of the island I came across a deserted orchard of citrus fruits, mainly small oranges. It did not appear to be looked after and I helped myself to a few pocketfuls - these turned out to be delicious. That evening the kingfishers and fruit bats again visited us.

On arrival at Neiafu the rally skippers had been given a copy of some pilotage notes prepared for their clients by the 'Moorings' Charter Company. These were most helpful and identified numerous anchorages, giving each a number. At the radio net that evening we heard that a lot of the other boats were heading for No16, we looked this up, it was at Vakaeitu.

Before leaving for Vakaeitu's intriguing anchorage No16, we went for a snorkel over the reefs in the unnavigable entrance to the lagoon between Fofoa and the southern tip of Hunga itself. There were some magnificent shoals of fish there and numerous bright blue starfish. At the foot of the cliffs on Fofoa we found several rock layers full of fossil clams.

A big attraction at Vakaeitu was a sort of 'escape' hotel, for those who like holidays on the wild side and are prepared to rough it a bit. The place was called the 'Lighthouse Café' and was run by an Austrian, Hans, who was delighted with the large number of visitors from the rally boats (18 in the bay) and laid on a 'uma' for us. This was a sort of hors-d'oeuvre with a lot of small bits and pieces but, for my money, rather insubstantial. However we enjoyed it well enough and the wine was good which made getting back through the woods to our dinghies all the more difficult.

Back on the boat we decided to have a bit of a game, knowing that nearly all our boats kept a listening watch on Channel 77 VHF. With my best imitation of that well-known TV sit-com 'Allo Allo' I transmitted.

'Allo London, zees ees night 'awk, are you receiving me, over'

Of course, the whole fleet was!

'Listen vary carefully, I shall say zees ornly wunz. Zere are crabs in ze coconut trees.'

A commendable Herr Flick soundalike came on. 'Zees improper use of ze radio waves vil not be tolerated'

Eileen joined in, egged on by all of us. 'Herr Flick, zees is Helga. 'ow is ze beeg sausage? You vant I should vear ze black stockings tonight?'

It got worse!

Next day we all went off to Lisa's beach on Pangai Motu for a Tongan feast. This was more enjoyable in the prospect, while the pig was slowly cooking in a hole in the ground, than when it was finally served up. A great stretch of ground was covered with palm leaves and decked out with dishes of fruit, kasava, bananas, and other plentiful but excessively bland dishes. I found the meal rather unappetizing and tasteless. Afterwards there was some singing and dancing by a local group of very substantial ladies (they like them that way in Tonga) and this, in my view, was more enjoyable than the feast.

Back in Neiafu next day there was a party in the Paradise Hotel. It was to celebrate the halfway point of our trip. After all we had seen and done it was hard to believe that we were still only halfway round the world. The Shantymen, that splendid group of volunteer singers that had first performed back in San Cristobal at the navy party, entertained us with their usual gusto, but what was to follow seriously upstaged them. Four of the young ladies on the rally and four fellows had been secretly practising the art of Polynesian dancing. Announced as 'The Coconuts', on they came in traditional grass skirts and coconut bras and gave an impeccable display to the enduring delight of all of us. The fellows were pretty good too.

Next day, after a hurried last shopping expedition, we left for Fiji.

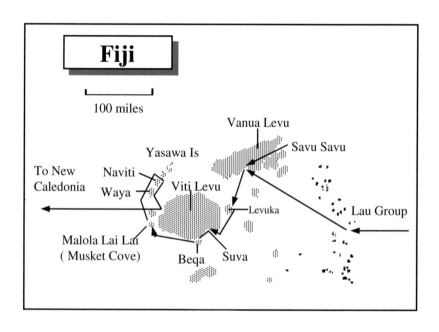

12 FIJI
The Fijian Homeland, Invaded by Missionaries and Indians

We departed from Neiafu on the 13th of June for the 420-mile journey to Savu Savu, a small town with a harbour on the south coast of Vanua Levu, the smaller of the two main islands of Fiji. Our route took us through a narrow gap in the Lao group of islands, about 100 miles south-west of Vanua Levu. We had enjoyed easy downwind sailing since Tonga and we approached the gap in the Lao group in the last of the daylight on our second day at sea.

On each side of the narrow passage through the islands there are reefs and rocks, so we had to be certain of our position before going through in the dark. I considered 'heaving to' and waiting for daylight to return; but with the GPS and our radar to help, this seemed unnecessarily cautious. The trouble is that charts of these remote areas can have significant errors; they are based on surveys done in the last century by the likes of Captain William Bligh. Even though the GPS gives an accurate latitude and longitude, this can lead one into disaster if the landmasses are inaccurately drawn on the chart. A one-mile error is serious when negotiating a narrow channel such as we were approaching that evening. The way round the difficulty is to set a waypoint (or position) on the GPS that is, say, 5 miles off the entrance to the channel according to the chart. When you get to this position you use the radar to measure the distance from some good solid object, such as an island. If the radar suggests you are closer to, or further from the island than the chart indicates, believe the radar. After all the radar is looking directly at the hard stuff!

All this has to be done with care because the radar will not always pick up a coral reef or low-lying coastline. But if there are good, hunky islands around, giving good radar reflections, the system works well. On

139

this occasion our chart turned out to be fairly accurate and we navigated our way through the Lao group without any difficulty.

Next day we enjoyed splendid fast sailing and arrived at the pretty anchorage off Savu Savu in the early evening. It was a beautifully protected spot, lying between the waterfront of the town and a small wooded island opposite. We cleared through customs and immigration, where we were expected to fill up every form in triplicate. Worse still, we found out later that one has to repeat the process at every harbour one visits. 'But we've already cleared into Fiji ,' I would protest, but it was to no avail. Many of the huge Indian immigrant population, outnumbering the native Fijians, are employed in government offices and they are not about to volunteer up their jobs.

Savu Savu had a High Street of assorted shops, a small market and not much else. On the quayside there had been an old copra hut, which was now converted into a yacht club, with showers, a bar and an excellent little café. This was much enjoyed by all of us after the expensive drabness of Neiafu. An Indian in the town gave me a haircut which Janet declared to be a catastrophe, but at least it would last a few weeks even if it did look more like a shave!

On our second evening we went by dinghy over to the small island

The water front at Savu Savu

opposite the Copra Hut, for a curry buffet on the beach. There were Indian dancers to entertain us - I was beginning to realise that just about everything here was run by the Indians. Where, I wondered, could one find real Fijians doing their own thing? A journey inland might have found some, but visits organised by the tourist office always seem a bit artificial to me. We planned to go later to some of the smaller islands in the Mamanuthas and Yasawas where we had heard we could find a little bit of Fiji, relatively untouched by colonisers and immigrants. For now we were content to enjoy the facilities of the Copra Hut and restock *Greylag* with stores from the town.

On our third day we went to clear out with the officials, completing another pile of forms in the process; patience was wearing thin by now. Some of our colleagues on other boats were unfortunately having even more trouble. They had confessed to large amounts of alcoholic ship's stores. Normally this would not be a problem as long as they were not taken ashore. One skipper was charged treble duty and reluctantly paid up rather than invite trouble. But David Buckpitt, on *Nefertiti*, would have none of it.

'This is a British ship,' he declared, 'a registered British ship, just like the QE ll, and entitled to have stores aboard without attracting duty.'

Well he did have a very big yacht! But the customs man said they had made a rule that excluded boats smaller than ocean liners. David stuck to his guns and in the end they gave up. We kept very quiet indeed, as the customs had not looked in *Greylag*'s hold!

From Savu Savu we sailed southward in a brisk east wind to Levuka, on the eastern side of Ovalau Island, just off Viti Levu. The harbour there was horribly uncomfortable in the east wind and we considered going straight back to sea as an alternative to spending an uncomfortable night. However Levuka is the old capital of Fiji and steeped in British colonial history; we wanted to see it so we decided to put up with the conditions.

Next day we looked for a place to land our dinghy but everywhere was difficult, big surges of water making any landing hazardous. Then John, who had struggled ashore with difficulty earlier, produced a postcard - an aerial photograph of the town. A little to the north of where we were anchored, it showed a small boat harbour. Although it didn't look as though it had enough water to take *Greylag* in, at least we could land the dinghy more easily where there was some protection from the surge. We moved the boat and soon got ashore in comparative comfort.

In spite of the wet and windy weather, we enjoyed a short walk around the town. The High Street looked like the film set for 'High Noon', wooden fronted houses with balconies and stable doors reminiscent of the Wild West, lined both sides of the street. At the southern end of town there was a massive tuna-canning factory, and beyond that we found a monument commemorating the visit of HRH Prince Charles on the occasion of the granting of independence from the UK in 1970. We enjoyed an excellent lunch in 'The Whale's Tail', an institution much loved by visiting yotties.

After lunch we discovered the Levuka Club, an outpost of the old British Raj which seemed scarcely to have noticed the coming of independence. It lay a couple of blocks back from the High Street, alongside an immaculate cricket pitch and a rugby field. We approached the front door rather sheepishly, uncertain of receiving a welcome in view of the large 'Members Only' notice by the gate. We need not have worried, a native Fijian received us graciously.

'We were worried by the 'Members Only' notice', I said to him.

'Oh, that's just to keep out the locals,' he replied!

Inside the club the walls were covered with photographs of old British and New Zealand warships and those inevitable cricket teams. We were back in the nineteen twenties it seemed.

We left Levuka next day and sailed round the south-eastern corner of Viti Levu to the modern capital at Suva. It was still raining on and off, somebody said it always does in Suva. At the marina we were met by our good friend Keith Ellis, who had flown out to join us for a few weeks and was waiting on the quayside, resplendent in his Fijian skirt which he had purchased that morning.

Suva is a rather grubby town, with a splendid market and populated almost entirely by Indians. I was still hoping to find 'real Fiji', so we quickly did the shopping and refuelled ready to go to sea again. It was still raining. Our next destination was Beqa, a small island off the southern coast, where there was a genuine Fijian village, Naiseuseu. I had high hopes that this would turn out to be the real thing.

There is a custom in rural Fiji, the sevu sevu, which requires one first to visit the Chief or Headman of the village and present him with a gift of yanggona, the roots of a variety of pepper plant from which they make the slightly tranquillising kava drink. If he accepts your gift, and he nearly always does, he then grants you permission to visit his village and may even provide a guide. The custom is indispensable and great offence will be taken if you neglect it. With this in mind, I had asked John and Keith to purchase the necessary roots in town, sufficient for a few village visits. When they returned I looked at their purchase with an anxious eye. I thought I had seen yanggona back in Savu Savu and this didn't look quite right to me. However, we put the stuff down below and I thought no more about it.

That afternoon it finally stopped raining as we left Suva and headed along the coast to Beqa. The island is surrounded by a substantial coral reef, so we had to find the pass into the lagoon before crossing to Vaga bay, off the village on the western side. We arrived there in the last of the daylight and anchored alongside an Australian yacht *Sailmaker*. Next morning we planned to visit the village but I still felt uneasy that the 'roots' we had purchased might not be Yanggona. I decided to row over to the Aussie boat and seek advice. All they heard back on *Greylag* were loud peels of laughter. I rowed back to *Greylag* in due course.

'John,' I said, keeping as straight a face as possible, 'tell me again what the fellow in the market had said about these roots.'

'Well,' he started, 'I asked for kava roots and these are what he gave me. I queried him about them but he was adamant that these were k..ava.'

The light dawned on both of us at the same time, the fellow must have thought John had asked for kasava! No wonder the Aussies had thought it so funny, kasava is a sort of potato and the Chief would not have been amused by such a gift. Indeed he would probably have reacted like Henry V to that famous gift of tennis balls. A quick regression to the old custom of cannibalism might have seen me served up as 'long pig'! Very kindly, the Australians sold me some of their genuine yanggonna and rescued us from a social gaff of the first order.

We made the short trip over to the village and were immediately surrounded by hordes of excited youngsters, eager to help us carry our dinghy up the beach.

'Will you take me to your Chief,' I asked.

'OK,' said one young lad and led the way into the village.

The Chief invited us into his house and we sat on the floor, cross-legged, us on one side and he and his family on the other. I placed the yanggona on the floor in front of him and said how pleased we were to visit his village. Somehow this didn't seem quite solemn enough and I thought for a moment that I should have conveyed greetings from Her Majesty the Queen, I didn't though. He picked up the roots and passed them to his son on his left. There followed an intriguing little ceremony of acceptance in which they alternately chanted words of greeting, in a language I didn't understand, followed by gentle clapping of their hands. This went on for a minute or so while we sat there anxious that all would be well. As soon as this was finished there were smiles all round and we spent a while discussing village life and their problems, and telling them a little about England and ours.

After the sevu sevu ceremony, the Chief's son took us on a tour of the village. There were a few genuine Fijian houses, built mainly from palm fronds, but many were more solidly but less attractively built of blocks, with corrugated iron roofs. The whole place was spotlessly clean. We visited the church, which was clearly the centrepiece of the village. The early missionaries had great success in Fiji, persuading them to give up their cannibalism and turn to God. They have done this with great enthusiasm.

It was in the church at Naiseuseu that we first enjoyed the magnificent singing of the Fijians. The Chief had arranged for the choir to assemble specially for us and they gave us a short but delightful performance. They have marvellously powerful voices and a sense of rhythm and harmony that needs no musical accompaniment to guide it. The choirmaster gave a few preliminary notes, which he sang in tenor for the men and a true falsetto for the young boys and girls, and off they went in perfect tune, as he snapped his fingers to keep the time. It was a joyful sound that rang in our ears long after we had left to return to the boat.

The day when Janet was due to fly home was fast approaching, so we had to press on to Musket Cove, a resort complex on Mulola Lailai Island, from where she would take a small plane back to the main airport at Nandi. The island was more than a comfortable day's sail away and we had to negotiate a pass in the reef before running up inside to Musket Cove. I was concerned that we might run out of daylight before getting there. The pass provided access to the main Harbour at Lautoka and, conveniently, was one of the few with good lights to show the way in. But once in, the route up to Musket Cove was strewn with coral and definitely not to be attempted at night. So we settled on getting through the pass and anchoring for the night in a bay just inside. Next morning we ran up to Musket Cove without difficulty.

Musket Cove turned out to be a substantial resort complex, developed and run by an Australian, Dick Smith. There was a small marina, three restaurants and all the necessary facilities to have a bit of a holiday after the intense sailing of the last few months. It all proved a bit expensive, but we enjoyed the short interlude back in touch with western style and culture.

On *'Miss Molly',* David and Linda's son and his fiancee had arranged to get married here on the beach! It was a colourful occasion, a strange mixture of Fijian customs intertwined in a Christian marriage ceremony. The bride arrived in style, borne on a palm frond litter on the shoulders of four Fijian warriors, resplendent in their local dress. They were very big fellows; no wonder Fiji has such a fearsome rugby team! The happy couple were married beneath an archway of flowers, it was all very romantic.

The day arrived when Janet was due to leave. She flew off with Eileen from the little airstrip at Mulola Lailai, in a small 12-seater aircraft belonging to Sunflower Airlines. It took them to Nandi international airport for the long journey home. I felt very down after saying goodbye to them, I would not be seeing Janet again until Christmas time and that was six months away, the longest time we had been apart since we married 18 years before.

But now there were things to do. The boat had not had its bottom painted since Panama and was covered in barnacles and weed. We were back in a part of the world that has tides, albeit a good deal smaller than those in the UK. The difference between high and low tide was about 2 metres, just enough to dry the boat out on the sand and repaint her before the water came back. But it did mean we would have to go aground very close to high tide and it might be difficult to float off again if the next tide was not so high. Our calculations suggested that it wouldn't be, but the day after the tide would be higher, so at worst we would have to wait 24 hours. At low tide we surveyed a nice sandy area that looked suitable and, as we would have to be there in the dark before dawn, we made a careful note of various landmarks that would help us to find the spot accurately.

Next day we were up and off at half-past four in the morning, carefully finding our way to the pre-planned spot and going aground less than an hour after high water. As the water receded, *Greylag* settled nicely upright on her legs and we were soon scrubbing her off and getting her dry ready for the antifouling paint. By now the sun was well up and the warm breeze dried her quickly. It also dried the paint rather quickly, so we had to work fast and furiously before it became too sticky to brush out properly. The job was soon done and we settled down to await the return of the tide.

About an hour before the next high tide, we had still not floated off again and I became anxious that we might not get off that evening. This would not have mattered much had it not been for a rather worrying weather forecast, suggesting that the wind might get up and make things very bumpy on this rather shallow patch of beach. It was not a good place to be caught out by bad weather. We redoubled our efforts to get off the sand, setting an anchor in the deeper water and using our winches to try to pull her off. It didn't work. At this point I radioed some friends for help. We needed a dinghy with a good powerful outboard. I knew of a technique that was likely to work as I had seen it done before, back in the UK. One gets a dinghy to pull the boat sideways, using one of the halyards that go to the top of the mast. This gives a tremendous mechanical advantage and the boat can be heeled over far enough for the keel to come off the sand. At the same time the boat's main engine is used to drive her forward into deeper water. Nick Parker and his friends from '*Enarkay*' soon arrived with their dinghy, sporting a 25 HP outboard, just the thing!

'Don't be timid.' I advised him 'give it full welly as if you were trying to pull her right over.'

'Right,' he replied and did just that.

By then I had the main engine in full forward and with a gentle shudder she slipped off the sand and returned to an upright position. We all ate a hearty meal that evening, in one of Dick Smith's restaurants.

A few days later we left Musket Cove for a visit to the Yasawa islands, which lie in a fifty-mile long crescent around the north-west of Viti Levu. The navigation in the area was challenging with many patches of shallow coral to dodge. We slowly made our way north, through the Mamanuthas, until we reached a small group of three islands, Navandra, Vanua Levu and Vanua Lailai, running from west to east and more or less joined together by coral reefs. In the south-easterly breeze this spot offered good shelter for the night. We came round the north-east corner of Navandra and into the bay, to anchor off the middle island, Vanua Levu.

We were met by a sombre sight. The American yacht *Irish Mist* lay on her side, wrecked at the top of the beach. She was holed and dismasted, a motley collection of rigging and internal fittings lay on the beach. Alongside there was a temporary shelter from which a man emerged, aroused by our arrival on the scene. We were soon ashore in our dinghy and went over to find out how the wreck had occurred.

'Mbula', I said to the fellow by the wreck.

'Mbula', he replied, and then in perfect English, 'I hope your anchor is well dug in!'

His name was Beni. We asked him what had happened and he told us the yacht had been caught out when a 40-knot wind had come in

The wreck of *Irish Mist*, Mamanutha Islands

unexpectedly from the north. There is no protection from that direction in the bay and the fittings holding the anchor chain on *Irish Mist's* foredeck had broken. Before the owner could start his engine and escape, she was swept onto the shallow coral that lies all along the beach at Vanua Levu. Happily, the owner and his wife escaped unhurt. It was a sobering story, how often we must have been close to a similar fate. I made a mental note to check on our own fittings.

Irish Mist had been declared an insurance write-off, but Dick Smith (always quick to see a good opportunity) felt the boat could be retrieved and converted into an atmospheric pub back at Musket Cove. He and Beni had filled the hull with empty 50-gallon drums to provide flotation. They had fixed a large pulley to a coral head offshore and taken a steel hawser from *Irish Mist*, round the pulley and back to a chain winch attached to a palm tree on the shore. Beni was now waiting for the higher tides, due in a day or two, to attempt to pull the boat back into deep water and tow her away to Musket Cove. We heard later that this had been successful, so any future visitors to Musket Cove may now be able to enjoy a beer in a rather unique bar with an interesting story.

The coral at Vanua Levu was spectacular, the best we had seen since Tonga. It was all healthy looking and teeming with fish, such a contrast to the moribund and damaged reefs in much of the Caribbean. Ashore there were a few goats on the island but no people, other than Beni. We found a cave and alongside it was a circle of stones with several offerings of kava roots laid inside it. We had heard that one was supposed to leave these gifts, even on unpopulated islands, and that failure to do so would anger the spirits and bring bad luck. I wondered whether *Irish Mist* had failed to do this. A silly thought, as I am not at all superstitious. Or am I? I think I might have done it if I had had some to spare.

Next day we moved on further north to Waya Island. There we found a quiet spot off the western coast where there was a small resort, the Octopus resort, run by Wolfgang and Ingrid. We went ashore for dinner in their little restaurant and enjoyed a chat with some of the guests. Wolfgang runs the resort for people who want to escape for a while and it was certainly a good place to do just that. He had arranged for some singers and dancers to come over from the local village to entertain us. The dancing was rather dull after Polynesia, but the singing, as always in Fiji, was very good indeed. They had walked several miles across the hills, carrying all their instruments with them. Afterwards they returned in the dark by the same route.

Next day we were off again, this time to Naviti Island. Back at Musket Cove we had heard that there were manta rays to be found there, those huge fish, twelve feet across and more, that look so magnificent on

Manta Rays at Naviti Island

148

television wildlife documentaries. At Naviti we met up with John and Ruth on *Griffyn*, who had anchored their boat just south of the Tokatokauna Pass, which separates Naviti from Drawaqa Island to the south. They confirmed that they had seen the rays in the pass. We were soon off in the dinghy to find them. At the pass we found more very good coral and teeming hordes of fish, but no manta rays. Disappointed, we returned to the boat in the last of the daylight.

In the morning we returned and there they were, great dark shadows just beneath the surface of the sea, facing into the current flowing through the pass. Occasionally the tips of their massive wings would break the surface and waves broke on their backs as if they were but shallow coral patches. Some were only small, perhaps six feet across, but there were some huge fellows at least twelve feet across.

Mantas are completely harmless plankton eaters and they were clearly feeding, swimming just fast enough to hold themselves stationary against the tide. We understood now why we had not found them the day before. We had been there at slack water when they probably move away, feeding was easy when the current was flowing.

We drove the dinghy up alongside the rays and anchored in amongst

Griffyn at Naviti Island, the 'manta' pass is just beyond her bow.

them. They more or less ignored us and I soon donned my snorkel and fins and jumped into the sea beside them. What a magnificent sight they were, 'flying' like the old Vulcan bombers, their curving 'horns' protruding forwards on each side of their huge but toothless mouths. Their eyes seemed to watch me and I felt just a little nervous even though I knew they were harmless. Some of them had pilot fish, sometimes two, swimming along beneath them. They stemmed the tide effortlessly; just the gentlest movement of their huge wings seemed enough, whereas I found I had to swim hard against the tide just to stay with them. Keith had brought an underwater camera but, as he wasn't a strong swimmer, he lent it to me to take some photos. And then, quite suddenly, they were gone again. The tide stopped running and they moved off into the bay. It had been a wonderful experience, beyond anything else we had seen on our voyage so far. We returned to *Greylag* in high spirits.

Indenting the northern coast of Naviti is a large bay with two villages on its shores. To the east is Somo Somo, a large village often visited by tourists from the main islands - a situation amply confirmed by the presence of a cruise liner, anchored off! In the south-western corner of the bay was Ngunu, a smaller village, more natural and inviting. We anchored as close in as the depth of water would allow. Two young lads, Beni and Evi, came out to us in their tin canoe.

'Mbula', they called.

'Mbula' we replied, these *Hullo's* preface all contacts in Fiji.

'What is the name of your Chief?' I asked.

'John', they replied, 'John Neitau'.

'Is he in the village today?'

'He is having a meeting but you can see him at the meeting place.'

Beni and Evi had come in a tin canoe. It was made from a corrugated, aluminium roofing panel, folded in a semicircle and nailed fore and aft to a wooden stem and sternpost. We had seen many such craft in the villages and admired the skill with which the occupants remained upright in such an inherently unstable vessel.

We were soon on our way to the village, led by Beni and Evi, and carrying our gift of yanggona for the Chief. The meeting was already under way when we arrived and, though much would be discussed through the afternoon, we soon realised that the main purpose of the meeting was to have a kava-drinking session. It was too late to escape now, so we resigned ourselves to joining in.

The meeting place consisted of an area, perhaps thirty feet by twenty, covered over with a roof made from palm fronds. There were no walls. The men sat in a circle on coconut matting around a tanoa or kava bowl, made from vesi wood and approximately three feet across. I was slightly surprised to see that the *chef* was mixing the drink using white powder from a plastic bag, which I took to be purified extract of yanggona, rather than using the roots themselves.

We were warmly greeted and invited to sit down with them. Shortly Chief John arrived and sat down, cross-legged, alongside the three of us. He was an imposing figure with his traditional skirt and highly coloured shirt; he clearly commanded great respect from the other men around the bowl. I had better take the plunge, I thought, and fiddled nervously with the paper bag containing our gift of yanggona. I placed it on the ground in front of the Chief and watched anxiously as he inspected it carefully before handing it to a deputy on his left. The deputy then started the ceremony of acceptance with its incomprehensible chanting and slow hand clapping, liberally interspersed with 'vinaka's or 'thankyou's' - all of them joined in. We were accepted!

Then came the difficult bit. One of them, who appeared to act as server, went up to the fellow who was in charge of the kava bowl and collected a small wooden cup (half a coconut shell) filled to the brim with the unappetising, pale white drink. He presented it to the Chief who clapped his hands once, took the bowl and drained it in one go. He then clapped his hands three times more, muttering 'vinaka, vinaka, vinaka', and a few other things I could not decipher. The others also clapped. We watched all this intensely, knowing full well what was coming next and feeling that we had better get it right.

The next shellful went to Keith. He must have been paying attention as he went through the required motions without a hitch. I watched his face for any sign of faltering as he drank the awful potion, but he downed it in one long gulp. John's turn came next, he too did well. Now it was my turn. I took the shell amid a flood of inhibitions concerning the appalling lack of hygiene (everyone uses the same shell), to say nothing of the awful taste. Some events in life require a massive exercise of willpower to drive from one's brain all rational thought and sensibility and to cause one to react with robotic obedience. It happens to me when the dentist advances, syringe poised, and I'm sure it must happen just before the incomprehensible leap of the bungy jumper! I remember learning the technique at prep school when required to force down that indescribably disgusting cabbage, under threat of no pudding. I put the bowl to my lips, inhibited all my higher senses, thought of England and the Queen, and drained the contents. It wasn't as bad as I had expected, rather like diluted kaolin mixture with a slight hint of liquorice.

More rounds of kava followed and I began to wonder what was the minimum number we would have to accept before we could make our excuses and escape. The effect was not like getting drunk, one felt very relaxed, with a slight numbing of the lips, but not really intoxicated. I thought that conversation might delay the endless refilling of the dreaded half-coconut cup, and luckily Chief John spoke reasonable English.

'We have really enjoyed the singing in Fiji,' I said to him, 'your people have marvellous voices and everyone seems to enjoy it.'

'You like singing?' He asked.

We all nodded enthusiastically. He beckoned to three men sat at the other end of the mat, inviting them to entertain us. These three then sang in perfect three-part harmony, one tenor, one base and one falsetto. We didn't understand the words of course, but it mattered not at all, we were enchanted. I suppose the kava had made us especially receptive but I have the fondest memories of those three Fijians singing round the tanoa.

Outside the meeting place, another event was under way. It was a fund raising exercise, Chief John explained, in aid of their church.

'We would like to make a contribution,' I said, seeing this as an opportunity to escape from further rounds of kava.

We got to our feet without too much trouble, said our 'vinaka's and wandered over to a table where the fundraiser sat with a large accounting book. Somebody had just made a contribution and he was recording the amount, and the donor's name, as we arrived. He then got to his feet and, in a voice that would have drowned out a town crier, he announced to the assembled village that 'Arafin Fradesa has given ten dollars!' What a terrific system this was; anyone tempted to be stingy would have to face the humiliation of this public announcement. Imagine such a system operating in front of the neighbours when the lady from the RSPCA comes round to your door! It worked on me all right. So much so, that I coughed up twenty US dollars. This was obviously considered generous as the public announcement was greeted with cheers from the women.

Back at Musket Cove, we had been told that there was an old WW2 plane lying at the bottom of a shallow bay on the east coast of Naviti. We didn't have an exact position, only that it was in the bay just past the fourth island coming from the north! That sounded like a challenge, so we

Soso village on Naviti Island, Yasawas

decided to try to find it.

We left Ngunu on a beautifully calm and sunny morning, making our way under engine around the northern end of the island, before turning south again to go down the east coast. There are many small islands off this coast and we counted them off until we reached number four and then turned in towards the coast. The bay was a brilliant blue, with large sandy patches between the coral reefs each side. We could see what looked like a reasonably clear channel snaking in towards the shore, so we cautiously made our way in and dropped the anchor over a good patch of sand.

I went off in the dinghy to see what I could find, travelling up and down the bay in straight lines, about ten metres apart. Eventually I spotted the wreck, in fact you couldn't really miss it if you got anywhere near, because it was surprisingly complete and easily seen in the clear water. We returned for our snorkelling gear and swam back to the spot where the aircraft lay. It was only about sixty metres from where we had anchored *Greylag*. We were unable to identify the type of aircraft; it was a single-engined fighter, John thought it might have been an American Mustang. The fuselage was in two sections and the engine had been removed, but the tail fin was still attached and the tail plane and port wing lay on the sand, presumably where they had come to rest some 50 years before. It served to remind us again that this part of the world had not escaped the turmoil of the war with Japan. I wondered what might have happened to cause the pilot to ditch. Was he shot down? Or perhaps he ran out of fuel. Who knows? We hoped the pilot had escaped - given the apparent slight damage to his plane, we thought he probably had.

We were nearing the end of our time in Fiji so, after a short visit to another village, So So, at the southern end of Naviti, we left the Yasawas for Lautoka to complete our exit clearance. As luck would have it, the wind had turned into the south and got up quite a bit, giving us a windward slog down to Lautoka. The situation was made more difficult by our late departure from So So, where we had gone to church to hear the singing. This is exactly how trouble starts, - late start, slowed by unexpected headwinds, daylight running out while still in reef strewn waters!

We knew we were getting late so we decided to stop at Vomo Island, which we thought we could reach in the last of the daylight. We could then move to Lautoka next day. When we got to Vomo it really was in the last of the daylight, virtually twilight, and I felt very uneasy as we tried to identify a way in through the reef. It was not at all clear. I was becoming anxious, with a strong feeling that I ought not to be where I was, and regretting a plan that had been too optimistic in the prevailing conditions. Suddenly there was a terrific bang and the boat lurched ninety degrees and came to an abrupt stop. We had hit the reef in a place where the chart suggested it shouldn't be! Our keel was cast iron and very strong but I was desperately worried that we would damage the rudder if I couldn't get her off quickly. I turned the boat ninety degrees to face back the way we had come and heaved a sigh of relief as she wriggled off the reef without any serious damage other than that wire between the keel and rudder, which had broken again. It was not until many weeks later, in Darwin, Australia, that I found some minor hull damage where a hillock of barnacles on the top of the rudder had been forced upwards when we hit the reef.

It had been a stark reminder that these are dangerous waters and one should avoid travelling except between the hours of ten and four. As soon as it had become obvious that we couldn't get to Vomo in time, I should have returned to Naviti, but it was too late to do that now. We had a problem. We were off the reef but still at sea in gathering darkness, with plenty of other reefs we could hit if we got careless. I studied the chart with John. There was a sheltered bay on the west coast of Viti Levu, if only we could identify a clear passage through the reefs with a big enough margin of safety to enable us to rely on the GPS and the radar. It would soon be completely dark. Luckily, there was just such a route, even though it meant travelling a considerable extra distance so as to remain safe. We set waypoints into the GPS and steered the boat as precisely as we could so as to avoid straying from the exact course. We arrived at the bay safely and crept slowly in until the echo sounder showed 5 metres. Then we dropped the anchor, had a stiff drink to steady the nerves, and went to bed.

When dawn broke, I looked out to find that we were in the middle of the bay, in mirror calm water. There were some more yachts further into the bay but nobody we knew. I repaired the wire under the boat; not a difficult task with a snorkel as the water was warm and clear.

We were soon on our way up to Lautoka where we refuelled and restocked our stores before clearing out with customs and immigration, the latter exercise being as tedious as ever. The next day we left Fiji and headed westward for New Caledonia, our last stop before Australia.

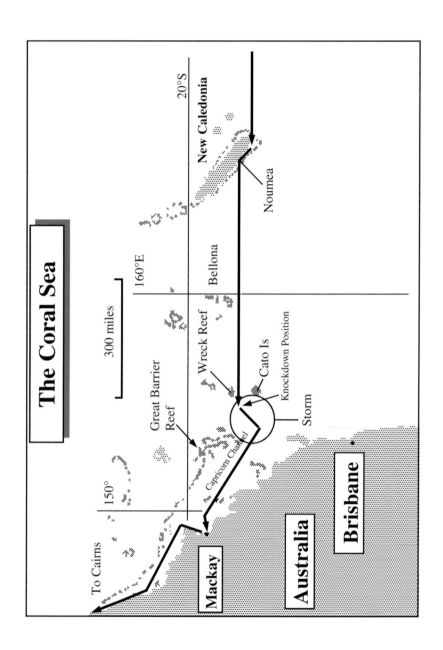

The Coral Sea

13 A Stormy Passage to Australia

On the 9th of July we set out from Lautoka for Noumea, the capital of New Caledonia, where we planned a brief stop before the final leg into Australia. Most of the Tradewinders followed a more northerly route to Vanuatu and then to Cairns, but we were keen to visit the Whitsunday Islands and this meant a more southerly landfall in Australia at Mackay.

As a parting gift from Fiji, a dog had bitten Keith on his way back to the boat from town. John and I had been vaccinated against rabies but Keith had not and we were just a little concerned. However there was nothing we could do until we reached the good facilities of Australia, so we put it to the back of our minds.

In flat calm conditions, we motored out to the Mulola Pass and departed from Fiji via the same gap in the reef through which we had entered, on our way to Musket Cove. As soon as we were out in open water, a breeze came in and we made good progress over the next four days along the 614-mile route to Noumea, with only short periods of motoring. Early on Bastille Day (14th July) we had just over 100 miles to go.

We planned to enter through the reef at the Havannah Pass and needed to get there by about 2030 hours to avoid the stiff 4-5 knot adverse tide that would start about then. As luck would have it the weather turned wet. It was not too windy but the continuous heavy rain threatened to make visual navigation through the pass extremely difficult. However, the chart showed a good lighthouse on one side of the pass that should be visible on the radar, even if we couldn't see the light. We pressed on.

As we closed on the pass the rain became torrential and to make matters worse, the wind got up to 20 knots. I was just beginning to think that perhaps we should lay off the coast until next day in the hope of better weather, when we spotted the light. Flashing at 3-second intervals - this was definitely the lighthouse. We also had a good picture on the radar that confirmed the lighthouse at 4 miles range. This gave me the confidence to navigate through the pass in the dark.

Once inside the reef there was an easy route, free from dangers, into Baie du Prony, just a few miles to the west. With careful use of the radar we found our way into the bay and in the quieter conditions we nosed up to the shore, just inside Pointe des Pins, and dropped the anchor. Although it seemed an extraordinary thing to do in the tropics, I then fired up our diesel heater. The boat was dripping wet after that dreadful last 24 hours and we were glad to have a real fug-up in the cabin. We slept soundly.

Baie du Prony was a large bay and provided access to quarries at the head of the bay. The shores near the entrance were attractive with pine-covered hills and a rocky foreshore. There was more than a hint of Scandinavia in the surrounding countryside. If it had stopped raining we might have enjoyed it more, but it didn't - not all day. We read and played chess. Keith and I had a musical session - me on the piano and him on the recorder. This later descended to 'rugby' songs. I had been reading Gavin Young's *'Slow Boats Home'* and came across a passage with a Chinese prostitute's song - to be sung to the tune of the old hymn 100. It seemed to suit our mood at the time and we all joined in with gusto...

> Me no likee Blitish sailor,
> Yankee sailor come ashore,
> Me no likee Blitish sailor
> Yankee pay one dollar more.
>
> Yankee call me 'Honey darlin',
> Blitish call me 'fuckin whore'
> Me no likee Blitish sailor,
> Yankee won't you come ashore.
>
> Yankee always wear Flench letter,
> Blitish never wear fuck all,
> Me no likee Blitish sailor,
> Yankee won't you come ashore.
>
> Yankee sailor fuck and finish,
> Blitish fuck for ever more,
> Me no likee Blitish sailor,
> Yankee won't you come ashore.

Just right for the Salvation Army wouldn't you say? It cheered us up a bit.

Next day the rain showed signs of abating for our move along the coast to Noumea. I felt we should try to get there as we hadn't cleared in yet, although we reckoned no one would see us in all that rain! We emerged from the bay and passed between the Ile des Pins and the mainland, through a delightful channel with attractive scenery on both sides. I remember wishing we had more time to spend there, the whole place looked inviting. At Noumea we found a modern marina at Moselle Bay with finger berths and lovely hot showers, we were certainly ready for them. The town had many facilities and good shops but everything was expensive, similar to Papeete in Tahiti - about 3x home prices! *Saullitaire* and *Best Respects* from the rally were there when we arrived, but were planning to leave next day. We met up with a New Zealander, Rob Lockett, on a Sadler 34 *Jeanne,* named after his wife, who sadly had died recently, and Dik and Ulla from Sweden on *Mundi-Mundi.* I mention these two boats because in a few days they were to be caught by the same storm that was lying in wait for us all in the Coral Sea.

It was at Noumea, for the first time on the voyage that I began to feel rather tired and worn out. Partly this was emotional, I missed Janet and Christmas still seemed a long way off. I found myself questioning why I had opted to undertake this journey; the long separation could not be good for a marriage. I thought how it must have been the same for thousands of couples during the war. Perhaps it was all that rain, I certainly felt rather down in spirits.

After five days, our strength recovered, we motored out of the harbour and out through the Passe Boulari, at the start of the 1100-mile journey to Mackay. As soon as we were clear of the reef, a stiff Force5-6 headwind came in to give us an uncomfortable first night. It remained on the nose all next day though it moderated to Force 4. After that first 24 hours we had made only 72 miles towards Mackay.

On the third day out, the wind showed signs of freeing and we were able to retrieve the 40-mile cross-track error built up during the headwinds. By the middle of the third night the wind had died altogether and we were back on the engine. Dawn broke over a flat calm sea and we enjoyed sunshine and easy conditions.

We had our fishing line deployed behind the boat, with one of those multi-coloured lures on the end. At teatime there was a loud splash, way off on the starboard quarter, as a huge mahi-mahi leapt from the water. Immediately I spotted my highly coloured lure dangling from its mouth. I grabbed the rod from the back of the boat and wound in furiously but there was nothing on the end. There had been no sign of a fish taking the lure, the rod hadn't moved and there had not been the usual screech of the reel as a fish runs off the line. I will never know what had caused the break, perhaps the fish had bitten straight through the line, but this was unlikely, as the last section was wire. More likely perhaps was a poorly-made knot coming undone - rather embarrassing for a sailor. I muttered a few curses and one might have thought that would have been the end of the matter, but not a bit of it. After a few minutes I noticed a vivid blue flash in the water alongside the boat. I looked again carefully and sure enough it was another mahi-mahi. No, it was two of them! And then I saw that one of them had my lure hanging from its mouth. How strange that was, I would have thought the fish would have been scared off by the experience. The two fish stayed close to the boat for several minutes; time enough for me to catch them on video. They are such beautiful fish, all the colours of the rainbow down their sides and that pugnacious, blunt-nosed head that looks so innocent on the front of such an unremitting predator. They were obviously a pair, the big one perhaps 50 pounds and about 4-5 feet long. A silly thought passed through my mind, perhaps they were looking for revenge - I had visions of 'Jaws' grabbing that fellow from the back of the fishing boat!

By the evening of the 27th of July, after a fast day's downwind sailing, we had just less than 400 miles left to get to Mackay. But there was an ominous forecast, a deepening trough was heading towards us and Rob, on *Jeanne*, had radioed that he already had 30 knots of wind from the east. We had just passed between Wreck Reef and Cato reef and were clear of all dangers downwind for several hundred miles.

.........*bad weather was on the way, just how bad none of us could have guessed. Australia was only a few hundred miles away to the west, a safe haven snug behind the Great Barrier Reef. We had all but crossed the vast Pacific Ocean* ....but I have already told this part of the story.

After the storm had abated enough for us to feel we were probably out of danger, I had slept fitfully. We had all gone to bed cold, wet and exhausted and left *Greylag* look after herself, lying ahull with the helm lashed. She had managed very well. Consciousness returned as the grey light of dawn began to filter into the cabin. I glanced around at the mayhem. Despite the large screws I had put in the floors to hold them down, they had come partly adrift and large hunks of the spare anchor chain had fallen to the starboard side of the boat. Several items that were once in the fridge were now strewn around the starboard side lockers - coke bottles, cartons of long-life milk (miraculously unbroken), containers of butter etc. Crockery lay all over the place, lucky it was plastic. Everything was sprinkled with peppercorns from a large bag that had burst. There was a tear in the cabin top lining where the fridge lid had hit it as it fell out during the inversion. Although it was a depressing sight there were things to be thankful for. Nothing important had broken. The hatches remained secure, the windows also and we still had a mast and a rudder - not always the case when boats suffer serious knockdowns. The VHF aerial had been bent at right angles but we still had a working GPS. I was thankful I had made strong fixings for the batteries and we still had power. The engine had remained on its mountings despite what must have been tremendous strains.

We emerged from our bunks and started the slow process of tidying up. I checked the bilges and was surprised to find how little water had actually entered the boat, barely three bucketsful. Our charts and several books were sodden and would have to be carefully dried out, as we would need them.

Outside the wind was still fairly strong but moderating fast now and the sun was about to emerge. The canvas dodgers and the main spray-hood lay in tatters, still joined to the boat by occasional surviving turnbuckles. The stanchions on both sides of the boat had been bent inwards. Both solar cell panels had been ripped from their fixings but the lashings had kept them with us. The windvane cover was shredded, luckily we had a spare one. The horseshoe life buoy with its light had gone. Up the mast the VHF aerial stuck out sideways at right-angles to its normal position and the Firdell radar reflector was bent sideways - telling evidence of the force with which the mast must have hit the water. The mainsail cover hung in pieces from the boom that was still lashed down to the deck where we had secured it at the height of the storm. Although it all looked dreadful, in fact there was little or no serious damage, nothing that couldn't be repaired over a few days in harbour.

The sun finally came out that morning and we set about getting the boat going again. Our GPS position showed that we had drifted downwind, slightly south of east, for about 40 miles while we were running before the storm and then lying ahull. Thank heaven we had the necessary sea room to allow us to do this. We put a new cover on the windvane, poled out the genoa and we were sailing again, and in the right direction.

As the sun dried things out and we got on top of the clearing up, one could feel morale improving. I think all of us had had a severe fright and we all recognised that we had been a little lucky to get off so lightly.

At the ten o'clock net I reported our problems to the other boats on the rally. Inga was running the net on *Calidris*, how often we'd had cause to be grateful to them. Inga was most sympathetic and passed on our news to Peter Seymour who was already at Cairns awaiting the fleet's arrival. He later confirmed that he had contacted the authorities at Mackay and asked them to expect a rather battered small yacht with an exhausted crew in a couple of days or so. We also managed to contact Rob on *Jeanne* who had been 50 miles ahead of us and had experienced similar weather. Dik on *Mundi-Mundi* said he had experienced 60-80 knot winds but was still in one piece.

We reset our course for the Capricorn channel that would take us in behind the Great Barrier Reef and up to Mackay. Mid-morning on Tuesday the 30th of July we sighted Townsend Island, our first glimpse of Australia, and, shortly after, High Peak Island. We still had a fair way to go to Mackay but we reckoned we would get there next day.

A considerable reception committee was waiting for us at the quay-side of Pier No 1 at Mackay. The harbour master, Wayne, the customs officers, the Australian Quarantine and Immigration Service officers, together with reporters from the Daily Mercury and the local radio service!

Diana, the customs officer, and Steve from AQIS were quite the most efficient and courteous officers I have ever met. They got us through the formalities quickly and without fuss, although I recall Diana having to be rather firm with the press who were trying to get interviews while we were still filling up the forms. As soon as they were done we moved the boat onto some pile moorings in a quiet part of the harbour and went ashore by dinghy.

Our first call was to the Mackay Cruising Club, for a huge beef burger lunch and a lot of helpful advice on local facilities for our repairs. Then I went downtown by taxi to call on David and Margaret Hope who ran Hossack's Chandlery. They were able to get us virtually all the spares we needed and offered to fly them in from Melbourne to save time. They were most helpful.

That evening we enjoyed steaks in the Club and had an early night - I think we were still suffering the aftershock of what had happened. What we hadn't realised was how cold the nights there could be. Although the latitude of Mackay is 22°S, it was the Australian winter and temperatures at night fell precipitously. We froze, despite all our efforts to cover ourselves with anything and everything we could find. We had been in the tropics for a considerable time and there were no such things as sleeping bags or jerseys on the boat.

Next day we were straight downtown to the camping shop to buy sleeping bags! In town we soon found out we were front-page headlines in the Daily Mercury…

Yachtsmen tell of beating death…

Dr Dick Allan, John Anderson and Keith Ellis dried off in Mackay yesterday after mountainous seas nearly claimed their lives in the Coral Sea.

Ah well, that's the press for you! Mind you, the huge colour picture of us on the front page made for instant recognition in the various shops we visited and we received terrific service.

That afternoon I did an interview for the local radio station. At the end the interviewer asked me what I most looked forward to, now that we had arrived in Australia. I replied 'the biggest steak in town and a bottle of Cab Sav'. 'That's easily arranged', he said, and gave me directions to turn up at a well-known, downtown hostelry where, he assured me, one could find the best steaks in Australia. We went there with Rob and each of us ordered a 'medium', which turned out to be 600 grams. I am ashamed to say that I was unable to finish mine but the others all managed. With full stomachs and our new sleeping bags, we slept well that night.

Next day I collected the spares from Hossacks and we repaired the stanchions and guardrail, replaced the broken navigation lights and mended the VHF aerial. The leads on the solar panels had to be re-soldered on and the frames repaired. I decided to leave the canvas work until Cairns, where there would be more time. While John and I were busy with the repairs Keith kindly volunteered to do all our laundry. He sat by that washing machine for five hours - well beyond the call of duty!

That evening in the Cruising Club we had a dinner of garlic and chilli prawns and a bottle or two of that splendid Aussie wine 'Nottage Hill'. To the great amusement of my colleagues and the waitress, I ordered this as

'Notting Hill'. Perhaps I was still feeling the after effects of the storm. Earlier in the evening we had all purchased raffle tickets and when the draw took place after dinner, we found that Keith had won the star prize - a dozen T-bone steaks!

Next day, substantially mended, we were off. The whole idea of going to Mackay had been to visit the Whitsunday Islands and after paying such a price for the detour, we jolly well were going to do it! Our first night stop was at Brampton Island, not a very special place but peaceful enough. Next day we pressed on north to Goldsmith Island. On the way there we finally got close to some whales, a pair of humpbacks lounging around just off the Bullin Rocks, south of Goldsmith Island. We managed to get quite close enough for some good photos but I confess to being just a little nervous of getting too close to whales - they are such enormous creatures and they smell. After lunch at Goldsmith we moved to Shaw Island where we anchored in a beautifully calm bay at the southern end. There we met up again with Rob on *Jeanne* who had left Mackay just ahead of us.

After a calm night at Shaw Island, we pressed on north in a flat sea, through the Dent Channel, past Hamilton Island before stopping for lunch at Sawmill Bay on Whitsunday Island. En route we had passed a large marina with an airstrip alongside. Although many of the islands are uncrowded, this one did look rather popular. We saw several turtles but all were a long way off, but we hoped to get closer to one soon.

After a short stop for lunch we were on the move north again to the Nara inlet on Hook Island. Our pilot book said there were some aboriginal paintings on the rocks there. Rob was there ahead of us and invited us to dinner on *Jeanne*. He was expecting to pickup his parents soon and this was probably the last time we would meet up with him.

The Inlet ran into the island for about a mile with steep rock cliffs each side. Some of the rock formations were spectacular and there were several caves. Beyond the cliffs, the scrubland rose gently towards the centre of the island, covered with eucalyptus trees of several varieties. On some rocks close by the anchorage we could see elaborate paintings and wondered if these might be the aboriginal rock paintings we had read about. Next day, we had all taken photos of them before someone enlightened us that they were only *grafiti*! Subsequently we saw more grafiti around the Nara Inlet, a sad disfigurement of what was, in all other respects, a beautiful place.

The Nara Inlet, Hook Island, Queensland.

Next day we headed for Townsville for some more rest and recuperation in the big marina there. On the way over we finally found a large turtle, paddling slowly on the surface. As soon as we got close it dived , but we got some photos just before it disappeared. Townsville is one of the larger towns on the coast of Queensland and the marina had all the facilities one needed.

This was just as well, because on the way from Nara we discovered a fuel leak. It appeared to come from the bottom of our reserve tank in the cockpit locker, it must have shifted during the storm. This was going to be a big job as the whole tank had to come out. Downtown in Townsville we went for dinner at Buckaroos, steaks again but not as good as those we had had in Mackay. I was amused by their loos - Jackaroo and Jillaroo! I phoned Janet and heard that she had been suffering from sciatica. I had asked her to contact John Weaver who had expressed interest in coming out as crew when we had met him in Antigua; the time was fast approaching when we would need to find a third person. Janet said he was interested. We were all right for a bit since we had Keith with us and, when he left from Cairns, John's daughter Kate would be joining us until we got to Darwin. Then we would need a recruit.

We left Townsville and headed north, up past Great Palm Island and on to Orpheus Island where we anchored for the night. Here we had our first meeting with the shrimp boats that fish along the Queensland coast. They lie up in the daytime before moving off at dusk for the night's work. They have large arrays of powerful lights deployed on long booms each side of the boat to attract the shrimps into their nets. At night they can be seen for miles. When we arrived there were several of these boats anchored close by, but they soon moved off to their fishing.

From Orpheus we headed next morning up into the Hinchinbrooke Channel. This Channel is a very sheltered waterway but quite shallow near the southern entrance, so we planned to be there around High Water. Unfortunately we fell behind schedule by about an hour and, approaching the channel, our anxiety was increased further when we spotted a large yacht, *Under Capricorn*, hard aground and heeled over on its side. We proceeded carefully, past the 3-mile long pier which services the local sugar cane industry, and as we got closer we saw that the yacht aground was well out of the channel marked on our chart. We tuned in the VHF and could hear the fellows on her talking to the coastguard and trying to arrange for a tug to pull her off. She was a big yacht and there was no chance that we could have done anything useful to help, so we pressed on. During our transit of the channel (about 2 hours after HW) we never saw less than three metres depth on the echo sounder.

That morning there had been trouble with our loo, so I planned to find a nice quiet spot and deal with it. There was just such a spot at Bluff Creek. The loo problem turned out to be quite serious, we found that all the pipe-work had furred up inside, including some of the stainless steel pipes welded into the holding tank. This was a perfectly disgusting job and John kindly helped me with it. Eventually we managed to clear all the pipes and the re-assembled loo worked perfectly. John and I soaped ourselves from head to foot and got into the sea to get clean.

By four o'clock we were ready to move on but when I went to start the engine, nothing happened. This was going to be a day of disasters. Out came the Avo, that magic circuit testing device, and we checked over the entire engine starting circuits and found corrosion problems behind the engine-starting panel. This was yet another problem attributable to the knockdown as the panel, being on the starboard side, had been completely immersed. We cleaned it all up and she started. By now it was rather late so we moved just a few miles up the Channel to a calm anchorage at Haycock Island. We were alongside a mangrove swamp there and during the evening and night we heard crocodile sounds emanating from the swamp. We never saw one.

Time was now pressing to get to Cairns as Keith had a plane to catch and Kate would be arriving there, expecting to find us. So we made an early start next day and headed in perfect weather for Mourilyn. This was a deep water harbour at the mouth of a river; its main trade was in servicing the huge sugar cane industry that thrives all along this part of the Queensland coast. We went up the river for half a mile or so and found a good anchorage in flat calm conditions. It was good holding ground for which I was grateful as the flow in the river on the ebb tide was quite high.

We were now just a day's sail away from Cairns. Conditions along this part of the Australian coast are conducive to fast sailing, the fresh to strong south-easterlies making it easy to complete dayhops of 50 or 60 miles. By teatime we had arrived off Yorkey's Knob, just north of Cairns, where there was a substantial new marina complex. As we motored into the marina all the rally boats, who had heard of our troubles, gave us a terrific welcome - sounding their horns and claxons and generally making us feel they were pleased to see us in one piece. The facilities at Yorkey's were terrific with excellent showers, a laundry, superb bar and restaurant. A signpost on each pontoon warned

'There are salt water crocodiles in the marina and it is dangerous to swim'!

I phoned Janet, it was great to hear her again. She agreed to talk to another potential crew Richard Rhodes, Peter Seymour had given me his name, and then I would have to make up my mind between him and John Weaver. It was easy to get all one needed in Cairns and in no time flat I had obtained the necessary acrylic canvas to make new dodgers and repair the spray hood. I was glad to have our old industrial Singer sewing machine and this made short work of the dodgers that were completed and fitted in a day. This saved a lot of money, but more importantly it saved the long wait for the overloaded local sailmakers to catch up with the large number of repair jobs that had arrived with the Trade Winds fleet.

A few days later Keith departed for home after a day trip sightseeing in the hinterland and Kate arrived from Sydney, where she had spent a few days at the start of her visit to Australia. We were going to stay in the marina for a bit and hire a car to explore the local countryside. What a nice thought that was. I had grown just a little weary with the sea and looked forward with enthusiasm to a spell on dry land.

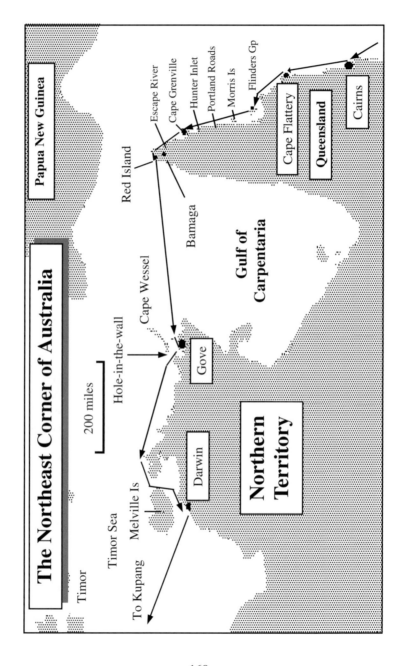

The Northeast Corner of Australia

Papua New Guinea

Timor

Timor Sea

To Kupang

Melville Is

Darwin

Northern Territory

200 miles

Hole-in-the-wall

Cape Wessel

Gove

Gulf of Carpentaria

Red Island

Bamaga

Escape River
Cape Grenville
Hunter Inlet
Portland Roads
Morris Is
Flinders Gp

Cape Flattery

Queensland

Cairns

14 Around the Top Right-hand Corner of Australia

The repairs to *Greylag* were now more or less complete and there was time to explore a little of Queensland. I went off for a day on the Brompton bicycle with my painting kit in the bag. Behind the Yorkey's Knob marina there were a modest number of private houses and a few shops. I was quickly through those and out on the open road going north to a place called Smithfield.

The first thing that struck me was how green everything was. One thinks of Australia as a rather barren place, as if the whole country was like Alice Springs or Ayer's rock. But the coastal fringe of Queensland is lush and fertile. The flat areas near the coast are heavily cultivated with sugar cane, huge fields that stretch as far as the eye can see with only an occasional line of eucalypts to break the monotony. Further inland the cane fields gave way to forested hills surrounding the high tableland around Atherton and the northern end of the Great Dividing Range. My guidebook described the many rivers and waterfalls that drain the water off the high land, flowing both east to the Pacific and west to the Gulf of Carpentaria. I looked forward to our tour in the hire-car when there would be an opportunity to see some of these. In places the slopes of the hills, especially to the north of Cairns, were covered with protected tropical rainforest. This too would be on our itinerary for the weekend.

For now, I settled down in a quiet corner and painted the view across the cane fields to the blue-green hills beyond. A fine eucalypt, its white bark glistening in the sun, made a good foreground and gave some perspective to my painting. One of the joys of painting is the ability to move things around a bit and to edit out the odd telegraph pole or overhead power line of which there were a few. Exact topography is not important, it is as if one is trying to make a picture of how one feels about a place. I felt good about Queensland; it had a certain grandeur. After completing my painting I visited the shopping centre at the Smithfield University

Campus to get a few stores before riding back to the marina.

First thing on Saturday John took delivery of our hire car and we were soon off to the north again. Of course one sees a lot more country from a car, but somehow it lacks the closeness and feel of a smaller piece seen from a bike or on foot. Things rush by that would catch your attention at a slower pace.

We travelled there along the spectacular coastal road to Mossman Gorge, one of the areas with tropical rain forest. The forest was a protected area and there were good paths enabling walks of various lengths; we went on a 2½-kilometre circuit. A fast flowing river ran through the forest with many small waterfalls. Some of the trees were most striking with huge buttressed trunks, others had branches returning to the ground and re-rooting to form massive arches. There were many birds and butterflies. One fellow whose blue shirt was obviously being mistaken for a flower particularly amused us - he had two or three butterflies at a time settling on him.

A few miles north of Mossman Gorge, the Daintree River meanders towards the coast through some relatively flat country. We had heard that this was a veritable haven for wildlife and there was a good chance to see a crocodile. At Daintree we boarded a small, flat-bottomed boat, driven by an outboard. The boatman was also our guide and turned out to be a thoroughly knowledgeable fellow. We soon appreciated the reasons for the flat-bottomed boat; the river was quite shallow in places - no chance to bring *Greylag* up there!

At first none of us saw it. The boatman had nosed into the edge of the river and was waiting to see if any of us realised why. And then we saw it; well camouflaged, half submerged and partly under some bushes, lay a large, saltwater crocodile. It remained utterly still, never batting an eyelid but nevertheless creating an aura of menace, at least in the minds of those of us with eyes focussed on those impressive teeth. There are two varieties of crocodile in Queensland, the saltwater or estuarine crocodile, known locally as 'salties', and the smaller freshwater crocodiles. A decade before, our guide explained, a local woman had disappeared from the riverbank one day. A posse of local men had then shot every crocodile they could find, up and down the river. In one they discovered the woman's remains. In response to this and similar episodes, the government made the crocodiles a protected species and they have thrived so well that at the time of our visit, there was some concern that the protection may have gone too far. The crocodiles had increased in number alarmingly and attacks on humans and animals were becoming more common. I recalled reading an article in Reader's Digest describing the horrific experience of a young woman and her boyfriend who were walking along a river bank. Suddenly there was a splash and a rush and a crocodile had grabbed her by the arm. Her boyfriend held on to her other arm and there ensued a long tug-of-war between the two of them. Eventually the crocodile did what they often do to tear flesh. It twisted itself round and round until the young woman's arm came away from her body. Her life was saved at the cost of an arm. Everywhere we went along the coast of Queensland and around the rivers we saw notices warning of the dangers of swimming - we took them seriously, including that one in the marina.

We saw several more crocodiles on that trip, and a couple of pythons resting in the branches of overhanging trees. There were many birds, mainly egrets and a few ibis and spoonbills. A pair of frogmouths, they looked like small owls, sat side-by-side on a branch. At $15 each, the trip had been very good value and we returned to Yorkey's Knob feeling the better for such a good day out.

On the Sunday we decided to go further inland and took a steep winding road up into the hills to the Barron Falls at Karimba. The gorge was most impressive but we were disappointed with the falls. One could see how spectacular they might have been, but when we were there was very little water flowing. Much of it is diverted into local irrigation schemes on the Atherton Tablelands. There was a narrow-gauge railway running up the side of the gorge, it looked a bit nerve-racking in places where the ground fell sheer away from the track, but the views must have been spectacular.

We tracked across the flat Tablelands, a vast fruit and vegetable garden criss-crossed by man-made irrigation channels, then south past Lake Tinatoo to the Millstream Falls. These were the best we had seen, curved almost to a semicircle they looked like a miniature version of the Horseshoe Falls at Niagara. It was a steep climb down into the gorge but worth the effort and the only way to get close to the falls. The gorge was a mass of blossom and butterflies. After struggling back to the top we found an ambulance parked by our car. Some athletic-looking men with climbing gear and a stretcher were preparing to go down into the gorge. A very large, German lady had fallen and broken her ankle, about halfway down. We had every sympathy with the rescuers who were going to have a difficult time retrieving her. We returned to the boat having had another good day out.

The next three days were spent preparing the boat for her onward journey and generally enjoying the facilities of Yorkey's Knob. One of the Trade Wind skippers, Geoff Fielden from *Lucky Seven,* gave us all a splendid party to celebrate his fiftieth birthday. It was held at a restaurant with the unlikely, but typically Australian name 'Elwood Dowd's'.

It was now the 21st of July and we had been among the fleshpots of Yorkey's knob for nine days. I rang Janet who had bad news for me on the crewing front. Richard Rhodes had sounded rather unhappy about *Greylag*'s small size and John Weaver had family problems that prevented him from coming out. We were back to square one on this, but it would have to wait until Darwin. We had a final dinner out, back at Elwood Dowd's, and made a firm decision to set out next day on the long voyage around the top right-hand corner of Australia.

Our first destination was the Low Islets that stood just offshore from the estuary of the Daintree River, half a day's sailing to the north-east. The anchorage there was good and fairly calm despite the 20-25 knot south-easterly breeze. We saw several turtles. For dinner I cooked Delia Smith's recipe for pork chops with mushrooms and cream, but using lamb chops. It seemed to work.

Kate had a return flight booked from Darwin for the 16th of August so we were going to have to keep up the pressure in order to do the 1350-mile journey in time. We were keen to do as much day sailing as possible and to anchor for the nights. This partly reflected our growing fatigue, I certainly was feeling quite tired and the thought of watch on-watch off with John was not very attractive. Kate was an intelligent young lady with a fair amount of experience but probably not enough to stand watch on her own at night, in waters that had their fair share of dangers. Once round Cape York, however, she stood watches on her own and never gave me any cause for concern.

We were off at six o'clock next morning and made a fast passage to Hope Island where we arrived with plenty of sun left to help us in past the coral heads. We anchored close to the eastern of the two islands where we found two other boats. Hope Island was only small and we walked right round it in about an hour. At the southern end there were a number of sea eagles and some pairs had nests in the trees at that end of the island. There were a lot of terns and egrets. The night was not very restful as the wind

The old pier at Cape Flattery, Queensland

got up a bit and sleep was fitful. Near to Hope Island was the famous Endeavour Reef where Captain James Cook had run aground during his search for a way through the Great Barrier Reef. *Endeavour* was retrieved and taken to Port Douglas, a little to the south, for repairs.

I was glad to get going again early next morning, as we had a 50-mile trip to make to Cape Flattery. It seemed a long way in prospect, but the strong south-easterly breeze, which seemed to be almost guaranteed when we were there, made for very fast downwind sailing. The coastline had changed, now there were long stretches of white sand between occasional headlands of rock. We arrived at Cape Flattery with plenty of daylight left and found an excellent calm anchorage around the corner to the north of the Cape. There was a large silica mining operation there and we anchored alongside an old derelict wooden pier. This was no longer used to ship out the silica, they had built a more substantial pier for that purpose on the other side of the Cape, where the water was deeper and allowed the berthing of bigger ships. We had a much needed, good sleep.

Another early start next day was necessary to get us the 60 miles to Ninian Bay. We had the usual stiff breeze and made fast time. When we arrived we were disappointed to find conditions were quite rough in the bay. We edged in as close as I dared - the whole bay was rather shallow -

to get a little shelter from a small headland. It turned out to be a bit too close, as we went aground in the night at low tide. It wasn't a serious problem, the bottom was soft mud and we only just touched at low water. But it did cause another rather restless night. We had heard there were dugongs here, those large aquatic mammals, sometimes referred to as sea cows. There was a lot of their favourite, green grass-weed around but we never saw one. We heard from David and Jill on *Sooty,* that they had seen some just around the corner in the next bay to the north of us, so perhaps we were just unlucky.

Our next stop was at the Flinders Group of islands, another long day sail away. I was beginning to be impressed with the sheer size of Australia! So far we had completed only about 180 miles of the journey to Darwin. On our way we spoke on the radio to *Sooty* who were headed for the same destination. The pilot book suggested an anchorage off a sand spit at the south-west end of Flinders Island. When we got there we found the anchorage untenable. The island is quite high and the strong south-easterly winds were generating powerful gusts coming down from the high ground. These gusts are a common local phenomenon and are known as 'bullets'. We heard later in Darwin that it was here that *Sheet Lightning* had damaged her rudder when one of these gusts blew her onto some coral. Our friends on *Sooty* went to the west side of Stanley Island, which was very near, and radioed through that conditions there were much better. We moved round to join them, and enjoyed a peaceful night. In the morning we all felt relaxed and decided to stay for a day's rest.

Ashore, Stanley Island had interesting rock structures but was otherwise not very inspiring. I came across a long column of ants and followed it all the way down to the foreshore. It ascended a mangrove bush there via the extraordinary roots on which they stand at low tide. In the bush they had woven leaves together with their own silk to make nests. This established one end of the column, the other was somewhere in the outback. The mangroves at Stanley Island were not as dense as most and I was able to study them closely. Our guide at Daintree had explained that the open-ended, tubular stems emerging from the mud all around the trees are important devices providing aeration to the root system at low tide.

Refreshed after our day off, we set out early next morning for Morris Island. The wind was lighter that day and we were able to hoist our spinnaker for the first time on this journey. It was a long day and we finally got to Morris Island at 1600 hours. It was only a small Island with a single palm tree - lone survivor, the pilot book said, of some the British planted to help ship-wrecked sailors. There were brown pelicans out on the sand and a sooty tern that was trying to decoy us away from its nest. Just behind the foreshore we came across a grave. It was neatly set out with stones and decorated with seashells. The inscription recorded that the dead man had been a pearl diver. Diving for pearls was a lucrative business at one time and in those early days little was known about decompression sickness. Fatalities were quite common and the victims were usually just taken to the nearest island and buried as this man had been.

Next morning the wind was still light and we again had the spinnaker up for the day's passage to Portland Roads. Many of the local names had English counterparts - Sidmouth, Weymouth, Portland, Newcastle. At Portland we anchored in among the shrimp boats, but by dark they had all moved off for the night's work. The bay was well protected from the prevailing wind. That evening we discussed plans and decided it would be interesting to try to enter one of the local rivers, most had shallow entrances so we would need to be careful. The Pascoe River was our first choice but the bar looked shallow and was exposed to the south-east wind which might make things difficult. At the southern end of Temple Bay our chart showed the Hunter Inlet and the pilot book gave a few details as to how to get into it. That was where we would go next day.

The Hunter Inlet lay 25 miles to the north of Portland roads, an easy sail compared with many of recent days. As High Water was at 1000 hours we left early to be there at the top of the tide. On the way we noticed several huge termite mounds ashore, but mostly the coast was a mass of mangrove. The Inlet was not difficult to navigate, we found a least depth of 2.7 metres over the bar and once in the river there were a few spots that showed 1.9 metres on the echo sounder. The next day's HW was expected to be about 0.2 metres lower so there should be plenty of water for *Greylag* to escape - she needed 1.5 metres for safety. This sort of calculation is always a bit of a worry because changes in the atmospheric pressure can cause significant changes to the height of the tide and this was no place in which to be trapped.

We pressed on up the river for nearly 3½ miles and anchored the boat just inside a small branch running off the main river. We were reluctant to go further even though the water was still quite deep, because it looked very easy to get lost in there. I frequently glanced over my shoulder to see how it looked from the opposite direction and to make a mental note of the few recognisable landmarks. The place was a maze of small, mangrove edged channels and it would be easy to take a wrong turning and be lost forever! Surprisingly the mosquitoes were no more prevalent in that swamp than elsewhere along the coast. We saw a snake swimming along the edge of our creek and there were plenty of interesting birds to watch. We were expecting to see a crocodile but none appeared. The night was flat calm and peaceful as far as the weather was concerned, but there were some eerie noises emanating from the mangroves and one found oneself conjuring up all sorts of monsters.

Next morning we made our way back down the river well before high tide and made the entrance, with only one short spell ploughing mud. At the entrance some idiot from a large powerboat, that we could see off the bar, had put a net right across the river and then gone back to his boat. I suppose he was not to know that there might be other idiots actually up that river! Again I was pleased to have the wire between our keel and rudder to keep the net out of our prop. Nevertheless we put the engine into neutral as we ran across the net, just to be sure.

Safely out of the river, we made our way north again to Margaret Bay, just around the corner at Cape Grenville. This was an excellent anchorage and we were pleased to see *Magic Dragon* appear round the Cape shortly after our arrival. We were rather short of water by then and Steven Thomas very kindly gave us a can full from their water maker. This was the only time we came near to being short of water which was surprising so close to land, but this coast is very sparsely populated and supplies were few and far between.

We risked a swim over the rocks at Margaret Bay and found some interesting fish. These included a lionfish - an extraordinary sight, all stripes and whiskers. We later had a visit from one of the local fishermen who said that he thought we might like to know that a salty had been seen in the anchorage recently. We asked him whether there was trouble from sharks.

'No mate' he replied 'the salties have 'ad 'em all!'

Ashore I found large numbers of wild oysters. It was possible to break them off the rocks with a hammer and screwdriver and I enjoyed half a dozen before dinner.

Our next destination was the Escape River and we anchored there along with *Sooty* who had been with us for several days. We were now just a day sail away from Cape York, the northernmost tip of the Australian

Continent and the end of our long journey to the north. From there we would be turning once again to the west to head for Darwin. The first problem was to time our arrival at the Albany Passage so as to catch the favourable tide through there and round the corner. For once this was conveniently at nine o'clock in the morning and made for a leisurely start. The route took us along some impressive coastline and we saw more of those huge termite mounds. At the very tip of Australia we found a narrow passage and hurtled through on the tide. As we went by we saw a large notice board, facing away from us, which John recognised as the one he had seen on a postcard. We knew from the postcard that the other side said 'You are standing at the most northerly point of the Australian Continent.'

After rounding Cape York, we passed round Peak point and then sailed south-west between Possession Island and High Island and on to Red Island. There we found several pleasant surprises. The anchorage was good and well sheltered behind a small island. There were some showers at a camping site and a small food shop, a restaurant and a garage for diesel. There was even a 'laundromat', and all this in a place as remote as you could imagine. In the centre of the Seisa village, as this tiny settlement was known, we came across a memorial to a local man who was 'sadly taken by a crocodile'. This sort of thing concentrated the mind and reinforced our cautious approach to swimming. We heard that Nick Parker on *Enarkay* had taken a dinghy to explore the small island and been chased by a salty!

A few miles inland from Red Island was the small town of Bamaga with a supermarket and a booze store. We decided to go there by taxi but when the time came the taxi was *caput*. However, this was the sort of place where everybody helps everybody else, a real frontier spirit, and in no time flat a local man had stopped and offered us a lift. It turned out that he was the one who had built the road between Bamaga and Seisa village. It was the only bit of tarmac road for hundreds of miles, after Bamaga there was nothing but dirt track until one got almost to Cairns. Once a week a ferry came to the village with supplies for the whole area, this being an easier method than bringing the stuff up the dirt track. We found everything we needed in Bamaga and got a lift back from the same fellow. Considering the extreme isolation of this corner of Australia we were both surprised and grateful to find this civilised tip on the end of the largely wild Cape York Peninsular. Rested and re-supplied, we were ready for our trip across the Gulf of Carpentaria.

On the opposite (west) side of the Gulf is Arnhem Land and tucked in behind Cape Arnhem is the small town of Gove, with its huge aluminium works and a harbour. Our voyage across the Gulf was fast and uneventful, some of the best sailing we had in Australia; we were across in 2½ days. Once past the aluminium works and the large quayside there for the ships to be loaded, we found a pleasant sandy bay with numerous moorings and room to anchor. Ashore was a club-cum-restaurant, a sort of water sports facility provided by the aluminium company for its staff. Visitors, however, were more than welcome to use the facilities. We soon discovered that just about everything at Gove was associated with the aluminium company, it was a very large employer on whom the whole local economy depended.

In the club at Gove I found a small advertisement. I cannot recall the exact words but as far as I can remember it said 'Hi fellas, I will crew for you. Not much experience but a quick learner and prepared to do anything! Contact Bec on 04638 or at the bar.'

I am not sure what her mother would have thought of this but Bec sounded quite a girl. However, I couldn't imagine that she would want to go on a boat with a couple of sixty-year-olds. I asked the lady behind the bar whether she knew this Bec and she said she was a very nice girl and well-liked around there. In spite of my reservations, not least concerning the ribbing we would get from other rally boats if we turned up in Darwin with a young lady crew, I rang the number and asked for Bec. The person who answered said Bec wasn't there at the time but agreed to pass on a message to meet me in the bar later that day. Bec turned up on the dot. She was an attractive, lively young lady, tomboyish, full of enthusiasm for our trip and madly keen to opt out of her employment with the 'Company' and come with us on *Greylag*. She thought she could get her affairs sorted out in time to join us at Darwin in a few weeks. I agreed to take her on at least as far as Bali, and further if things worked out well on both sides. And so our crew problem appeared to be solved, we had found someone in the most unlikely of places.

Going west from Gove, one has either to go round or through the long chain of islands that form Cape Wessel. They stretch out north-eastwards for more than a hundred miles, so the option to go through a gap in the islands is very attractive. The problem is that the most convenient gap is a fearsome place, known locally as the 'Hole-in-the-Wall'. Arrive there at the wrong time and so fierce was the tide that you would either find it impossible to go through or you would be swept through the narrow gap at about 10 knots, like bath water going down the drain, and with about as much control. John worked out that we would need to be there at about 0800 hours to catch a quiet period, so I decided to move to a nearby spot so that we could time our arrival accurately.

We left Gove Harbour in quiet weather, amid a huge school of dolphins. I got some wonderful video of them. We were soon around Cape Wilberforce and through a gap between Cotton Island and Wigram Island, to an anchorage in the lee to the north-west of the latter. This was not an easy anchorage because although well sheltered, the coral was continuous and shallow for the last 150 metres to the shore. We had to anchor a long way out and trust to luck that the anchor would not get ensnared in the coral.

These islands belong to the Aboriginals and they do not always welcome visitors. We found some evidence of human occupation, some tracks on the sand, but we didn't see anyone there. *Sooty* anchored close by after several aborted attempts. Like us, *Sooty* had no anchor winch and we felt sorry for poor Jill who often found herself doing the hard work of pulling up long lengths of chain. Once may be OK, but when you have to do it two or three times before finding a secure hold it can become distinctly unfunny! However, both boats persisted with the difficulties because this anchorage was only 17 miles from the Hole-in-the-Wall and made it easy to time our arrival.

We were off at five o'clock in the morning and arrived off the 'Hole' as planned at eight o'clock. There was still an adverse current of about 1½ knots when we arrived but this was probably better than a favourable current. It is always easier to keep control of the boat against the tide rather than with it, especially if there is a risk, and there was, of the tide increasing rapidly after turning. As it was we went through that place comparatively easily. On the way through we passed several areas of swirling water and one could see that it might be nasty at the wrong time. We heard on the radio that *Pale Moon* had touched 16 knots when she went through the day before. At that speed any mistake, or getting caught in a strong eddy, might sweep one into the rocks either side.

The next three and a half days took us along the coast of Australia's Northern Territory, around the Cobourg Peninsular and across Van Diemen's Gulf to Darwin. There were long periods of flat calm along that route and I was pleased we had been able to start the journey with full fuel tanks. During one prolonged period of motoring we ran into a huge area where the sea was smothered with a reddish-brown algal bloom. An Australian research vessel was there taking samples. *Sooty* reported seeing a three-foot long sea snake and we saw numerous dolphins and turtles. It was a little frustrating that we were tight against Kate's deadline for her plane home and did not have time to stop and explore. Perhaps it was just as well because most of that territory is an aboriginal reserve and one is supposed to have permission before visiting.

Luckily the fuel lasted to get us into the magnificent new marina at Cullen Bay, with just a day to spare before Kate's flight home. The marina had every facility and lots of shops and restaurants. It looked a good place to recuperate and gather our energies for Indonesia. Bec was due to join us at Darwin in a few days so once again we would have a crew of three. I still regretted my falling out with David but it was by no means an isolated experience. Many of the other boats in the fleet had suffered breakdowns among their crew. Each time we all arrived at a major port it was a matter of great interest, and a lot of gossip, to see who would be swapping boats. The strain was beginning to show in places, even among the married couples. A new illness emerged among one or two of the older gentlemen who appeared to have found young lady partners. We called it PSV for 'Pre-Senile Virility'. By now everybody knew each other rather well - we were like a small village community and characteristically enjoyed talking about the neighbours. There were no secrets that lasted more than a few days before the bush telegraph spread the news.

After a few days at Darwin, David and Jill on Sooty invited us to share their hire car for a visit to Lichfield National Park, about two hours drive inland from Darwin. This was a fascinating day out. Our first stop was in an area covered with termite mounds and at last we were able to get a close look at them. Some were as much as twelve feet high and we heard interesting stories as to how they were used as hiding places by various animals looking for protection from the bush fires that were common in the area. Another type of termite mound was flattened in one plane and the longitudinal axis lined up with the earth's magnetic field. There was no obvious explanation for this extraordinary arrangement, in some places we saw dozens of these mounds and all of them were lined up in this way.

As before at Cairns, we visited a lot of waterfalls. But the highlight of the day was a visit to a billabong. In spite of familiarity with the words of 'Waltzing Matilda', I never knew what a billabong was until then. We all tumbled into a four-wheel drive vehicle and were driven off through several miles of wild country. We saw plenty of kangaroos and wallabies and at one spot the driver stopped to show us the nest of a lyrebird. The structure consisted of rows of sticks stuck in the ground and then bent over to form an arched roof, open at both ends. Inside there were all sorts of 'trinkets' put there by the male bird in an effort to attract a female. There were attractive little stones and shells but also a number of man-made objects like the rings from beer cans!

The billabong was a lake formed on the route of a river; it was only about 200 meters wide but several miles long. We boarded a flat-bottomed boat and our guide took us around the billabong to show us some of its rich wildlife. There were a lot of crocodiles, and unlike the Daintree River, here there were the freshwater crocodiles as well as 'salties'. Huge flocks of egrets decorated some of the trees and in one spot a flight of several thousand whistling ducks took off as we approached. A pair of white-bellied, sea eagles had nested in a dead tree. The sides of the billabong were often fringed with weed beds and there we saw the little 'Jesus' birds, so-called (our guide said) because of the way their large feet enabled them to walk across the water! It was a good day out.

Back at Cullen Bay there were a few more days to relax before Bec was due to arrive and we would need to start thinking seriously about the next part of our journey which would take us north to Timor and then through the Indonesian islands to Malaysia. Of all the legs on our circumnavigation this was then the most unknown.

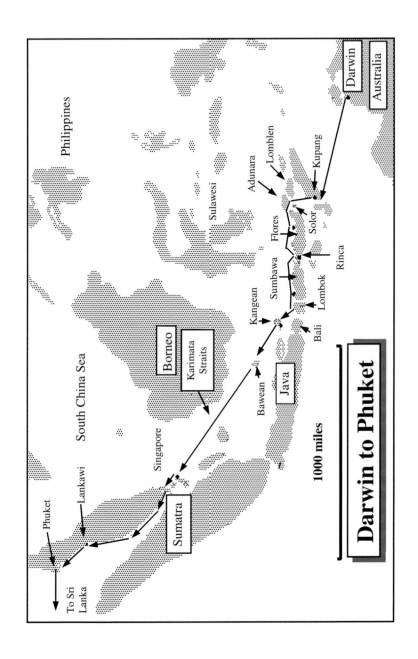

Darwin to Phuket

1000 miles

Australia

Darwin

Kupang

Lomblen

Adunara

Solor

Flores

Rinca

Sumbawa

Lombok

Bali

Kangean

Bawean

Java

Karimata Straits

Borneo

Sulawesi

Philippines

South China Sea

Singapore

Sumatra

Lankawi

Phuket

To Sri Lanka

182

15 Indonesia - A Continent of Islands Stretching Forever

Bec, our new young crew, arrived in Darwin on the 23rd of September. She bubbled with enthusiasm, reminding us just how exciting such a trip could be for someone who had never done anything like it before, and Bec had never been out of Australia. Her boyfriend Warren had come to Darwin to say goodbye, he said, but I wondered whether he was angling to come as well. This was not a possibility given the space limitations on *Greylag*, anyway something told me Bec was looking for a break from the relationship. That said, the two of them and John set about a major clean up of the boat prior to our planned departure for Indonesia on the 28th.

It was during this clean up that I found trouble in the stern locker. I had emptied everything out, gas bottles, fenders, the endless bric-a-brac that always seems to collect in these places, when I discovered a small amount of water at the bottom. Closer inspection revealed a crack in the hull just behind the rudder that was clearly leaking, albeit slowly. I probed around some more. Yes, there was a crack in the hull that would have to be repaired before we could leave.

Unfortunately there were no facilities at Cullen Bay marina for lifting boats out of the water, so we had to try to do the repair afloat, no easy task for a hole below the waterline. But we had a good idea - we would move the waterline. If we were to transfer as much weight as possible into the front of the boat we might be able to tip the stern up clear of the water, to allow us to mend the hole which was quite near the surface. We piled everything we could onto the foredeck, including our five 25-litre jerry cans filled with water. This did the trick perfectly; the stern came up about eight inches with the hole well clear of the water. I was now able to look at the damage from underneath and I soon found what had caused it. On the top of the rudder was a large cluster of barnacles. It was probably when we hit the coral, back in Fiji, that this hard little lump had punched a hole when the rudder was forced upwards. I purchased a fibreglass repair kit downtown and soon had the hull repaired good as new. But now we had another small problem. Epoxy resin takes a little time to cure thoroughly, even in a hot climate, so it was necessary to keep the stern out of water for at least another 24 hours. The extra weight would have to stay on the foredeck overnight, leaving the back end sticking up in the air like a stalking cat.

'All sleeping in the forepeak now are we?' Remarked some passing wit, leering at Bec. I protested our innocence but he would have none of it!

We were now into our last few days at Darwin and my thoughts turned to the next stage of our journey. Along the one thousand-mile track from northern Australia to Singapore lie the many thousands of islands of Indonesia. Large ones you have heard of – Java, Sumatra, the romantic Bali whose reality never quite lives up to the image created by the tour companies. But for the most part the islands are small, unknown, beautiful, always interesting and populated by some of the happiest and most welcoming people one could wish to meet. Have you heard of Solor, Flores, Sumbawa, Bawean or Lingga? To me at that time they were just names on a chart. But now I can tell you about these islands that lie across the equator, lush, green and inviting, where exaggerated tales of piracy and well-founded reports of bureaucratic zeal have served only to keep the area wild and unspoilt. As we prepared to leave Australia, we were full of excited anticipation for this land that none of us knew.

Partly because the rally skippers had a few nagging worries about piracy and other aspects of security, various informal arrangements were being made to travel through Indonesia in groups. We talked to some of the smaller boats and decided to set up STING - The Small Tradewinders Indonesia Group. Initially it consisted of *Greylag, Sheet Lightning, Aditi, Sooty, Papa Golf* and *Hilda* but it grew more popular as the days went by.

At first light on the Saturday we left Darwin and slipped quietly out into the Arafura Sea, heading for Kupang at the western end of Timor. This was to prove a quiet trip with hardly any wind for the first two days of the 440-mile journey. It was a gentle introduction for Bec as we motored most of the way. In spite of her inexperience, she took everything in her stride and quickly picked up the basics of running the boat and keeping a watch. She took her turn in the galley and produced a welcome change of menus; John and I had become a bit bored with our limited repertoire.

We passed close to one of the many new oilfields just south of Timor, the huge flame of burning gas lighting up the sky like a gigantic Roman candle. Luckily we were upwind of it and avoided the big plume of black smoke drifting away downwind on the other side from us.

Daylight on the fifth day saw us just off Selat Semau, the strait running between Pulau (an island) Semau and the western tip of Timor. Grey-green mountains rose majestically from the sea, their foothills clad in the mists of early morning. We saw a turtle ambling along on the surface as we made our way between the many small fishing boats drifting about on the glassy sea. Inshore there were numerous fishing huts, built on stilts, and we had to be careful steering a way through them towards the anchorage at Lassiana beach. It had been an enjoyable landfall to start our visit to Indonesia, yet only a tiny taste of the many magic moments still to come in that beautiful but almost unknown country. I wondered how much different it must have been for Captain William Bligh and his few faithful sailors. They had been set adrift by the *Bounty* mutineers shortly after leaving Tahiti and eventually arrived at Kupang after an astonishing 4000-mile journey across the western Pacific in an open boat.

Next day we cleared ourselves through customs and immigration with the (expensive) help of an agent. We were already armed with our $200 cruising permit and 60 day visas, obtained from the High Commission back in Darwin after interminable form-filling and tedious nit-picking over minor details. It had taken much patience, a lot of ink and a broad sense of humour, of the kind that can see the funny side of walking through deep mud!

The next job was to obtain some local currency and replenish our stores. We were soon on our way into Kupang on one of the ubiquitous 'bemos'. These are the local twenty-seat buses that career around with about forty occupants. You hail one down and fight your way in, hoping that it is going in the right direction. The fare is fixed at 500 rupiah however far you are going. Kupang was a noisy, jostling little town where we did the shopping after quickly learning to adjust our dietary preferences to what was actually available and didn't look a serious health hazard. The fresh meat lay around in the open, covered in flies; we didn't think it worth the risk even though we probably ate something similar in the local restaurants. Oh for a British supermarket! In the end we settled for fresh vegetables and various things in tins, mostly the dreaded tuna. The banks had not yet caught up with plastic cards but luckily they understood dollar traveller's cheques. To obtain cash with a card involved a three-hour wait while they phoned through to Jakarta to obtain clearance. The local currency would be sensible if one could remove about three zeros from the end of each figure. Mind you, I enjoyed the transitory illusion of wealth.

'How much would you like?' The girl in the bank asked.

'Half a million please!' I hadn't had this experience since Galapagos where the situation was much the same. I always get a bit of a fright in restaurants when the bill comes for 10,000 whatsits; I never quite get used to it.

After the noise and bustle of Kupang, we were keen to move on to the Nusa Tenggara, the chain of islands running east to west from Alar to Bali. We left the Lassiana anchorage in the afternoon so that we would arrive at Lomblen, about 100 miles north of Timor, early in the morning. It was nearly always essential to plan journeys this way as it could be highly dangerous to make a landfall at night, given the extensive coral and inaccurate charts. When we arrived off Lomblen, we heard from a boat ahead of us that the anchorage we were heading for was unpleasantly rough in the blustery wind, so we changed our plans and went to Solor instead. After the bustle of Kupang, here was the real, unspoilt Indonesia. Lamakera on Solor was our first experience of an Indonesian fishing community. Even before we had dropped the hook in a quiet bay just west of the village, we were greeted loudly by Badarhudin and his young friends who had paddled out in their dugout canoes to welcome us.

'Hello Meester', he called, the greeting echoed by his friends. 'Come to Kampong' he added, indicating the village with a wave of his paddle.

Next day Bec and I set off along the mile-long track which ran along the low cliff top to the village. Long before we got there, we acquired an entourage of children – smiling, noisy, welcoming. We soon learnt that 'Hello Meester' was the only phrase of English they all knew. Follow-up conversation was more difficult but smiles and sign language got us by well enough.

'Nama saya Dick' I introduced myself, 'Nama saya Bec' I said pointing to Bec whose long hair seemed to fascinate them.

The communities in Indonesia are mostly Muslim and one dresses conservatively for visits, long trousers and not too much bare flesh, especially for the girls. Not a lot of sexual equality round there! Although hot, the covering had the advantage of frustrating the local insectivora. The villagers seemed delighted to see us and invited us into their homes. These were simple wooden structures with little in the way of services. Water came from the village well and there was a basic electricity supply from numerous small generators. One could buy eggs and bananas, other items looked a bit iffy on health grounds. On the beach the fishermen showed us their boats, each insisting that we take a photo of his particular pride and joy. A sad note was struck when we came across large pieces of

Enarkay at Solor

manta ray set out on the rocks to dry in the sun. It seemed a sad end for such magnificent creatures, especially as our memories of swimming among them in Fiji were still fresh. One has to accept that these communities survive on what they can grow or catch and western judgements can be unrealistic. It saddened me all the same.

The anchorage at Solor Island was wonderfully protected, from the south by Solor itself and from all other directions by the high hills, mountains almost, of Lomblen to the east of us, Adunara to the north and Flores to the west. Way off to the north-east, when the clouds allowed, we could see a smoking volcano, a reminder that this part of the world is no stranger to natural disasters. The volcano at Krakatoa is perhaps the most famous recent example. The sea was warm and clear and full of fish. Sometimes we were surrounded by shoals of small squid, all making their way east purposively albeit for reasons unknown to us. In the evenings we watched the sun go down behind the mountains of Flores, creating as it went some memorable sunsets.

After a couple of days it was time to move on westwards through the Larantuka Narrows and along the northern coast of Flores. These Narrows, separating Flores from Adunara, are barely half a mile wide off the little town of Larantuka and we had been warned that the current could be fierce.

187

Solor fisherman

It was important to get there when the flow was northwards or one could spend a lot of time going nowhere very fast. Unfortunately for us, the tide on that day would be right between five and eight o'clock in the morning, so we had to leave Lamakera in the dark to cover the thirteen miles to the Narrows before the tide turned against us. It wasn't an option to wait until the evening favourable tide because that would have left too little time to get to a safe anchorage on Flores before dark.

What we hadn't reckoned on was that everyone and his friend was out fishing that night in their small unlit boats. They were very difficult to see in the dark and this was one of many occasions when I was glad to have our radar which usually picked them up in time to avoid collisions. Sometimes we heard them shout a warning and a few had torches. Happily there were no collisions as we picked our way through. Dawn soon came to make things easier, and now at least we could see the fishermen. Infuriatingly, however, we discovered that our information on the tides was wrong and we had to struggle against the current for several hours before escaping north into the Flores Sea.

The eastern end of Flores curls northward to form a substantial peninsula. We were hopeful of finding a place to stop at the northern end of this peninsula, failing which we would have to press on overnight to reach 'Sea World', where there was a known safe anchorage. We were lucky. Just around Telung Kapondai, the most northerly tip of the peninsula, we found Telung Gedong, a small headland sticking out about half a mile from the coastline with an attractive bay on its eastern side, well protected from the westerly breeze. As we had no information about Gedong, we approached cautiously over the extensive coral patches towards the coast. Close in we found a few patches of sand and dropped our anchor into one of them. Our friends on *Hilda* and *Aditi* followed us in and managed to find other patches of sand to anchor. In this they were considerably aided by John and Bec, who were quickly into the water to survey the bottom. Although safely anchored on sand, we found ourselves surrounded by beautiful coral gardens, easily the best we had yet seen in Indonesia. The water was crystal clear so that one could watch the fish from the deck. A cave full of small bats ran deep into the headland and we watched a troop of monkeys in the trees that cloaked the low cliffs. A small village nestled among the trees on the shore and very soon canoes full of youngsters visited us, curious to inspect such rare visitors to this out of the way spot.

The coral at Gedong was truly spectacular. Although on a smaller scale than some we had seen in Tonga, the variety of types and colours and the shallowness of the water made this a special place. I lay on the surface with my mask and snorkel, marvelling at the marine miracles covering the seabed for as far as one could see.

A day sail west of Gedong, we stopped at 'Sea World'. The name conjures up unattractive images of California-style marine circuses, but actually it was a small resort with a couple of restaurants and a few thatched huts for rent. The day after we arrived we hired a minibus and driver to take us into the hinterland. Flores is mountainous and the few roads wind round the hills and valleys in terrifying hairpins with sheer drops on one side, or sometimes on both. The scenery is stunning; everywhere is green and lush. One finds valleys with tumbling streams, dammed here and there to divert water into the rice fields which climb into the valleys like giant flights of steps. Flores is about 200 miles long, but the road from one end to the other is 400 miles long. This gives some idea of the tortuous terrain.

We climbed into the mountains to find the three big volcano craters at Kelimutu, inactive but still emitting sulphurous fumes if you happen to be downwind. Each crater is filled with water of a different colour – green, turquoise and brown. From this vantagepoint we looked out over the glorious mountain scenery, not snow covered like the Alps, but no less grand for that. It was still early in the morning when we were there, and the mistiness in the valleys added an ethereal quality to the view. Later, as the day warmed up, the warm moist air would rise up the mountains and condense into thick cloud. After that the view was gone for the day.

'Sea World' had been a brief glimpse of organised tourism, but we were soon moving on westwards to wilder places. We found a near perfect anchorage off a small island close to the little fishing village of Riung. Many of the *STING* group joined us there - *Sooty, Hilda, Papa Golf, Aditi*; also *Alb, Excess Line* and *Taos Brett*. Here was some more excellent snorkelling and one could climb the hill on the island and look down on the boats apparently suspended in mid-air, so clear was the water. For me, the chief interest was the stilted village about a mile and a half from the anchorage. We took *Greylag* over there to look around and get some fuel if possible.

The contrast with Lamakera was most interesting. That village had been built on high ground; Riung was at sea level or a little below. So the houses were built on stilts, surrounded by the sea at high tide. The welcome was the same here as it had been at Lamakera and nothing was too much trouble for them. The main street at Riung was a dirt track running at right angles away from the sea. We were amused to see the white line painted down the middle, presumably for the guidance of both the local vehicles! On each side of the road were rows of houses on stilts. Each had a front balcony with steps going up to it from the ground. These were favourite spots for the families to sit of an evening to discuss events and, no doubt, village politics; or simply to while away the time. At high tide the seas would just about reach the houses but the stilts were longer than would have been necessary simply to stay dry. Perhaps they had other purposes; the basement seemed to be where the animals were kept, though I'm not sure what happened to them at high tide. We watched one fellow carving a new canoe out of a solid tree trunk. He used an adze with extraordinary skill and precision, with never a care that it might take him six months to complete the job.

We asked about the possibility of buying some diesel and soon found that there was no difficulty about this provided that one didn't haggle about the price too much. At 650 rupiah per litre, about half the price at home, they were happy to sell you all you wanted because at that price they made more money than if they used the fuel for fishing. When they ran out of local supplies, they were even prepared to drive into the local town to fetch some more.

The foreshore by the kampong was alive with fiddler crabs. I was fascinated by their extraordinary sensitivity to the slightest vibration on the ground. One could creep up close and then the merest tap of the foot would send them scuttling for their holes. For such ungainly creatures, their one huge claw grotesquely out of proportion with the rest, they were surprisingly nimble, disappearing backwards into their holes, neatly followed by the big claw to plug the entrance.

We made our way back to the island anchorage, crossing the coral reef in the last of the sunlight. The next day we would finally leave Flores. It was hard to believe that we had travelled three hundred miles since leaving Kupang and most of that had been on this one island, a great long mountain ridge rising up from the sea bed with only the last few thousand feet showing above the water.

Between Flores and Sumbawa, the next main island to the west, lies dragon country. The islands of Komodo and Rinca have small populations of the largest lizard in the world, the Komodo dragon. Komodo is the more famous site and consequently more crowded with tourists who go there by boat from Lombok. We decided to go to Rinca which, although still part of the Komodo national park, was more remote and therefore more likely to let us see those extraordinary creatures, so reminiscent of the dinosaur age, in their natural surroundings. There are believed to be only a few hundred left in Indonesia, the only place in the world where they are found. They measure about 3 metres long and have big teeth and fearsome, flesh-tearing claws. They are carnivorous and lie in wait along the animal tracks to ambush their prey. Like crocodiles, they can move with astonishing speed when a meal presents itself. And they won't reject the odd careless human. We heard of one fellow in a nearby village who would show you his scars for a few dollars – he had to have 400 stitches!

We employed a guide to take us to the place where we were most likely to see the dragons; local knowledge seemed essential if we were not to be disappointed. We assembled at six in the morning for the long trek into the hinterland, at least at this time of day it was fairly cool, it would have been unbearable to do it in the heat of the day. On our way through the scrub covered hills we saw several other animals, a wild pig snorted off into the undergrowth and there were several deer and monkeys and a pair of the wild horses for which this island is also famous. Our guide explained that, on Komodo, the tourists were invited to purchase a goat, which would then be walked to the dragon territory, slaughtered, and hung from a tree. The dragons would leap for a jawful of the unfortunate beast for breakfast. We were happy not to be on Komodo.

The landing stage, Crocodile Bay, Rinca

'Sssh', our guide's hand went up to warn us to move quietly.

We had arrived at a dried out riverbed with one or two water holes remaining. At one of these an old water buffalo, half-blind and life-weary, stood motionless. And then we saw them. One huge creature, fully three metres long, lay on a ridge above the buffalo. He did not move but his eyes were focussed on us and a foot-long tongue snaked out at intervals. I fully expected to see a plume of fire and smoke as he breathed out! He had the countenance of the devil, leathery, scaly skin lying loosely over an obviously powerful body, and claws. Those claws could rip one apart in seconds. Tyrannosaurus Rex would have been pleased to have such claws! I felt a little nervous as I zoomed in with the video, asking John to warn me if the animal showed any signs of moving in my direction. It was difficult, looking through the telephoto lens, to judge how close they were.

Below the ridge and nearer to us, another dragon was definitely on the move, his gait slow and ponderous, but menacing. I felt for the poor old buffalo, they were just waiting for it to weaken a little more before going in for the kill. The scene was gruesome, even though nothing had yet happened one's imagination conjured up visions of the most appalling, primitive and bloody carnage as the buffalo met his inevitable end. There was no way of knowing whether this was minutes or hours away, we didn't feel like waiting anyway.

A little further down the riverbed we came across a buffalo skull, evidence of earlier horrors. Our guide also showed us the holes where the dragons spent the night and where they laid their eggs during the breeding season. The cool of the night slows them down and, in common with most reptiles, they rely on the sun to warm them up and get them going of a morning. Mind you, I've known some crew like that! We left Rinca later that day, each with his own private thoughts about those primitive inhabitants of the riverbed.

Westward again, we stopped briefly at two places along the northern coast of the next island along the chain, Sumbawa. Labuan Sumbawa is a small port, too shallow for yachts to enter, but the anchorage off the beach was reasonably comfortable in the predominently south-east wind. The local fishermen who were pushing large, fine-mesh nets along the edge of the water fascinated us. They were having no obvious success in the way of a meal. Later they showed us their quarry, tiny fish fry which they transferred into pools behind the beach. There they fed them and grew them on to plate size. Five miles inland from the port is the town of Sumbawa Besar; we hired a bemo to go there for supplies from the substantial market.

Our second stop on Sumbawa was at Poto Paddu, a tiny hurricane hole which one enters via a narrow channel with a tight S bend in it. Hurricane holes are common in the Caribbean where they provide a refuge for boats to ride out the storms of the hurricane season. In the western Pacific, hurricanes are called typhoons but their origins are the same and they are no less devastating. Once into Poto Paddu, we were surrounded by hills and very well protected. The local village was a mile or so inland but that didn't deter the usual entourage of canoes coming out to greet us. Next day we moved on, west as always, for Lombok.

We sailed overnight in a fair breeze and, at dawn, we were off the Gili islands to the north of Lombok. The imposing north face of Mount Rinjani towered above us as we found our way carefully between the islands of Ajer and Telung Sirah. But the most impressive sight was the view of Mount Agung on Bali, climbing skywards in the morning sunshine. The slight mistiness around the foothills cloaked it in a greater majesty; one could see how it came to be regarded as sacred.

There are many who claim that Lombok is a prettier island than the more famous Bali, a few miles further westward. Some friends on another boat, who went on a tour around the island from Sengiggi, where we had anchored, confirmed this. Sengiggi, on the west coast of Lombok, is a pulsating, rather garish tourist centre, whose only real assets are a large choice of restaurants and access to supplies and banks. In retrospect we wished we had stayed in one of the quieter anchorages on the north coast and this feeling was reinforced by our first and only confrontation with a corrupt official. He described himself as the harbourmaster and a colleague of his, not in uniform, explained to us that in return for doing the paperwork with a minimum of delay, the harbourmaster would like to receive a 'present'. This turned out to be a few thousand rupiah! No doubt our clearance would have taken days to complete if we had not given in, all the same I resented paying the bribe and it left a sour note.

At Lombok we had reached the end of our journey from east to west along that magnificent chain of islands. Now it was time to start moving north towards Singapore. We had decided against going to Bali, partly because the harbour area is unattractive, surrounded by high rise buildings, and partly to avoid more contact with bureaucratic and sometimes corrupt officials. Instead we turned north-westward from Lombok and headed for the island of Kangean. Here the Muslim faith was strong and prayers echoed round the bay at dawn and sunset. Soon after anchoring in a sheltered bay at the south-west corner of the island, a fisherman came by in his small canoe.

'Can we buy some diesel in the kampong?' I asked him. He looked blank. 'Solar', I said, using one of my few Indonesian words, 'we need solar.'

'Ah! Solar. OK I get you solar'. We were making progress.

'You give me these' he said, pointing at our plastic cans which we had been waving in the breeze to assist the communications, 'I go get solar'.

Now fuel cans are valued possessions in the islands and we were unhappy to part with them in case we never saw them again.

'We will come with you in our dinghy', I said, but he seemed unhappy with that proposal.

'You give me rupiah, I get solar for you,' he said.

This was getting more difficult, now he wanted the money *and* the fuel cans. I didn't like to show distrust but it would be a serious matter if we lost our only means of getting fuel, to say nothing of the money. He could see we were concerned and started rummaging among his belongings in the bottom of his canoe.

'I give you this', he said, holding out a motley collection consisting of an old teapot and a dilapidated primus stove, 'I give you this and when I bring solar you give me tings back.'

What could one say, he looked almost hurt by our evident mistrust.

'OK', I said, it wasn't in me to distrust him further. 'How long will you be?'

' I get back quick' he said, pointing at his watch and indicating four o'clock.

Thirty minutes seemed very quick indeed. We handed over the cans and the money and off he went, paddling furiously towards the shore as if his life depended on it. On the dot of four he was back with our cans full to the brim. Without a hint of resentment, he took back his teapot and stove, beamed a generous smile and paddled off for a night's fishing.

'Terima kasih' I called after him.

I felt much humbled by this man and we all felt badly for mistrusting him. It was an episode typical of all our experience in those islands, to find that the villagers were honest and trustworthy. Neither ourselves, nor any boat travelling with us, suffered any robberies, which is unhappily more than one can say of Portsmouth harbour.

It was time to start making serious progress northward towards Singapore, across the notorious South China Sea. This part of the world has a bad reputation for piracy and hearing of a recent attack between Belitung heightened our nervousness and Bankka islands only a short distance west of us. Most of the attacks, including the one we had just heard about, were on big ships rather than yachts - big time piracy, more interested in a shipload of Toyotas than a few hundred dollars. Nevertheless one couldn't help feeling just a little anxious. We carried no guns, the local advice being that to do so would simply provoke a shooting match at which they were more expert than we were. Best not to take Henry V's advice to 'imitate the action of the tiger ...stiffen the sinews, summon up the blood.' Emulating the cringing style of Uriah Heap was more likely to prolong one's life!

We decided to break the journey at Bawean Island, just north of Java. The voyage to Teluk Promalion, at the northern end of the island, was straightforward and although we spent much of the night surrounded by thunderstorms, none came overhead. Approaching Bawean in the evening of our second day at sea, we came across numerous bamboo fish attracters. These consisted of bundles of large bamboo poles, about five metres long, lying horizontally on the surface. Some had flags but many did not and one had to keep a very good lookout to avoid hitting them. It would have been impossible at night. We heard on the radio that a Swedish yacht had collided with one of these devices that ensnared their propeller and caused the engine to break its mountings.

Teluk Promalion provided a beautifully calm anchorage that night, the peace being disturbed only by the regular prayers broadcast from the mosques with their arrays of powerful loudspeakers. Thank Heaven the Church of England hasn't yet tried to emulate them!

Next day we visited the small village, sprawled loosely along the shore, itself adorned with row upon row of brightly painted fishing boats. Anchored just off the beach were some larger vessels, even more brightly painted. They reminded us of Phoenician galleys. Ashore we bought some eggs and filled four cans with fuel at 650 rupiah per litre, the price we had discovered they were happy to accept instead of using the fuel for fishing.

From Bawean, we made our way north through the Karimata Straits and into the South China Sea. We never saw anything remotely resembling a pirate; the major hazard for yachts was the large number of unlit fishing floats. We had seen them before, in the area around Kangean and Bawean Islands, extending offshore for ten or twelve miles. The only safe course was to cross these areas in daylight or keep well offshore. Heavy showers and thunderstorms, with spectacular but worrying displays of lightning plagued our passage through the Karimata Straits and across the South China Sea. We were travelling in company with two other yachts, *Sooty*

Bawean boats

196

A house on the shore at Teluk Promalion

from the rally and *Grace* from Australia. Sometimes the rain was so torrential, and the visibility so poor, that we had to separate to avoid colliding with each other. After a 220-mile journey, we arrived at a tiny island, Pulau Penoh, lying off the beaten track just south of the much larger Pulau Sebanka.

The island's only village was a classic stilted kampong, built half on and half off the island. I am not sure of the reasons for building the houses out over the sea, but I imagine it makes sewage disposal somewhat easier. The villagers took a great interest in our arrival and soon gave us a tour of the village, its school, the mosque and several of their homes. These were mostly simple huts with little in the way of furniture. We sat on the floor to drink the sweet black coffee which they offered and learnt a little of their way of life and about their families. By most standards they are poor, but the simple life they lead, where survival occupies most of the day, had its attractions in the eyes of one work-stressed westerner. Mind you, there were a few surprises, like the satellite dishes nestling among the huts, as if newly arrived from outer space.

Northward again, our next destination was Senayang at the south-western end of Sebanka Island. At Penoh, we had been 5 miles south of the equator. Senayang is 5 miles north of the equator. As the wind was north-westerly for this trip, we had an interesting time tacking to and fro across the equator, from the Southern to the Northern Hemisphere, for a total of seven crossings. We dispensed with the usual ceremonies – one small spray of shaving cream would hardly have done justice to the occasion. It was nice to think that after 18,000 miles and 18 months of sailing we were back in the Northern Hemisphere again.

Senayang is a small strip of island, 2 or 3 miles long, lying just off the south-west corner of Sebanka, a much larger island. Between the two is a narrow sound, very well protected from the wind. The town was much bigger than Penoh and there was a modern concrete wharf for supply ships to berth. As everywhere, the locals were very friendly and pleased to take us round the town. As at Penoh, most of the houses were built out over the edge of the water on stilts. We made friends with the local teacher, Beran, and his friend Lena who had been particularly helpful in showing us around the town. Lena stayed for dinner on *Greylag* and I cooked buttery kedgeree as per Delia's recipe.

'Ah!' Said Lena, 'fish fried rice!'

We stayed for only one night at Senayang. It was now the 8th of November and our plans required us to be in Thailand for Christmas when Janet would be coming out to join us. So we departed early next day for Temiang, a small island at the southern end of the Riau group. There were numerous coral reefs all around the small islands off the southern extremity of Temiang, but in good daylight we had little difficulty in finding our way into a quiet anchorage just south of a small island called Selebah. I'll always remember Selebah for one of the most glorious sunsets of the whole circumnavigation.

The Riau group of islands stretches for a hundred miles from Lingga in the south, up to Singapore. Here one begins to see the influence of proximity to the thriving and wealthy city of Singapore, with sophisticated resort development, numerous hotels and restaurants, and even a smart new marina complex at Nongsa point on Batam Island. Luxury power boats, out from Raffles marina, and ferries full of day trippers began to appear; it is only 10 miles across the Singapore Strait to Batam. To encourage the lucrative trade, the Indonesian government had greatly simplified the paperwork for visitors from Singapore, who can get year-long cruising permits for visits to the Riau group as often as they wish. What a contrast to the situation at the other end of the country! All this had its inevitable consequences on the local economy. It was the end of cheap meals out and quiet, deserted anchorages. Our heads were full of such pleasant memories of our voyage through Indonesia – Solor, Gedong, Riung, Bawean – precious memories we did not wish to dilute with others of this brasher northern edge. We stayed only briefly before slipping across the Strait, around the eastern end of Singapore Island and up the snaking river Sungi Santi to Sebana Cove in Malaysia.

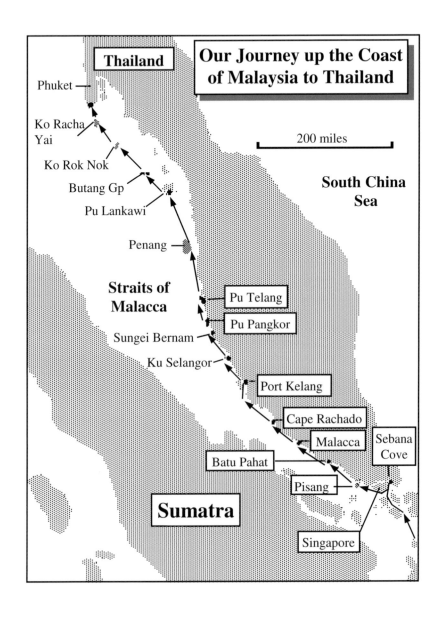

Thailand

Phuket

Ko Racha
Yai

Ko Rok Nok

Butang Gp

Pu Lankawi

Penang

**Straits of
Malacca**

Sungei Bernam

Ku Selangor

**Our Journey up the Coast
of Malaysia to Thailand**

200 miles

**South China
Sea**

Pu Telang

Pu Pangkor

Port Kelang

Cape Rachado

Malacca

Sebana
Cove

Batu Pahat

Pisang

Sumatra

Singapore

16 River Hopping up the Coast of Malaysia to Thailand

Our arrival in Malaysia found us motoring up the Sungai Santi River to the east of Singapore Island. It had been a short but interesting trip across the Singapore Straits, dodging in and out of the vast number of anchored merchant ships - convincing evidence of the huge commercial success of that small island. By contrast, the Santi River was a winding, muddy waterway, its banks wooded and largely undeveloped, only the modern channel marker buoys gave a hint that it led anywhere special. But it did.

Four miles up the river we arrived at the Sebana Cove development. A large marina had been dug out on the side of the river. Alongside were several substantial buildings, a hotel, restaurant, shops, a swimming pool and sports facilities. An 18-hole golf course had been constructed nearby. It was like a small Port Solent in the middle of the jungle and a very welcome sight after our long trek through Indonesia.

On the evening of our first day at Sebana, Bec delivered a bit of a bombshell. She had decided she would prefer to be on a boat with other young people and would be looking for an opportunity to move. This was not altogether surprising, having had her first taste of adventure she was definitely now going to have her fling. We were probably rather dull company for her and it was 3 months since she joined us - a long time in the life of a twenty-two year old! I couldn't really blame her but I felt the break should be made quickly; having a crew member who wishes to leave is not a good basis for harmony. Besides that, John and I needed a third member for our crew and we were more likely to find one if we could offer 'vacant possession'! I explained this to Bec and asked her to make arrangements to leave before *Greylag* departed Sebana Cove on the following Friday. In fact she went on *Calidris* where there were no other young people, but I think that was just a stop gap and she finally left the rally altogether when we got to Thailand and eventually joined an Australian racing boat called *Australia Maid*. Given her thirst for adventure, she probably did the right thing. Anyway, before leaving us in Sebana Cove she bought us a splendid lunch in the restaurant and we parted friends.

On the evening of our second day at Sebana, there was a magnificent reception given by the regional government of that province of Malaysia. It was easily the best buffet I have ever enjoyed. It was arranged in sections, one corner decked with sea food, another had various roasts - carved as you waited, a third had curries and spicy stews. Finally there was a huge table of desserts. What a feast it was after the privations of the previous few months! Some important people came and each skipper was given a gift of a small pewter bottle opener, nicely engraved with a picture of a hornbill, and a rather distinctive hat.

John and I discussed the problem of losing Bec. There was little likelihood of finding a replacement at Sebana Cove except by poaching other people's crew and that seemed an unfair thing to do. We studied the charts and worked out that we could probably make the whole distance to Thailand in short day-sailing hops. Although this would involve us in some interesting 'gunkholing' up some of the river estuaries, it did not seem an unattractive proposition and would save us from an arduous watch-on-watch-off routine. We agreed to give it a go.

On November the 15th, as soon as there was sufficient light to see our way, we slipped out of the comforts of Sebana Cove and back down the Santi River. There was little breeze as we motor-sailed across the southern side of Singapore, marvelling at the huge development all over the island. I recalled my visits there when I was in the Army. How different it all looked. Back in the early 60s, Changi had been but a small village strung out along the road. Now it was a thriving metropolis with one of the biggest airports in the world where the old RAF station once stood. There were ships anchored all over the place and we kept a keen eye for any that were on the move, as we would not have been popular getting in the way. At the eastern end of the main island there were several smaller islands and most of them appeared to have extensive oil refining and storage facilities. Once through the channel between them we were out into more open water and on our way north to Pulau Pisang, a small island about 60 miles from Sebana Cove. There we found a reasonable anchorage in the lee of the island and we were soon joined by *Magic Dragon, Brandy Cove, Ocean Gypsy , Griffyn, Gambatte Go* and *Jonathan*, all from the rally! Most of the others were heading for Port Kalang where they were planning to enter a race for the Raja Muda Cup, run by the Royal Selangor Yacht Club. We thought it a strange thing to want to do, though we had heard that there were going to be some big parties.

The night at Pulau Pisang was peaceful but we had to make an early start next day to get to the estuary at Kuala Batu Pahat at High Water which was around noon. Most of the river estuaries had shallow bars and patches of sand at Low Water so it was important to plan our journeys around the tides. We arrived there in good time and proceeded cautiously up the river and round a sharp right hand bend about a mile in. Once into the river proper the water became deeper and we anchored in a depth of just over 4 metres. John calculated that this would leave us plenty of water when the tide fell. It was a marvellously calm spot and we enjoyed watching a troop of monkeys in the trees alongside our anchorage. There were two sea-eagles courting each other nearby. The only sign of humanity we saw in that place was when an old fellow came down river in a small boat and deployed a net all along the edge of the mangroves beside us. He then departed, we assumed to return next morning.

Sure enough, as soon as we arose from our peaceful sleep he was there collecting in his net. There didn't seem to be many fish in it. By 9 o'clock we thought we could try to escape from the river even though it was only just after low tide. There was plenty of rise left in the tide so it would not have mattered if we had gone aground, the flow in the river was quite small. As it was, we saw one small patch on the echo sounder with only about 1.3 metres. We didn't feel her touch bottom but this was soft mud and we might not have noticed. Out in the open sea again we headed north towards the Water Islands just off the old Malaysian capital at Malacca. This was a shortish trip of 38 miles so we were soon settled on an anchorage to the north of Pulau Besar. We were joined by an Australian yacht *Baghera* and *Calidris*, complete with our Bec on board! I wished we had time to visit Malacca but it was now November 17th and I had a firm commitment at Phuket in Thailand - Janet was coming out on the 6th December for Christmas. How I looked forward to that day!

Interestingly enough with just the two of us on board, there was a distinct air of tranquillity on *Greylag*. I am not sure why this was, although I have heard people say that things can work better with two than three, even though it is sometimes harder work. Several of the rally boats were now being sailed by just a husband and wife crew who were finding it better without the inevitable hassle and loss of privacy one gets with crew. Perhaps with John and I it was just that there was more room in *Greylag*, but I suspected there was a bit more to it than that. I remember my friend

Mike Stroud, who made several arctic and antarctic trips with Sir Ranulph Fiennes, recording in his book 'Shadows on the Wasteland' that he couldn't really understand the concept of leadership when only two skilled individuals were involved. The relationship is too equal to identify one as leader and the other follower. When we were three I somehow felt I was the skipper, and sometimes needed to be, but now there was no such feeling. All our decision making emerged from genuine two-way consultation. It was, in many ways, more relaxing than at any previous period of the journey.

The anchorage at Pulau Besar was not very comfortable at night. A strong tide swept through the gap between the islands and caused some rolling. We were happy to be on our way at first light, this time heading for an anchorage just south of Cape Rachado - another shortish trip of 35 miles. There we were again anchored alongside *Magic Dragon, Ocean Gypsy and Griffyn.*

The Cape provided an attractive view, covered in trees and with the occasional monkey to be seen. The lighthouse appeared to be under re-construction. John and Ruth on *Griffyn* invited us over for drinks and a good party ensued - as it so often did on the hospitable *Griffyn*! The drinks party developed into a dinner party and John, who had already prepared a curry for our meal, fetched it over as a contribution to the evening meal. We slept well for half the night but then things got less comfortable as the wind got up a bit and the tide held *Greylag* stern into the waves. It is an annoying characteristic of yachts with low overhanging sterns that the waves cause slapping if the boat is moored stern to the sea or held there by the tide, as on that night. My cabin in the stern became distinctly unrestful and I was reinforced in my view that going up the rivers was an excellent arrangement for peace even if not always for peace of mind.

Next morning dawned calm and sunny and we had to motor all day to get up to Port Kalang, a busy, major port serving Kuala Lumpur. A good deal of shipping plies up and down the channels that lead between the islands lying just outside the port. John and I were keen to find a peaceful spot to recover from the poor sleep of the night before, so we chose a little backwater running off the main channel. We anchored the boat in perfect calm and had just settled down to our evening drink when a small ferry, packed to the gunwales with locals, came careering up to the entrance of our creek and turned in, passing by uncomfortably close and ridiculously fast. For a while we wondered whether we had made a mistake in our choice of anchorage, however that ferry turned out to be the only one that night. Somewhere up that creek there must have been a small village and the ferry was for those commuting to work in the port. We slept like logs.

Next morning I took a careful look at our gearbox. For a couple of days I had experienced difficulty engaging reverse gear. I would put the lever in reverse and nothing would happen until I put some revs on the engine, when it would engage with an unhealthy clunk. Often one relies on reverse gear to pull an anchor in or to stop the boat in a berth, so it was rather disconcerting to find that I could not rely on it. My inspection revealed no obvious cause of the problem so I contented myself with a small fiddle with the Bowden cable that connects the gear-lever to the gear box, and hoped the problem would go away.

Over breakfast we looked at our charts and worked out that we could get to Phuket Island in eight easy day trips. We still had twelve days before my deadline so this gave us four days for stops. The route would be Kuala Selangor, Sungei Bernam, Pulau Pangkor or Pulau Telang, Penang Island, Langkawi Island, Ko Lipe, Ko Rok Nok, and into Phuket.

That day's trip was another easy one and we motored the whole 20 miles to Kuala Selangor. The entrance to the river was a similar depth to Batu Pahat and posed no problems around High Water. About a mile up the river we came across a huge sprawling kampong that stretched for more than a mile along the northern bank on our port side. Above the kampong was a newly constructed bridge which would definitely prevent any further excursion up river for the masted *Greylag*. The kampong was a seething mass of humanity right to the water's edge and beyond, since many of the houses were built out into the river on pilings. Numerous wooden fishing boats were moored all along the waterside.

At about the middle we spotted a sign for fuel, this was a relief because we were getting low after so much motoring. I pulled over alongside the fuel wharf and a fellow passed down a dirty rubber hose. The Heath Robinson contrivance on the end failed to deliver fuel when pressed until one of the men there attacked it with a hammer. This seemed to do the trick. When we were finished at the fuel jetty, I called to John to release our warps and then put the boat in gear. We moved forward at a snail's pace. I pushed the throttle further forward. Nothing happened. There was clearly a problem and with a knot or so of flow in the river this was no place to lose power! As we were in fact creeping forward against the flow on idling revs, albeit slowly, I decided the best thing to do was not to touch anything and sidle across the river to the opposite, quieter side and drop the anchor. This we did successfully. Investigation revealed that the

The Kampong at Sungei Selangor

Bowden cable, joining the throttle to the engine, had snapped clean across at the throttle-lever end so that one could put her in gear but only on idling revs. The metal terminals on Bowden cables are quite complicated devices and not easy to repair, so we poured ourselves a beer and sat down to consider the problem. It was then that I had the idea to turn the cable around, since the unbroken engine end would fit on the throttle-lever and the broken end could be joined to the engine with a rigging clamp for which there was more room down there. We soon completedthe work and I can now recall that I didn't finally replace that cable until we returned to the UK eight months later! Although this cured the immediate problem, the difficulty with reverse gear persisted.

We went ashore to the small town situated opposite the kampong. There we found a good range of shops, a post-office and a very useful little metal workshop. They were capable of fabricating all sorts of one-off metal parts and would be tremendously useful if one had a serious breakage. I made a note of this in the log. We found a Malaysian equivalent to the Colonel's Kentucky Fried Chicken and bought a whole cooked chicken with liberal chips for our dinner. It was delicious.

The river was quiet at night and the only worry was over the occasional small tree floating downstream. We could see how one of these might snag our anchor and cause us to drag but it didn't seem too big a risk as most of them were out in the stream. As we sat around in the dark after dinner I suddenly heard some splashes on the muddy banks alongside the anchorage. At first I thought they were dogs. We got out our powerful spotlight and shone it towards where the noises had come from. The beam was reflected by four pairs of bright red eyes. They were otters.

Next morning, after removing a small tree from our anchor warp, we sat in the cockpit for our breakfast and watched some brilliant kingfishers and a lot of red kites circling around overhead. This had been a nice spot but we had to keep going so we were soon off down river and out to sea.

We spent the next night peacefully tucked into Sungei Bernam. It was an easy river to enter, plenty of depth and well sheltered. There was not much else to be said for it and we left early next day for Pulau Telang. On our way there we stopped for a quick lunch at Pulau Pangkor. This was a substantial island with quite a bit of holiday centre development. It looked a good place to spend a few days but we didn't have them to spare. While at Pangkor we heard on the radio that one of the rally boats had helped a local fisherman who had been struck by lightning while at sea. It was a grim story as the lightning had travelled down the poor man's arm and grounded through the metal tiller, blowing his hand off in the process.

North from Pulau Pangkor there is a steep headland at Teluk Telang ,with a small island of the same name just offshore. On the lee side (north on that day) we found a good anchorage and had a splendid view of several hornbills on the island. They look so unbalanced with that huge beak although it doesn't seem to present any problems. They are extraordinarily adept at tossing a berry around until it is in a satisfactory spot to swallow.

Next day I awoke with a cold, something I could have done without at that stage. We left early for Penang Island and had to motor the whole way in order to keep on schedule for the 56-mile journey. At Penang we opted for a tiny little marina at the southern end of the island where we were able to moor alongside and visit the small Chinese restaurant on the pier. The marina had a facility for lifting boats from the water and I seriously considered whether we should take the opportunity to repaint the hull and generally check over things below the waterline. After John had worked out that there would be good tides at Langkawi, where we would be in a few day's time, I decided to postpone the painting job until then. At Langkawi there would be sufficient tide to dry out on our legs and save the high cost of a lift-out.

We stayed put next morning, as I had intended to have a serious go at finding out the trouble with our reverse gear. I started the engine first, just to check out the problem, and Glory be, the problem had disappeared!

This was indeed good news and I was relieved at not having a big job on my hands as I was feeling distinctly unwell with the cold.

After lunch we moved on north between Penang Island and the mainland, under the huge new road bridge that crosses the Straits and on to a new marina at the Penang Yacht Club. There we very nearly had two disasters. Just before entering the marina I thought I had better check the reverse gear, as there appeared to be quite a tide flowing through the marina and stopping could be tricky. The bloody thing had gone wrong again! I crept in towards the berth we had been allocated, with my fingers crossed that I would be able to stop. I suppose it was because of this worry that I put her in reverse rather early and while we were still a good six feet off the pontoon, the tide took hold of her and I knew we were not going to make it. With supreme self-sacrifice, John took a brave but futile leap for the pontoon and missed. He is not a strong swimmer but luckily he managed to struggle ashore - losing reverse gear was one thing, but losing John would have been seriously inconvenient! Meanwhile *Greylag* was swept to the other pontoon where she made a very firm landing - what is known in the RAF as a 'controlled crash'. Happily there was no significant damage and we later winched *Greylag* across to her proper berth.

The marina at Penang Yacht Club was awful. Not only was there the difficulty with the tide running through, but the buildings ashore were not completed and there were no facilities. And that tide through the berths brought every kind of flotsam and jetsam imaginable - endless bits of wood, even trees, gathered around the boats and threatened to snag rudders and propellers. One boat said they had seen a dead dog go by! We were keen to get away as quickly as possible but decided to wait for *Enarkay* to arrive next day. Tom Parker had said on the radio that he had a servicing manual for a Volvo engine like ours and that would have been a great help to us. Unfortunately, when they arrived the manual did not include details of the gear box. I did an oil change on the off chance that it might cure the problem - it didn't. I decided to leave it all alone for a while. After all, we still had a forward gear and that could get us home if necessary. Better not to risk heroic fiddling with the gear box, I thought, in case I wrecked it completely. We spent a relaxed afternoon around the swimming pool - one of the few completed facilities at the club.

Our next intended stop was at Pulau Paya, an island at the centre of a protected marine park which offered the promise of some good snorkelling. On our way up there we met up with Graham and Mary on *Hilda* and Jean and Valentine Thierry , a Belgium couple on *Excess Line* (You might have guessed he was in insurance!) On arrival there was a problem. Anchoring was prohibited and there was only one spare buoy which was taken by *Excess Line* who had arrived first. We tied up to *Excess line,* and that would have been fine in settled weather. However, not long after, a terrific squall came through and swung both boats towards the buoy. *Excess line's* warp sagged into the water and we overran it. When we drifted back again we found that the warp had snagged around our propeller. *Greylag* had what is known as a 'sail-drive' arrangement in which the prop is mounted directly on a downward extension of the engine, like an outboard motor leg. This was very worrying as it left *Excess line* hanging on our engine leg with the whole force pulling against our engine mountings. We quickly got our flippers on and swam a spare line back to the buoy to take up the strain. We were then able to release the other line and free ourselves. Cruising is full of these little tests.

We reviewed our options. It was clearly not going to be a good idea to stay alongside *Excess Line* even though we had an nice invitation to dine with them that evening. The Bass Harbour at Kuah on Langkawi was about 4 hours sailing away, but there was a good entrance from the south, well lit with buoys and probably OK for a night arrival. We opted for that plan and left immediately, Valentine very kindly handing over a container with the dinner we would have had with them.

Sure enough the entrance into Bass Harbour was straightforward and once inside we found conditions were calm. We anchored close to some other boats which we could see quite well in the light from the town.

Next morning we met up with Roy Newey from *Gaviota* and he gave us the good news that the marina at the Langkawi Yacht Club was free to Trade Winds Rally boats. We moved in there in a flash. Later on *Excess Line* and *Hilda* arrived from Pulau Paya where they reported having a restless night on those buoys. To make matters worse the sea had remained too rough for pleasurable snorkelling, so none of us had seen anything of the marine reserve.

Not only was the marina free but there was also a free buffet and booze for each of the next three evenings. On the second of these there was a big party for us, attended by the Malaysian King's brother. The Langkawi Yacht Club had certainly done us proud.

Ashore on our second day, we made a massive purchase of duty free booze, as Langkawi is the cheapest spot in the area for this. I had a good look at the beach alongside the yacht club. There was an area of flat sand where we could dry out and do that overdue painting job. I had almost decided to go ahead with this when a large power boat went by at speed and sent waves right through the marina and onto the beach. That would cause trouble if we were on our legs, so once again the job was postponed. I rang Janet to confirm that we were now within spitting distance of Phuket and would be there in good time to meet her plane on the 6th of December. I checked in and out at the customs and immigration office a day late, lying about exactly when we had arrived!

We left Langkawi early on the 29th November and headed out north-west to Pu Lipe in the Butang Group of islands. This would be our first stop in Thailand. We wouldn't be able to check in there, but we had heard that there was no objection to a visit to the small islands ahead of checking in later at Phuket. On our way out of Langkawi we enjoyed the magnificent scenery in the environs of Bass Harbour. The small islands around the bay are wooded and there are some dramatic rock structures. It looked like a place to spend time if only we had more of it. Along the coast we came across Malcolm McLaren in *Malmac*. He was barely sailing, drifting really, towards the finish line of the Raja Muda cup race. We made encouraging noises over the VHF but unfortunately he didn't manage to finish within the time limit for the race. I had to admire his tenacity though, it must have been tedious sailing.

We anchored in the bay at the southern side of Pu Lipe and spent a quiet night. Well, most of a night, because at first light the breeze got up and pushed us inshore to the limit of our anchor rode and we bumped a coral head. We moved offshore for morning tea and then got going north through the Butang Islands and on up to Rok Nok. This was a rough passage for the first half but then the wind freed and eased down a bit and when we arrived at Rok Nok everything was tranquil. There are two islands there and we anchored just south of the gap between them. This was an excellent anchorage in some of the clearest water we had seen. I went for a snorkel after first inspecting the rudder to check if we had sustained any damage from the bump on the coral that morning. There was none.

Ko Racha Yai, our next destination and the last stop before Phuket, is 47 miles north of Rok Nok. We left via the passage between the islands and made fast time to Racha Yai. On arrival there, we ran around the southern end of the island and then up the west coast, intending to stop at the Racha Yai Bay. When we got there , the wind was south-west and was causing a fair amount of swell to enter the Bay. It didn't look comfortable so we decided to move round to the north-eastern side of the island. There we found a delightful little bay about one third of the way down the eastern coast of the island. The night was peaceful.

Next morning we awoke to find ourselves anchored close to some of the very best coral we had seen since Tonga. The water was gin clear and we were soon in for a snorkel. This was an excellent spot, full of fish - some of them quite large - and lots of spectacular coral. I found a large moray eel. Unfortunately, as you might have guessed, the local dive boats also knew about this place and three or four of them turned up during the morning with their loads of tourists. Happily they didn't stay long. That afternoon we departed on the final short 12-mile leg into Nai Harn Bay at the southern end of Phuket Island.

The Phuket Yacht Club was not really a yacht club as we know them. In fact it was an expensive 5-star hotel! The anchorage opposite the 'Club' was distinctly uncomfortable, so we moved to the next bay along, where the Jungle Beach Resort lay in among the trees and the water was a little bit calmer. The night was peaceful.

Next day we went ashore and made contact with Peter Seymour and Tony Diment. We checked in with the authorities and then Peter and Tony drove us round to Chalong where we found a Volvo agent. He had a complete set of workshop manuals for our engine and, after a little persuasion, he let us take one down the road to a photocopier and copy off the pages with the gear box details. It looked awfully complicated! After that we went out with Peter and Tony for a splendid lunch at the 'Old Siam' restaurant - said to be the best Thai food on Phuket. It was certainly very good; mind you I was beginning to realise that one has to be cautious in selecting things from the menu, some of the dishes were hot and spicy almost to the pain threshold.

Things were no calmer next day at Nai Harn Bay. Each time we landed or launched the dinghy on the beach we had to confront the surf and usually got a soaking. We had been impressed with the brief glimpse of Chalong Bay the day before so we decided to move round there. It was a much more sheltered spot and we anchored well inshore in calm water. This gave me a chance to take another look at the gear box. I emptied out all the oil and to my surprise found that without the oil the reverse gear seemed to engage normally. The plot thickened. I comforted myself with the thought that it couldn't be all that serious, as it was so intermittent. With the help of the new manuals, I removed the gear change mechanism from the side of the gear box ; there was nothing obvious wrong with it so I put it back and replaced the oil. Back to square one - the reverse had

211

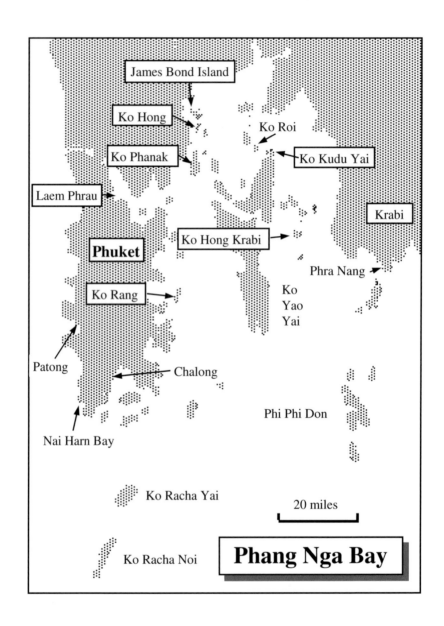

James Bond Island

Ko Hong

Ko Roi

Ko Phanak

Ko Kudu Yai

Laem Phrau

Krabi

Ko Hong Krabi

Phuket

Phra Nang

Ko Rang

Ko
Yao
Yai

Patong

Chalong

Phi Phi Don

Nai Harn Bay

Ko Racha Yai

20 miles

Ko Racha Noi

Phang Nga Bay

gone again! The only time it seems to work is first thing after engine start when everything is cold. This was all beginning to be a bit frustrating.

At Chalong we soon discovered Jimmy's Lighthouse Bar and Café, a veritable Mecca for 'yotties' and a good place to start my hunt for a replacement crew. There was an advert there from one, Steve Bazzard, and we called on him to talk it over. Unfortunately he had also been in touch with David Macmillan on *Arabian Sands* and it didn't seem likely that poor old *Greylag* could compete with the luxury of the Hallberg-Rassy 53. As it turned out we were lucky not to get him as the poor fellow developed a kidney stone soon after.

Back in Jimmy's Lighthouse bar, John had met a young Canadian student, Chee Chan, who was looking for a berth on a boat. We met up and he seemed just what we had been looking for. His father was Chinese, hence the name, and his mother English. He had been back-packing up from Singapore and now fancied a spell on a boat. He was obviously very intelligent and articulate, and extremely athletic. He was a keen rock climber but had only a little experience of sailing. I said we would give him a try out over Christmas and, if it all worked out satisfactorily, then we would take him on from here.

The great day arrived at last, Janet was due in on the flight from Bangkok that morning. I had arranged a taxi with 'Boomerang' taxis (they always come back, they said!) She arrived on time and the taxi took us to the outrageously expensive Amari Beach Hotel at Patong. We had decided to give ourselves a couple of days there as a treat. It was a super hotel and our room looked out through the palm trees to the bay. The gardens of the hotel were extensive and every tree and shrub was covered with tiny white fairy lights, Christmas was upon us. On the headland just beyond the hotel we found some elephants. There were rides on offer but Janet wasn't keen so we settled for feeding them with bananas. They seemed grateful for these, indeed as we went to leave one of them followed us down the path. We visited the local shops and a butterfly farm near-by where there were thousands of exotic coloured insects and ponds full of koi carp. We thoroughly enjoyed those two days of shore-based luxury.

After two days at the Amari Beach we moved to a cheaper hotel in Patong for another two days. That was the end of my shore spell as it was now time to rejoin *Greylag* and start our cruise around the islands of Phang Nga Bay. John had been looking after the boat while I was away, I suspect he enjoyed the peace on his own for the first time for many months. Back at Chalong the wind had gone into the south and produced a moderate chop in the anchorage. This made it difficult to get Janet and her luggage out to the boat and I am afraid she got wet as we struggled out in the dinghy. At least one could dry out quickly in that climate. We had to spread Janet's US dollars out on the engine to dry them out.

One of the other nice things about Chalong Bay is that one can anchor either side. To escape the chop on 'Jimmy's' side, we crossed over to the south where there was some good shelter. There we found *Hilda* and *Ocean Gypsy* and joined up with Graham and Mary for drinks. We all went ashore to Froy's for a miraculously cheap meal out.

Next day we had arranged to pick up Chee at Jimmy's bar. He was there waiting and looked very enthusiastic at the prospect of joining *Greylag*. Janet liked him immediately and I had, as always, great faith in her judgement of people. John did some shopping before we moved off again, this time out of Chalong Bay and then north to the lee side of Ko Rang Yai where we found a nice sheltered anchorage.

Ko Rang Yai was an attractive island with a firm sandy shore that looked ideal to dry out on and do the painting job. The problem was that there was a narrow strip of coral just off the beach which we would have to cross to get onto the sand. Luckily this looked possible at high tide. At the next low water I went ashore and identified a good firm spot to dry out on and marked it with an anchored plastic fender. At high tide we could bring *Greylag* across the reef and anchor her alongside this marker fender.

In the evening we were joined by David and Barbara Wardle's big Oyster 55 *Baker Street* and Chris and Gill Mounsey on *Pale Moon*. Meanwhile, in a last determined effort to cure the gear box I drained out the oil again and filled the gear box with diesel. I then ran the engine for a short while in the hope that this rather drastic action might clear the gubbins or whatever it was that was preventing reverse gear from engaging.

The next morning we took the boat in across the reef and anchored alongside my marker buoy. By lunchtime, she was safely aground on her legs. As soon as the water had gone down a little we were all out there with brushes to scrub her clean. Next we washed the salt water off with our 'Hozelock' shower system and very soon the hull was dry and ready for painting. On went the masking tape and in a short while we had painted the whole hull - long before there were any signs of the returning tide. I then drained the diesel out of the propeller leg and refilled the gear box with oil. In all of this, I was delighted with Chee's willingness to join in with the chores and his general cheerfulness. He really was a most engaging young man.

In the middle of this work, some locals emerged from the trees with an injured child. The little girl had been bitten on the hand by a dog and they wanted us to take them across the water to where their men were fishing, so that the child could be taken to hospital. I examined the wound and it looked quite severe with large puncture wounds where the animal's canine teeth had sunk in. She clearly needed to go to hospital but our dinghy was tiny for that job and we desperately needed to finish our painting before the tide came back. David Wardle very kindly came to the rescue. He had a larger dinghy with a bigger outboard than ours and took the family to the opposite shore. We never discovered the outcome.

When the tide returned we floated off without trouble and anchored in deep water for the night. The reverse gear was still not working. I felt exasperated with it. However, we were pleased to have successfully repainted the hull at last.

Next day we went on our way north towards Koh Hong. Just short of Phanak Island, disaster struck. The engine suddenly ground to a halt. I bled the fuel system - the usual cause of sudden stoppages - and tried to restart her but the engine would not even turn over. I took the engine covers off and everything seemed rather hot, I had the dreadful feeling that either the engine or the gearbox had seized. Things looked very serious indeed. We sailed on to Phanak Island to find a safe anchorage while we sorted things out. Once safely on our anchor I put a large spanner on the crankshaft and was relieved to find that I could turn it, although it did feel very stiff. At least the engine wasn't seized. Next I checked in the data book and realised with horror that the oil capacity was 2.6 litres and not the 1.6 litres I had replaced after draining the diesel out. To this day I do not know how I had come to make such a simple error, perhaps I was more tired than I thought but it was still a most careless mistake. I was now even more convinced that something had seized up in the gear box but even with the engine in forward gear I could still rotate the crankshaft and this gave me a little hope.

I added the missing litre of oil and turned the crankshaft with the spanner several more times. It seemed a bit easier after this, so I decided to have a go at starting the engine. It went like a dream! Never have I been more relieved than I was at the sound of that engine going. Then, as if to cap it all, I tried reverse gear and it was working normally. The problem never returned, but to this day I do not know which of all the remedial actions I had taken was the one to effect the cure. I suspect the diesel flushing may have removed some sort of gunge, or perhaps running it really hot with the low oil level had got something to move. We will never know.

A local fishing boat, one of those known as 'longtails', with the enormous long prop shaft sticking out at the rear, came by and sold us some magnificent tiger prawns. With a huge sense of relief, we pressed on to Ko Hong where we anchored alongside *Magic Dragon, Griffyn, Brandy Cove* and *Gambatte Go*. The scenery looked stunning but we could enjoy that next day. It was now time to have a celebratory drink and enjoy those prawns. We slept soundly.

In the morning we went off in the dinghy to explore the hong. Hong is Thai for a room and one can find them on several of the islands in Phang Nga Bay. They are large chambers, open to the sky overhead and often almost completely surrounded by high cliffs of rock, with only narrow entrances into the 'lagoon'. This one, which gave the island its name, was particularly dramatic. We drove our dinghy in through the passageway to the north of a high pinnacle of rock on the eastern side of the hong. Inside the rocky cliffs rose vertically to about 180 feet. I could see Chee eyeing up these faces for some rock climbing. There were caves in several places and we ran the dinghy into one of them. It was an eerie place with stalactites hanging from the ceiling and a lot of bats. The cliffs both inside and outside had been etched away by the sea at their bases so that they overhung the water by several metres. Stalactites had formed on these overhangs - huge, jagged excrescences, hanging down for two or three metres. Most of the islands exhibit these structures, giving the whole area an extraordinarily dramatic appearance. There was a tunnel at the eastern side of the hong and, halfway along, it opened up into a large, vaulted chamber. There were more bats. Outside this tunnel we found a small beach to land on. Chee was soon demonstrating his skills as a rock climber. I was a bit concerned that he might fall but the face overhung the water and sure enough, when he missed his footing, he made a dramatic back-flop (if that is the opposite to a belly-flop) into the water. Only his pride was slightly injured, and that mainly because I had the video on him at the time!

Later that day we moved on north to Ko Yang, an island within easy range of the famous James Bond Island which we planned to visit the next day. Meanwhile Ko Yang provided another dramatic anchorage right up close to a colossal pinnacle at the western end of the island. The scenery was quite the most impressive I had seen on the whole trip. Although not as big as, say, the Pietons of Saint Lucia, these island pinnacles were more dramatically steep-sided. The overhangs and stalactites added a further dimension, and the colours in some of the rock faces were also very beautiful. Beyond the island, one could see into the distant reaches of the northern end of Phang Nga Bay. Dozens of similar tall, green-clad islands as far as the eye could see - the more distant of them fading into the haze. This was a place with more than a touch of magic.

I sat there in the cockpit painting the view over an evening drink. Everything, I thought, had gone wonderfully still. Then I realised the tide had dropped and we had gone aground. Luckily the bottom was soft mud so it didn't really matter. Later we moved a bit further out for the night.

Next day we headed for Koh Phing Kan or James Bond Island, as it has always been known since the film 'The Man with the Golden Gun'. The water at this end of the bay is shallow and we had to feel our way to an anchorage just off the landing pier. Ashore, we walked around the western side of the island and there, tucked in to a bay on the north side, was that famous pinnacle of rock around which J.Bond had sped in his longtail boat. It was an extraordinary sight, that rock, indeed I found it a little difficult to see how it remained standing, so undercut by the sea was its base. It looked hugely top-heavy. The dramatic scenery there had to be seen to be believed but having said that, there was not much else to commend this particular island. The bay was crowded out with small trader's huts and stalls, ready for the massive influx of tourists that came daily from the mainland in the longtail boats. They sold a miscellany of shells, butterflies, beetles and T-shirts, emblazoned with gaudy pictures of the famous island. How glad I was that this depressing scene was pretty well confined to this particular island. Most of the others were relatively uncrowded and undeveloped.

From James Bond Island we moved south to Koh Pak Bia. Some people there on an 'adventure' holiday had been delivered by boat, with some tents and a few stores, and left to fend for themselves. We invited Will and Mary, two doctors from Bristol and Alison from Church Crookham (just around the corner from our home!) back to the boat for a drink. They were envious of our circumnavigation and I suppose it would appeal to the sort of people who go on adventure holidays.

Next morning we made the short journey across to Koh Hong Krabi where we enjoyed some excellent snorkelling at last. Most of the northern part of Phrang Nga Bay has rather cloudy water and is not good for snorkelling, but the more southerly islands are much better. Koh Hong Krabi was a destination for boat loads of day trippers so we didn't stop for

James Bond Rock

long before moving off north again to Koh Kudu Yai. It was surprising how many of the islands existed in pairs, named 'yai' for the larger and 'noi' for the smaller. At Kudu Yai there was a large hong with a pair of small entrance channels either side of a large pinnacle of rock on the western side - much like the hong at Koh Hong where we had been a few days before.

We anchored in very deep water outside and went in by dinghy to probe around with the boat hook and see if it might be possible to take *Greylag* right into the hong. It was High Water and we found the depth was about 2.1 metres at the shallowest points, easily enough for *Greylag*. So in we went and anchored in the middle. At the northern end of the hong there was a nice sand beach and I reckoned we could have dried out there on our legs. However, the place was alive with mosquitoes and this put Janet off the idea. While we were there another dinghy arrived with Bob and Sally. They were from South Africa and had anchored their boat *Seerose* in the lee of the Koh Kudu Noi, just to the north. We got some magnificent photos of *Greylag* in the hong but then we had to leave before the tide fell and trapped us in that very beautiful, but mozzie-ridden hell-hole.

We anchored for the night at an island to the west, Koh Roi. I suppose we might have expected it, yet we were still surprised to find 'Roy' Newey there with *Gaviota*. We renamed the island Koh Roy. Roy and his crew Hugh Cassidy and Roger came over for drinks that evening. Interestingly they had taken on our David Reynolds after he had left *Sheet Lightning*, but the arrangement didn't work out for them either and David had departed from the rally in Darwin.

By now we were getting short of a few supplies, including fuel, so next day, the 17th of December, we had to plan a quick return to Phuket Island. We headed for the marina at the Phuket Yacht Haven which was under construction at Laem Phrau on the North-east coast. The pontoons there were fine except that they were not yet joined to the shore so we had to commute by dinghy! However , there were most facilities available and we were soon refuelled and supplied. We took a taxi to Patong to go to the supermarket Janet and I had spotted during our break in the hotel. Next day we discovered a much better supermarket, Robinson's in the centre of Phuket town. We had to go to town anyway because Chee's Visa had nearly expired and we needed to renew it. This was another opportunity to see the corrupt local officials at work! When we got to the immigration office we found we had to have three

Koh Roi

219

new photographs of Chee. However, this wasn't going to be a problem because the immigration officers wife ran a passport photo shop alongside the office! We paid over our 500 baht for the privilege. Back at the marina we were met with a terrific thunderstorm just as we got back to the boat. We ate on board on that damp evening.

Next day we returned to Koh Hong Krabi and anchored close to *Magic Dragon, Enarkay* and *Gambatte Go*. We were pleased to return as this was a very attractive spot and after the day trippers had gone home in the evening it was a very pleasant place. Our reverse gear was still working perfectly. Next day we moved off south-east to the spectacular scenery of Phra Nang. Perhaps this was the most dramatic scenery we had yet seen in Thailand. The high cliffs of Laem Nang and the pinnacle of Koh Nang towered over us, their gloriously coloured rock faces, red/brown and ochre, positively glowing in the evening sunshine. At their bases where the sea had under cut the cliff, the usual crop of gigantic stalactites hung from the edge like so many dragons teeth. It was a wonderful place to paint and photograph.

Ashore the peninsular was largely occupied by the Dusit Rayavadee Resort and we were able to go there for a meal in one of their restaurants. There were no roads out to the resort so everything came by boat.

Christmas was only a few days away by now and there was a loose arrangement for the Tradewinds fleet to gather at Phi Phi Don, an island to the south-west of Krabi. We moved there on the 22nd of December and found a lot of the other boats already there. Phi Phi Don was a more developed island than most we had visited, it had a veritable village of shops and restaurants. As it was Christmas, the general festive atmosphere was welcome and we enjoyed the company of so many of our rally colleagues. There were several good parties both on the boats and ashore. I still felt the same as I had back in Antigua for the previous Christmas, a good party but not the same as at home.

The rally boats held a collective meal at a local restaurant but, as is often the case with large parties, it wasn't a great success. The restaurant owners sold us books of tickets to buy drinks and we very soon discovered that we were paying more that way than if one went direct to the bar. Everyone was demanding refunds. This certainly gave us the feeling that we were being ripped-off and rather spoilt the party. On Christmas Eve we had a much nicer meal with a smaller group from *Griffyn, Aditi* and *Sheet Lightning* - a complete contrast to the night before. With one or two

Koh Hong Krabi

exceptions, I felt that most of the big rally parties were a bit of a flop. Maybe I just don't enjoy big parties.

Christmas Day started badly, Janet woke up feeling sick and feverish. She was definitely not up to joining in any of the celebrations. The rest of us went over to *Ocean Venture* where Ken Murray had invited the whole fleet for drinks. *Ocean Venture* was a big boat, 62 feet overall, but she still sank noticeably deeper in the water with all that lot on board. Ken and Heather did very well to cope with so many. Afterwards we all repaired to the beach for a barbecue, everybody taking their own idea of Christmas lunch with them, mostly determined by what was available in the local shops. David and Linda from *Miss Molly* brought vast quantities of turkey, enough to feed all of us it seemed. The inevitable party games followed. In the evening John and Chee went ashore while I stayed aboard to keep Janet company. She was feeling better but still a bit ropey.

On Boxing Day, with Janet now recovered, we set out from Phi Phi Don to return to Ko Racha Yai. John and I were keen to show Janet and Chee the splendid snorkelling we had enjoyed in that bay on the north-east coast on our way into Phuket. The bay does not appear to have an official name so we called it *'Greylag Bay'*. It was as good as ever and Janet, who

221

by now had become highly adept with fins and mask, thoroughly enjoyed it. I think the visiting divers must feed the fish and that may be why there were so many. We saw the large moray eel again, Janet gave it a wide berth!

Later we moved round to Racha Yai Bay and this time we found conditions tenable although there was still too much swell in the bay for comfort. We stayed for a couple of days and enjoyed the company of *Miss Molly* and *Excess Line*. We discovered a path across the island which led back to '*Greylag Bay*' and we returned there for another splendid snorkel.

There were only a few days left before Janet's return flight on the 30th December, so we needed to return to Phuket Island for that reason and to prepare the boat for our onward journey to Sri Lanka. Also we had heard that the fireworks at Patong on New Year's Eve were not to be missed. We went via Chalong where we called in at the fuel barge to fill our tanks before going round to Nai Harn Bay.

The next day there was a rather fractious skipper's meeting in the hotel. The rally programme had been slightly changed for the next few legs up to Eilat and some skipper's were unhappy because the new timings had clashed with their own arrangements for crew changes and visitors. Others had already changed their arrangements to fit in with the new plan. The problems were not resolvable, whatever the rally Commodore did would upset one group or the other! There was an air of disgruntlement. In the end, next day, a compromise was reached. Planning a rally as extensive as this one was no easy task and a few changes are unavoidable. However, once the plans become susceptible to changes as a result of pressure from individuals or groups, trouble is bound to follow.

Next day, the 30th of December, arrangements had been made for all the rally boats to complete their exit clearances at the immigration offices in Phuket town. This day had been chosen because New Year's Eve and the day after were public holidays and fees for clearance were doubled. We arrived at the immigration office in several minibuses only to find a large cardboard notice in the window announcing that the 30th was also a bank holiday! The fees were of course doubled. I hated this kind of endemic corruption among the officials in government departments but it was useless to complain to higher authority because it seemed that all of them were getting a share of the proceeds. Such a shame in a country that from all other aspects is so attractive.

Back on *Greylag*, we left Nai Harn Bay and made our way around the south-west corner of the island and up the coast to Patong Bay. Conditions there were much calmer than at Nai Harn and we anchored among several other rally boats who were there for the fireworks. Sadly this was Janet's last day and we took a taxi to the airport that afternoon to catch her flight to Bangkok. There were only two good things about that trip, one was knowing that Janet would be coming back soon to Eilat and the other was quite the best pizza we had ever had - and that was in the airport restaurant!

I returned to the boat with a heavy heart. Next day we all went off to Robinson's supermarket to restock the boat. In the evening we joined several other boats for a last Thai meal at a local restaurant and then returned to the boats to see the New Year in and watch the fireworks. They were quite spectacular and we had a very good view watching from seaward. It was a very professional show and was followed by several smaller displays in the streets of the town where individuals conducted their own personal celebrations.

Christine and Pat from *Papa Golf* joined us on *Greylag* and we fired off a few small rockets in the general direction of Alb where a noisy party had developed - well they are from Scotland. This led to reprisals later when they turned up in a dinghy and hurled buckets of water at us! It was rather unkind to soak poor Christine to the skin and only great good luck saved our cameras from serious damage. Ah well, boys will be boys!

At the crack of dawn, too early to decide how bad the hangovers were, we left Phuket and headed north-westwards for a brief visit to the Similan Islands before the long trip across the Bay of Bengal to Sri Lanka.

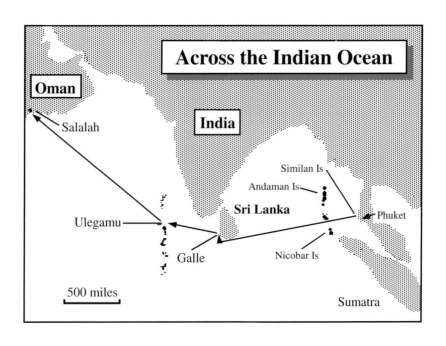

Across the Indian Ocean

Oman

Salalah

India

Ulegamu

Similan Is

Andaman Is

Sri Lanka

Phuket

Galle

Nicobar Is

500 miles

Sumatra

17 Sri Lanka - An Island Haunted by the Ghosts of Britain Past

Before setting out in earnest for Sri Lanka we planned to pay a short visit to the Similan Islands that lie in the Andaman Sea, a short distance from Phuket. After an early start from Patong Bay, we arrived there in the evening of January 1st 1997. There are nine islands (and a few big rocks) in the group - hence the name which is derived from the Malay word 'sembilan' meaning nine. We spent our first night at Koh Miang, at the centre of the group, and next day we moved on to Koh Similan, a larger island at the northern end of the group with an attractive bay at its northern end. On the way there we stopped alongside a group of large rocks, Hin Pasa - it would be an exaggeration to call them islands. There we found spectacular shoals of blue fish, many thousands strong. The water was so deep around the 'rocks' that we had to take it in turns to snorkel while the other one kept the boat slowly motoring in circles on station.

The bay at the northern end of Ko Similan was adorned with a white sand beach forming a crescent around the bay and giving way, at each end, to some extraordinary rocky outcrops. At the northern end stood the famous balancing rock, a massive structure that looked as though it might roll down the cliff at any moment. The sea at Similan had a most striking blue-green intensity; the whole area is a marine national park and is famous for its spectacular underwater scenery and marine life.

Best Respects and *Nefertiti* were there with us. Everyone was spending a quiet and restful day in readiness for the next morning when we would all depart for the long haul across the Bay of Bengal to Galle Harbour, at the southern end of Sri Lanka. This was a much longer trip than we had done recently - it would take 7 or 8 days - and I was glad to have Chee to enable us to revert to our well-tried watch system of 3 hours on followed by 6 hours in bed. This would be his first real test as we had only done short day trips since he joined us.

225

The distance to Galle Harbour was a bit over 1000 miles and our route would take us through the Nicobar Islands via the Sombrero Channel, before reaching the open ocean of the Bay of Bengal. I had vague plans to stop at Little Nicobar Island for a night's rest. Although we had been warned that the islands, which are administered by India, were prohibited territories for yachts except in distress, we wondered whether we might be able to find some lonely spot without making any contact with the authorities.

On the 3rd of January we set out from Similan Island at 7 o'clock in the morning. The Sombrero Channel was 244 miles away and we reckoned on getting there late on the Saturday. However things were very quiet for that first two days and we fell a bit behind the plan.

On the second day out, we heard on the net that *Griffyn* - she was well ahead of us - was getting close to Nancowry Island in the Nicobars and was planning to sail straight into the harbour, hoping there would be no trouble. John Roberts had a plan to plead generator failure if challenged. Later that day, Griffyn came through on the radio to say that they had indeed hit trouble. As soon as they entered the harbour at Nancowry they had been boarded by the Navy and police who inspected the boat thoroughly and took away their passports. Later they had been visited by three senior naval officers who had been impeccably polite but hidebound with bureaucracy. John Roberts had to choose his words rather carefully over the radio in case they were listening in, however we could 'read between the lines' and there was no doubt that he was in serious trouble. I decided that we would definitely not stop at Little Nicobar Island! Indeed I wondered whether we should be going through the Sombrero channel, since that would take us within a few miles of the islands. Other boats in the rally had decided to go a long way south of Great Nicobar to avoid any possibility of trouble.

Next morning the fleet again heard from *Griffyn*. They were still effectively 'arrested' and had now been told that they would have to wait for the chief of police to come down from Port Blair, up north in the Andaman Islands. They had told the authorities that there were a lot of other British boats in the area and, whilst it was emphasised that no one should stop for any reason short of serious emergencies, it had been confirmed that there was no objection to passing through the Sombrero Channel. A list of our boats had been given to the Navy in an effort to avoid further difficulties. That was good news for us and confirmed our plan to go through the Channel which was now only a few hours away.

Even so, when we got there we religiously kept to a course that put the greatest possible distance between us and any of the islands. We saw no sign of the Indian Navy.

The remainder of the trip to Galle was fast and furious. It was a splendid downwind sail in near perfect conditions and helped by a 2 or 3 knot favourable current around the southern tip of Sri Lanka, we arrived in Galle at midday on the 11th of January. The journey had taken just over eight days. So easy had the sailing been that I managed to get through three paperbacks - 'The Firm' and 'The Pelican Brief' by John Grisham, and Jeffery Archer's 'A Matter of Honour', all three had been obtained in a book swap back at Phuket. I still found the long ocean passages rather boring and I was reading more and more as time went by. Chee had done very well on this his first serious ocean passage and managed his watches without difficulty. We had discovered that he had a considerable talent for writing poetry, some of it was very good I thought - not that I am any kind of expert.

Our entry into Galle harbour was delayed for two hours while we waited patiently for clearance from the Navy. When they came they made a thorough inspection of the boat before allowing us to enter. Galle is a naval harbour, as well as serving commercial interests, and security was very strict because of the trouble with the Tamil Tigers. Although this was mostly in the north of the island, there had been the occasional incident further south and the authorities were taking no chances. In the harbour we joined several other Tradewinders, already there, to form a line of boats moored with bow anchors and stern lines to a large buoy.

Not long after arriving, there was a loud explosion nearby. Our colleagues explained that the navy dropped small depth charges into the harbour at random intervals as a deterrent to Tamil Tiger frogmen looking to sabotage the naval vessels. It was rather disconcerting and we were warned that it was dangerous to swim in the harbour. Apparently even a small depth charge can kill.

The first bit of good news we received was that *Griffyn* had been allowed to leave the Nicobars after being detained there for six days. We all felt relieved for John and Ruth; it must have been a worrying time for them. There were stories around that other boats had been detained for as long as three months. Ashore we completed the formalities quickly, thanks to Peter and Tony's excellent planning. They had arranged for a special detachment of officials to set up office on the quayside. There was even a tented outpost of the local bank to provide us with some immediate funds.

After that we went to the nearby Closenberg Hotel for the evening.

The hotel was straight out of a Somerset Maugham novel, one felt one was back in the 1850s. High vaulted rooms with oak beams and wickerwork armchairs. We had a passable meal for a very passable price. To get back into the harbour area past the guards at the gate, we had to produce the passes we had been given on arrival; one did not argue with them too much - they were armed with loaded Kalashnikovs! We heard an amusing story concerning this procedure. One young lady had forgotten her pass and when she returned the guard was reluctant to let her in. 'You will find my name on the list of Tradewinds people', she said to him. He got out the list and she cast her eyes down the page hopefully - baked beans, tinned tomatoes, dried milk, tinned butter... He had the list provided by the local ship suppliers! In the end she charmed him into letting her in, or maybe she just said her name was Peaches in Syrup.

Next day we went downtown to the 'Fort' area on the opposite side of the bay. Travel in Sri Lanka is very simple as the place is alive with tuk-tuks - small 3-wheel taxis with motorbike engines. They were unbelievably cheap and a great convenience. The tuk-tuk man drove us around the harbour and past the substantial town before arriving at the gates of the Fort. Alongside the gates there was a large cricket ground; I was beginning to feel at home. The Fort was an area of perhaps a square mile with a massive stonr wall around it. I was reminded of the old city of St Malo. We found the New Orient Hotel there, it was anything but new. A uniformed doorman guarded an imposing white façade, with large oak doors - only the right sort of people would be admitted! I wondered about our scruffy shorts and tee shirts but I need not have done so. Inside one could easily imagine one was back in the days of the British Raj. A waiter in a black sarong and smart white shirt came up to us.

'Would Sir care for a beer?' he asked. The ghosts of a British past certainly pervaded that place.

John and I had planned to go up to Kandy and the hill country for a few days. In a local bookstore I bought an informative book called 'Sri Lanka by Rail' by Royston Ellis, it was a veritable mine of information. Then we booked our seats for the initial journey to Columbo. This was about a three-hour journey and second class tickets cost the princely sum of 60p. One would never travel lower than second class after one look into a third class coach.

Chee made plans to go off backpacking with three of the young ladies from other boats, while John and I planned our trip up to Kandy. After a

228

The New Orient Hotel at Galle

night there in a hotel, we would catch another train and go on through the tea plantations and up into the hill country around Bandarawela. We had heard that this was an exceptional train journey, one of the most spectacular in the world, it said in 'Sri Lanka by Rail'.

The next morning John and I were ashore early and took a tuk-tuk for the station downtown. There are a surprising number of daily commuters into Columbo, so we reckoned we were lucky to find seats. The coaches were fairly ancient - rickety and grubby, with dreadful plastic seats that stuck to one's bare legs. Nevertheless we entered upon this journey in the spirit of adventure and made light of the many discomforts. There was a notice over one corner seat saying 'Reserved for Clergy'. I remember thinking that it might have been a good idea to carry a dog collar in one's luggage, in case the train was crowded.

The journey to Columbo closely followed the western coastline; indeed large sections of the track ran immediately behind the beaches. We rattled along through small villages, occasionally stopping for another group of commuters. One was able to study a wide cross-section of Sri Lankan village communities and their rural life. After three hours the train finally arrived at Columbo Fort station and we transferred to another for the four-hour journey up to Kandy.

The Kandy train was much the same as the Columbo one, just as noisy and grubby although somewhat less crowded. Built by the British in 1867, this line went through more interesting territory. After we had escaped from the Columbo suburbs we ran into open country, with wide expanses of rice fields interspersed with heavily wooded areas and occasional villages. In places the rice fields were arranged in terraces climbing up into the lower slopes of the surrounding hills. Farmers worked with oxen and were often knee deep in water. We saw groups of women planting paddy, one seedling at a time. The further we got into the journey, the hillier became the surroundings and everywhere was green and verdant, but as yet we saw no tea plantations. These, we knew, were much higher up in the cooler hill country.

Just past Mirigama, the train ground to a halt. John and I had noticed a package with suspicious metal objects protruding from the top which had been left by the seats opposite ours. It appeared to have been left there by somebody who had got off the train at Mirigama and evidently it had been reported to the guard who had halted the train. We felt just a little nervous; we were very close to this thing. *'Could it be a bomb, courtesy of the Tamil Tigers?'* we thought. There was talk of evacuating the train but no one moved. Then another guard appeared, picked up the package as if it were just groceries, opened the door and threw it out onto the embankment! John, who had served in Northern Ireland during the troubles, was not at all impressed with their technique for dealing with such an emergency. However, he hadn't been convinced that the object was a bomb and reckoned the objects in the bag were old-fashioned brass lanterns of some sort. Some poor fellow had probably lost something precious to him. The train trundled on amid a general sense of relief.

At Kandy we left the station and walked the short distance up the hill to the beautiful man-made lake. This is the dominant feature at Kandy and everything revolves around it. About a mile and a half long, it is surrounded by hills dotted with occasional luxurious houses and several hotels. The lake had been created by a dam built at the 'town' end in 1810 by the then King of Kandy. Our book recommended the Queen's Hotel, which was at one end of a square on the edge of the lake; at the other end was the famous 'Temple of the Tooth'. There were elephants in the square, demonstrating various trained skills under the encouragement of a man with a stick.

The Queen's was another place replete with ghosts of the British colonial past. The bedrooms had old-fashioned high ceilings and even more old-fashioned plumbing. A notice proudly announced that Margaret Thatcher had once slept there. My room was large and had an enormous bed with a canopy of mosquito netting. I had the best shower I could procure from the plumbing - a tepid trickle, and then joined John for a dinner that was more memorable for the small bill than the quality.

Next day we caught an early train to take us up to Bandarawela. Unfortunately we were unable to book ourselves seats in the observation car (first class). This car is at the rear of the train and has windows all round to give a splendid view on both sides and through the rear. It is always heavily booked by agents of the tourist companies. We settled for second class seats but luckily found some next to the windows. The line ran through level country for a while and then started the slow climb up to the 1,891 metres high spot close to Pattipola. This was a spectacular journey by any standards. As the track wound its way around the hills and valleys, it crossed wide river canyons, passed through pine forested areas and then, after Rozella, into the tea plantations. There were spectacular cuttings and embankments and numerous tunnels cut through the hills. One could hang out of the window as the train negotiated one minimum radius bend after another, and look forwards to the ancient diesel locomotive, bought a decade ago from Canada. Despite the sheer drop from the track in many places, there were young men hanging onto the outside of the third class carriages.

Up and up we went, past Nawalapitiya, Watawala, Rozella and then to Hatton. Each station had a notice giving its height above sea level. Hatton was at 1,271 metres and was the nearest station to Adam's Peak, a sacred mountain to which there are annual pilgrimages between late January and April, involving half a million pilgrims. That would not be a good time to be making this journey, luckily we were just ahead of the 'peak' time, as it is known. Beyond Hatton our train struggled ever upwards until, at Pattipola, we reached the summit of the track. After that the track followed more level ground, around more valleys, following the contours as far as possible, even though this sometimes involved a detour of many miles compared with the route a crow would take.

Eventually we arrived at Bandarawella. Our decision to stop there had been largely determined by a passage in Royston Ellis's book. He says there 'One of my favourite hotels in Sri Lanka, the Bandarawela Hotel, is next to the post office, superbly located on a bluff above the town so you escape the dross and have only the bliss of its garden setting, perfect for afternoon tea. In 1993 it was 100 years old but it seems rooted in the 1930s with its glassed-in terrace lounge and deep chesterfields, dining room with mixed grill fit for trenchermen, and atmosphere of a health resort. The beds have brass knobs on the ends, the furniture is practical antique and the whole place is designed for informal relaxation on the lines of a tea-planters' club, which is what it used to be.'

He forgot to mention the standard Sri Lankan plumbing! Nevertheless, we were not disappointed - the hotel certainly lived up to Royston Ellis's glowing account and we soon saw why he was so attracted by it. That first evening we were a bit tired after the long train journey, but not too tired to join in on the evening's excellent buffet dinner. The food really was very good indeed. Over dinner we discussed our plans for the next day - we had already decided to stay put for another day. John is a great walker and was planning to wander off into the hills and tea plantations to see Sri Lanka close to. For myself, I planned to do some sketching and painting locally - I felt like a less physically demanding day than John was likely to have and the surroundings of Bandarawela looked quite inspiring.

After a standard English breakfast, we each went our separate way. I wandered across the town and then along the road that ran parallel to the railway. It led back down the valley up which the gallant old diesel had hauled us the day before. I was finding the traffic on the road quite heavy, and the driving unpredictable, when I noticed that many of the locals seemed to be using the railway track as a footpath. I climbed up the small embankment to join them and I could see at once why they chose this route. The track was more even under foot than most of the local paths. It took a more direct route and, once one had adjusted one's stride to the 'standard British' distance between the sleepers, it was easy walking. And the trains were few and far between! After a while I settled on a corner of the track and sketched the marvellous view across the valley.

Bandarawela is 1,221 metres above sea level, so that although it is less than 6 degrees north of the equator the climate is pleasantly cooler than on the coast. At Nuwara Eliya, which is 1,898 metres above sea level, people sometimes complain that it is too cool, but sat there by that railway track in Bandarawela with my sketchpad, I enjoyed the beautiful surroundings in comfort.

Later I returned along the track to the station and did some more sketches of the railway buildings and accoutrements. It was all like a gigantic Hornby railway set and reminded me of my own, dating from just

Bandarawela
Sri Lanka
Jan 97

The railway side at Bandarawella

after the war. The signalling system must have been the original one built by the British in 1867, ancient semaphore signals operated by long cables from the signal box. There one could find the original brass-handled signal levers, and clocks and timetables from a bygone age. An old water tower still had the long hose dangling down to refill the tanks of the long-gone steam engines. An occasional goat grazed on the overgrown sidings, unperturbed by the ever-present stream of Sri Lankans walking along the track. I was back in my boyhood in that place.

John returned from the hills with accounts of the tea plantations. He had walked a very long way. We enjoyed another splendid meal in the hotel before retiring to our four-posters to recover. We never shared a room; perhaps part of our secret for survival together over those years in *Greylag* was that we never missed an opportunity to be at arm's length for a spell.

The trip back to Galle followed the same route in reverse, but this time we were lucky enough to get seats in the observation car at the rear of the train. This gave us a panoramic view of that beautiful country which I greatly enjoyed. It also added to the mild tension as the train negotiated steep-sided embankments or a rickety old wooden bridge across some gorge. Towards Kandy the land levels out and several of the stations

233

display notices marked with the height of the floodwater in various years when there had been serious inundations. At Gampola, for example, the flood of 1947 had completely submerged the station and its buildings. Similarly at Watawala, the same floods had caused an enormous landslide that washed away the track. There and at several other places along the track, one could see notices telling the drivers to go slowly because of 'weak sleepers' - they induced more of that slight tension, but it didn't last. Perhaps it added to the fun; perhaps it was even an aspect of our characters that we liked such feelings and maybe therein lay one of the reasons for sailing round the world - a slight addiction to adrenaline.

Back at Kandy, we spent another pleasant night in a hotel. This time we chose the 'Chalet', an interesting place built among the trees and well up the hill on the side of the lake. This was in fact our second choice. The first had been the Hotel Thakawela on the other side of the valley, but when we got there we found it was fully booked, partly by some coach loads of people who described themselves as Tradewinders! The 'Chalet' was owned by a family with an avid interest in art. The grandmother had been a student at the Slade School of Art and had filled the hotel with an extraordinary collection of pictures and 'objets' - some of them good pieces. John and I enjoyed a beer out on the balcony, watching the sun slowly setting behind the hills across the lake. Dinner was excellent and my room, with a splendid view over the valley, was comfortable in all respects except for the pl ... well, you can guess! There was an odd notice on the dressing table warning one to keep the windows shut because of the monkeys. I had noticed earlier that there were two-dimensional, metal 'cut-out' monkeys fixed around the railings of the first floor and I thought the notice was intended to add to the joke.

Breakfast brought an explanation. There were real monkeys all over the place and looking for any opportunity to beg or steal from the guests. They sat among the artificial ones creating an odd display - somewhere between a museum and a zoo. I was in the middle of a superb piece of close-up video of one especially aggressive male with his female entourage, when he got to his feet and copulated with the nearest of his 'wives'! Why does this always happen to me? Heaven knows what mother will think.

We walked around the lake and back to the station only to find that the train for Columbo was cancelled. We had to negotiate for a taxi to take us all the way, but this turned out to be a blessing in disguise. The driver gave us a running commentary as we wended our way through the countryside and persuaded us to accept his recommendation for several side visits. The first of these was to a spice garden from where the only way out was through the shop where the various potions were for sale. They were hard sell merchants all right.

'This one very good for the sex', one said, 'make you last 3 hours'.

He's probably selling Viagra by now! I expect the driver got a kickback for each visitor he took there, perhaps that was the explanation for the very reasonable starting price.

The next stop was at an elephant orphanage, a detour that necessitated a small renegotiation of the journey fare (up by 200 rupees) as it was a bit off the route - about 2 miles! A large herd of 70 or so elephants was bathing in the river; they obviously loved the water and we got some good photographs. One tiny baby elephant was only 2 months old.

At last we reached Columbo and after a slightly fractious argument with our driver over his proposals for further adjustments to his quoted fare, we paid him what we had agreed and he drove off looking slightly dischuffed. We hailed a tuk-tuk and asked him to recommend somewhere for lunch. He took us to a nice looking fish restaurant and in we went only to be greeted by a loud cheer. Inside was that coach load of Tradewinders again! How small the world can be sometimes, especially when one thinks one is getting away from it all.

Back at Galle we found that Chee had returned from his trip off base and had already done the major job of filling our water tanks. The next four days were spent dealing with some minor maintenance on the boat and getting in supplies for our onward journey. One of the troubles with travelling in a rally is that occasionally supply sources are overloaded with the demands of so many boats arriving and leaving together. This was the case at Galle where the local suppliers ran out of beer in cans. Disaster was averted by reluctantly accepting bottled beer instead. The trouble is the glass bottles are larger and heavier, serious problems for a small boat with enthusiastic beer drinkers.

The evening before we were due to depart from Galle it was Burn's night. Not surprisingly, the Scottish contingent among the Tradewinders organised the usual evening events although Heaven knows where they found a Haggis. Reluctantly we decided not to join in. Suffering from a serious hangover is not a good way to start a long sea journey, so we settled for a good night's sleep, with only minor disturbances as the revellers struggled with the navigational problems of returning to their boats. Before retiring to our bunks, we released the mooring line from the buoy at

The Church in the 'Fort', Galle

our stern to make it easier to get away quietly early next day.

We were up at six o'clock, released our lines from the boats on each side of us, started the engine and headed for the harbour entrance. What happened next could be described as mildly humiliating, more accurately as a diabolical shambles! I had completely forgotten that we were also anchored by the bow. *Greylag* accelerated quickly forwards for about 20 metres and then stopped abruptly as the engine cut out with the anchor rode round the prop.

Now normally this would not have been too big a problem as one would just dive under the boat and release it, but we remembered the warning about those depth charges. I tried to call the naval authorities on the VHF to get them to suspend their activities while I released the anchor but I could not make contact. By this time heads were beginning to bob out of hatches on the other boats, nobody likes to miss out on somebody else having a disaster. We gesticulated to some sailors who had appeared on the deck of one of the naval vessels not far away from us. They were the ones, we thought, in control of the depth charges. We thought they had understood what our problem was, but couldn't be absolutely sure. I decided to risk it and, though Chee offered, I thought I would do the job myself. After all, what would I say to his mother? The job turned out to be very easy and I wasted no time getting back on board. John quickly retrieved the anchor, and a small cheer went up from our audience as we left the harbour, red-faced but relieved.

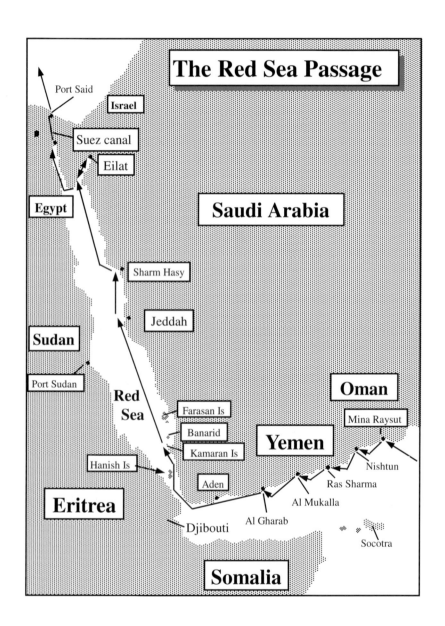

The Red Sea Passage

Port Said

Israel

Suez canal

Eilat

Egypt

Saudi Arabia

Sharm Hasy

Jeddah

Sudan

Port Sudan

Red Sea

Oman

Mina Raysut

Farasan Is

Banarid

Kamaran Is

Yemen

Nishtun

Hanish Is

Ras Sharma

Aden

Al Mukalla

Eritrea

Al Gharab

Djibouti

Socotra

Somalia

18 Arabs, Angst and Antiquities on Our Long Struggle up the Red Sea

We had all enjoyed Sri Lanka; it had provided a welcome break from onboard life and we felt rested and ready for what we knew would be a testing time on the next stage of our journey. Plans had been discussed with other skippers back at Galle. The rally plan was to sail direct to Djibouti and then to Port Sudan, before making the long windward sail from there to Eilat in Israel. Along with several other skippers, we wanted to visit the Maldive Islands and then take a shorter leg to Oman before tracking along the south and west coasts of Yemen and Saudi Arabia and into the Gulf of Aqaba for Eilat. This alternative plan avoided the long leg to Djibouti; it allowed us to see a bit more of the Arab world and would take us up the slightly easier eastern side of the Red Sea. We formed a group of boats as we had for Indonesia with 'STING', this time it was called the 'O-RING' (O for Oman) after an excellent suggestion from Inga on *Calidris*.   The boats involved were *Greylag, Calidris, Sooty, Ocean Gypsy* and *Nefertiti.*   After Oman, plans were less certain as one or two were keen to go to Djibouti, but the group were initially all set for a visit to the Maldives and then Oman.

Several months earlier we had been told that one could not visit the Maldives without prior permission from India and even then, one had to go to the tourist centre at Male. This involved a dogleg south, away from the direct route to the Red Sea, whereas the northern atolls were more or less on the direct route. At Galle harbour we had met several boats that were making their way eastwards and had already visited the Maldives. They confirmed that a small island, Ulegamu, in the northern Ihavandhippolhu group of atolls had welcomed them and there had been no bureaucratic difficulties.   This was good news and we were able to reciprocate with information on Thailand and Indonesia where they were headed. We had been given this information in good time to get hold of the detailed charts for Ulegamu - absolutely essential for safety in those dangerous waters.

A traditional hut at Ulegamu

The voyage from Galle to Ulegamu was 440 miles and easy sailing all the way. We arrived in daylight on the 27th of January and anchored safely off the reef that runs all along the south-west coast. Very soon a wooden boat arrived with a few officials and their leader, Judge Ahmed. They were most polite and asked us to fill in one simple form - what a contrast to Thailand! They charged us a mere $5 US for their trouble and said it would be possible to get fuel from the village. We felt pleased we had come.

Ulegamu was just over a mile long and lay on a NW-SE axis, giving a good lee in the north-east monsoon. The reef extended all along the island, about 150 metres from the shore. To seaward of the reef, there was good sand to anchor on and the few coral heads were easily avoided in the clear blue water. Once settled we sat in the cockpit with our rum and cokes, weary after the long journey, but enjoying the scenery, softly lit by the evening sunshine. A small wooden pier stretched out from the white sand beach. A few traditional huts built from woven palm fronds stood at the root of the pier, against a backcloth of palms and breadfruit trees. There was no hint of the village that lay hidden among the trees behind.

Between us and the beach lay three strips of coloured water, one of deep, deep blue, then the brown of the coral reef followed by the brilliant turquoise of the shallow water over sand. We had seen this a few times

240

before but it never lost its fascination. Exciting yet restful, it brought an irresistible urge to dive in, full of eager anticipation of the glories of the reef beneath. The mere sight of it dispelled all weariness from even the most water-worn sailor. It raised the spirits; it appealed to something deep within us, it was an image that remained in one's memory long after other details had faded.

Away from the shore we could see across the atoll to the other islands completing the 13 by 17-mile circle of Ihavandhippolhu. This atoll differed from others in the Maldives, and those we had seen in the Tuamotus, in that the circular coral reef is less complete, leaving a circle of islands with wide gaps between them, many of which are navigable. This made for easy access without the need to face the fierce tides so characteristic of the passes in the Tuamotus. Navigation into Ulegamu had been straightforward.

Next morning we awoke to a sparkling sunrise. A local boat with a lateen sail coasted by and open fishing boats, highly coloured and with large curving prows like Venetian galleys, lay at anchor inshore. At the pier Judge Ahmed met us. He was a sort of 'circuit judge' for the northern atolls - no murders he assured us, just the odd fight or quarrel over land, an occasional theft. The judge also controlled the fuel supplies! Refuelling took a good deal of patience. A 50-gallon drum appeared on the beach and the fuel was siphoned out into a 5-litre measuring jug and poured into our cans. This was a long process even for our 50 litres; I felt some sympathy for the bigger boats that wanted 300 litres.

The village had a population of 395 and the community was strictly Moslem. It was Ramadan while we were there, the month when devout Moslems refrain from eating and drinking (and other pleasures) between sunrise and sunset. Generously they offered us fruit drinks, even though they could not join in themselves - a stark contrast with, for example, Saudi Arabia, where the infidel is expected also to obey the rules. Behind the huts by the pier, most of the rest of the village was built of coral stone and mortar; the roofs were corrugated iron. There was a school and a mosque from which the sung prayers emanated at dawn and dusk. A small shop opened when required and everywhere was neat and tidy, the sand roads swept clean by the women each day. We were told that the beach was swept each day - it certainly looked true. Beside the mosque was a small graveyard, and alongside that was an area with the burnt remains of funeral pyres and others prepared for future use. Island villages cope unaided with the beginning and end of life's span, without the benefits of a health service

In the village at Ulegamu

or professionally run crematoria.

Someone had told them that I was a doctor and it soon transpired that Ahmed had lined up a small clinic for me. Doctoring is difficult when one is separated from the tools of the trade and the usual laboratory back-ups, to say nothing of the limited supplies of drugs and medicines one carries on a small boat. I prescribed much sympathy, a few aspirins and an occasional course of antibiotics. The latter introduced me to a problem I had not come across before in medical practice. Through Ahmed, acting as interpreter, I advised one old fellow with an infection to take some capsules at 6 hourly intervals. He shook his head.

'What's wrong?' I asked, 'these have come all the way from England. From the Queen!' I lied.

Ahmed explained that the fellow could not do this, because it was Ramadan he could eat nothing during the day. We settled for two capsules just before sunrise and one at sunset and midnight. I hoped that Allah would assist in the man's recovery after such a respectful compromise.

That evening we had a barbecue on the beach (after sunset, of course) with the other Tradewinders who were there. Alcohol is another of the proscriptions in the Koran, so we all exercised due reticence over our drinks. Mind you, it takes a sharp eye to distinguish a rum and coke mixed in a coke bottle from the unadulterated version! In any case, it is strictly

242

the fermented juice of the grape that is forbidden and there are Moslems who consider rum, gin and whisky are permissible.

After the barbecue we went along to the village where we had been invited to join in with some dancing. They arranged seats for us in a rectangle and a small group of drummers sat at one end. The dancing turned out to be an audience-participation event, done singly with no bodily contact between the sexes. The dancer would cavort around to the rhythm of the drums, holding a silk scarf in one hand. The girls did this with their heads completely covered; I wondered how they managed to breathe. When he or she had done their bit, the scarf was dropped on the head of one of the audience who was then expected to contribute his pennyworth. I must say our fellow Tradewinders rose magnificently to the occasion; I saw things I hadn't seen since the spinnaker was last released at both bottom ends! All this took place to the huge delight of the villagers who cheered and clapped. Young girls screamed for our handsome Chee - it was almost like a pop show.

We left Ulegamu on the 30th of January and headed north-west away from the atoll towards Salalah, a large port at the south-west corner of Oman. This was a longish voyage of 1,255 miles across the Arabian Sea. The wind was mainly northerly which enabled us to hold our course (304°), although we were fairly hard on the wind for much of the time. The days seemed to go by slowly with nothing very much to excite one's interest. We passed an oil tanker, apparently drifting. Perhaps he was killing time while waiting for a berth somewhere up the Gulf. *Miss Molly* reported seeing a red distress flare somewhere well ahead of us, happily all the Tradewind boats were accounted for, so it was not one of us.

I wanted to read Michener's 'The Covenant' again, in preparation for our coming visit to Israel, but discovered John had traded it back in Galle. For the first time I began to feel that life in this tiny plastic boat could become tedious, I felt weary and was probably rather poor company for my two companions. I became tetchy and complained of minor irritations, for example, over the way the log was being completed or the chart folded. I am not normally petty and I think these indulgences had their origins in the growing sense of frustration I felt with being cooped-up for so long. I settled for reading Gary Jennings' 'The Journeyer' in place of 'The Covenant' and came across a passage which very much suited my mood....

'I had hitherto supposed that a long sea voyage was the most unvarying and boring and interminable and monotonous sort of travel possible, at least when not made terrible by storm.'

By the 8th of February, after nine days at sea, we were at last approaching Mina Raysut, the harbour at Salalah. *Nefertiti* had radioed to say that she had lost her engine and might need a tow into harbour. We promised to keep in touch. *Ocean Gypsy, Sooty* and *Calidris* were all within range and it looked as though we would all arrive within a few hours of each other. But that last day was slow going and we soon realised that we would not arrive until the middle of the night. This was not too much of a worry as there were good lights to guide us in and *Nefertiti* had later called to say that she had got her engine going and the harbour entrance was straightforward - they were already at anchor there. Eventually we too entered the harbour and dropped our anchor alongside *Nefertiti* at one o'clock in the morning. It was surprisingly chilly and those sleeping bags we had bought in Mackay were again much appreciated.

Next morning, after a good sleep, I went topside for a look at Mina Raysut. It was a large harbour and the yachts were anchored in a quiet corner alongside some strikingly ancient looking wooden fishing boats. On a nearby quayside a serious(i.e. it had a gun) patrol boat was moored and beyond that, unoccupied commercial berths formed the perimeter of a rectangular inner basin. It was the last day of Ramadan and there was little sign of activity. A small motor boat came by with a fellow who introduced himself as the Coastguard. He took our passports away with him after explaining that it was a public holiday and the customs and immigration offices would not be open again until 3 days later, after the celebrations covering the end of Ramadan. Meanwhile, he added ominously, we would not be allowed to leave the harbour area. That was indeed disappointing, as we had not planned on staying for that long.

John Chapman, the skipper of *Calidris,* and I went ashore to explore. Water was available on the quayside but no fuel and the small snack shop, there for the harbour employees, sold only soft drinks in cans. We were not too worried about food supplies as we still had plenty on board, but we needed some fuel and *Sooty* was desperate for some. *Sooty*'s owners had gone home from Thailand and she was now in the charge of Roger and Teri Hyde who had previously been crew on *Papa Golf.*

We went off to the police at the dock gates to see what could be done and they phoned up the Port Captain who agreed to come and talk to us. Captain Hamud Ali, dressed in an immaculate white djellaba, arrived after a short while. He was a delightful fellow and went out of his way to be as helpful as he could be. He agreed that we could have our passports back next day and leave, effectively we would not have cleared in or out and the situation was not that different from the position if we had simply been turned away. Most generously he then lent us his car and driver to take us into the local town for some fuel. I volunteered to go and took with me a boot full of *Sooty*'s and our own jerry cans. Luckily the garage accepted US dollars in payment, so the fuel problem was solved. On the drive into town I caught my first sight of camels since arriving in Arabia, apparently free to wander around as they pleased, but I expect someone owned them. Salalah looked a nice town with all the right shops to replenish stores if only we were free to leave the port on our own. Another time, away from Ramadan, this would have been an interesting and enjoyable port of call. We had been unlucky.

That evening we hosted a bit of a party on *Greylag* for the other Tradewinders and also Alysia and Stefan from *Webefree,* a South African boat in the harbour with us. This passed the time pleasantly, as there was nothing else to do except stay on board for the evening. Next morning we collected our passports and all the boats left within an hour.

Our plans for the trip along the south Yemeni coast and into the Red Sea were flexible, to say the least. There were some useful notes in the Red Sea Pilot but things in the Yemen can change very quickly and we were not sure what we would find in the various small harbours. It was reasonably certain that we would be able to stop at Al Mukalla, about 350 miles to the west, and at Aden, which was another 300 miles beyond that. Other potential stopping places looked more doubtful, however we decided to give one or two of them a try.

The first of these was Nishtun, just inside the Yemeni border and about halfway to Al Mukalla. For the first 30 miles of the trip we had a spectacular sail, close inshore. The cliffs were 400-500 feet high with impressive rock structures and caves. A train of camels trekked along the skyline at one point, adding a picturesque reminder that this was Arabia. The terrain was so different from that in the tropics to which we had grown accustomed for the past year. Now there was very little green and much that looked barren. Yet the coastline had a grandeur of its own and was not unattractive. Where there were gaps in the high cliffs one could look further inland to the blue and grey mountains, successive layers of them, each less distinct than the one before as the haze increased with distance. The sailing was leisurely and by darkness on that first night we were back on the engine.

The next day we reckoned on getting to Nishtun by about tea-time, *Sooty, Ocean Gypsy,* and *Calidris* were also headed for Nishtun, but

245

Nefertiti had decided to press on to Al Mukalla. This, and the fact that we were now leaving the 'O' of O-ring led to a discussion of the title of our group, we renamed it the 'Y-front'! *Greylag* was first into Nishtun and headed in towards the harbour. Once around the end of the substantial harbour wall we found a good quay with one large wooden dhow alongside and several smaller boats further in. The latter were heavily armed with machine guns. We looked for some sign of welcome but the few people around seemed as confused as we were - they were clearly not used to visiting yachts. We went alongside and secured our lines. Very soon a jeep came roaring down to the quayside and screamed to a halt. I cast a nervous eye at the heavy machine gun mounted ominously in the rear of the vehicle; I remember wishing we had gone with *Nefertiti*.

The two men in the front, one in a captain's uniform, the other in a grubby white djellaba, got out and boarded *Greylag*. Without so much as an introduction, the fellow in the djellaba went below and started going through my cabin like a customs officer acting on a tip-off. After a while he seemed satisfied and ceased searching the rest of the boat. He muttered something unintelligible to the officer. After that the atmosphere warmed a little and my shattered nerves began to settle.

There were continuing hostilities between Yemen and Eritrea over disputed territory, including some of the offshore islands, and armed raids by small boats were not unknown. This accounted for their anxiety over a group of small boats arriving, notwithstanding our British flags. Once satisfied that we were bona fide visiting yachts they relaxed a little. They took our passports.

Once smiles had returned we asked if it would be possible to buy diesel and some stores and they soon produced a fellow who was ready to trade. He assured us he could get almost anything, but the prices he was quoting were silly. In the end, after negotiations that were made difficult by none of us speaking the other's language, we agreed a price for a stated quantity of fuel and fresh vegetables. When he returned he had only half what we had ordered but still wanted the $15 US we had agreed. We left the goods with him and, as it was now quite late, we told him we would talk about it in the morning. The night was peaceful, and given the two armed soldiers who were posted on the quayside to guard us, it was also very secure!

In the morning our trader accepted a reasonable price for his supplies and John went off in a vehicle for more stores from the local village. He returned with only onions. Later we were offered a trip to the more substantial town of Al Ghaydah, about 20 miles north of Nishtun. This sounded like a good opportunity to see a little bit of the interior of Yemen. The four boats shared the places available, leaving a good rearguard to watch over our interests in the harbour - this was not a place where one felt one could trust anybody. Indeed, knowing now of the recent kidnapping incidents I feel, with hindsight, we took a considerable risk.

The trip to Al Ghaydah took us across wide expanses of arid desert. We came across groups of camel here and there and some large flocks of goats. The goatherds were females, dressed head to foot in black as was characteristic in this part of the Muslim world. They wore tall black conical hats so that they almost looked like witches. It was obviously a hard life. Al Ghaydah was a ramshackle place with numerous street traders and a few small shops selling basic commodities. The town was untidy, half the population rushing around purposively while the other half sat around watching them. Goats wandered around freely, an occasional camel sat in the sun with the usual supercilious look on its face.

It was, however, a colourful place. We watched one fellow making pitta bread; the dough was kneaded and stretched repeatedly until it was formed into a thin disc about 15 inches across. With great dexterity this was then thrown against the wall of a fiercely hot stone oven where it remained stuck until cooked. We tried some for lunch and found it very palatable.

On our way back I was struck by the beauty of the distant landscape. As the sun went down even the desert became attractive; the sand seemed to glow, reddish against the backdrop of purple hills. Yemen is a surprisingly hilly country.

Back at the boats an obstreperous lieutenant arrived, we dubbed him Lieutenant 'Nasty'. He tried to charge us $150 for the vehicle that had taken us to town. In the end we beat him down to $50 which he accepted with an offensive lack of grace. By now it was clear that the army officers were taking a cut from all the traders they allowed on the quay as well as hiring out the army's vehicles and pocketing money for berths etc. It is difficult to deal with this in the presence of armed soldiers and I felt we had done as well as possible in the circumstances. But Lieutenant 'Nasty' hadn't finished with us yet. He turned up at four o'clock and ordered us to leave the harbour within one hour! I suppose he knew he had extracted all the money he was likely to get. We left the harbour and anchored for the night in a near-by bay.

We set off west early next morning. After a day and night sail we were a bit ahead of our schedule and would be arriving at Al Mukalla in the middle of the night. It seemed a good idea therefore, to take a few hours break and a convenient spot was quite close at Ra's Sharma. As we approached we noticed some fortifications with a flag flying and hoped that this did not herald another confrontation with the military. Our pilot book said this was Musa Fort.

The bay had a perfect white sand beach that gave way to a high rocky headland to the east and high cliffs of stratified rock to the west. The strata were of several different colours, creating a most attractive face to the cliffs. The water was crystal clear and the bay well sheltered by the headland. Ashore a group of Europeans arrived in a Landrover for a picnic. We talked to them and they told us they were installing refrigeration facilities for the local fishing industry - part of a contract between Yemen and the World Bank. It was a Thursday and this was the weekend in Yemen. They often came to this beach at weekends, they said it was probably the best beach in Yemen. We looked anxiously at some fast open boats with powerful outboard motors that were moored inshore of us. They were clearly military but lacked the mounted machine guns we had seen in similar vessels back at Nishtun. No one stirred in the fort; well it was the weekend after all!

In the last of the daylight we put to sea again to complete our journey to Al Mukalla, just 25 miles to the west. We arrived there at dawn. Al Mukalla was a big town with a substantial commercial harbour, Khalf

Musa Fort at Ras Sharma

Harbour. We anchored in a small corner of the bay to the west of the harbour, quite close to the town and protected from swell by some off-lying reefs. Apart from the 'Y-front' boats, now with *Nefertiti* again, there were several other yachts including *Lakmé* from Southampton (Mike and Rhona), and *Iron Lady*.

Ashore we checked in with Omar, an obliging fellow who seemed to be in charge of the yachts. He took away our passports (we were getting used to this) and organised some fuel for us. At 7 riyads per litre it was fairly cheap. The town was bustling and friendly and one could buy most things from one or other of the hundreds of small shops. The currency was a pain; it seemed they had paper money for denominations as small as a few pence. I made a phone call to Janet from the 'International Call Centre' and could have done with a wheelbarrow to take in the £23 it cost! All was well at home except that Janet had tennis elbow - this did not seem an undue threat to her visit to Eilat. We ate ashore that evening, chicken and chips.

Next morning I spent some time mending the loo for the umpteenth time. The plastic flange on the pump outlet had broken yet again. I then went on a tour of the town by myself. Increasingly I felt a need to get away

The Seafront at Al Mukalla

249

on my own whenever the opportunity arose. This is not a criticism of my colleagues; it simply reflected a natural reaction to being cooped up with them for so much of the time. I expect they felt it too and I know many of our friends on the other boats had the same experience. I worried though that this need to get away was becoming more pressing. Funnily enough, I had found another passage in 'The Journeyer' which described much the same thing...

'I noticed, at the first oasis halt, how we all soon separated and drew apart ... None of us had recently quarrelled, and we had no definable reason for shunning each other's company - except that for so long we had been in each other's company, and now it was pleasant to have some privacy for a change.'

There were no big stores in the town, just hundreds of tiny little shops, perhaps 6 or 8 feet wide and opening directly onto the pavement. The food shops were heavily stocked with sacks full of dried pulses of various kinds, pasta galore and tins of tuna - endless tins of tuna! The fresh vegetables looked good.

Women dressed in black went about purposefully, I wondered how they could see their way through the tiny slots in their headdress. Surprisingly they were still quite fashion conscious. I found a shop that appeared to specialise in women's clothing and was fascinated by the many subtle differences in design between black garments that looked superficially all the same. The town had several mosques. In the heat of the day they seemed to be used as resting places, I saw recumbent bodies all over the floor of the entrance halls. At dawn and dusk they would spring into life with the sung prayers, amplified many times over by loud speakers clustered around the minarets - such a strange mixture of ancient and modern.

On my way back to the boat I bumped into Teri from *Sooty*. She was in tears and explained that she had just phoned home to discover that her mother was dying of cancer. I took her back to their boat. She clearly wanted to get home as quickly as possible but this was not going to be easy as she and Roger were alone on *Sooty* and the nearest airport was at Aden.

On the quayside there was a growing crowd of Somalis sitting around. They were 'boat people' who had come over illegally, seeking refuge from the harsh conditions at home. The Yemenis had rounded them up and were waiting to load them on to a large dhow in the harbour which would return them to Somalia. They looked a forlorn lot and had been there all the previous night. Later they were loaded onto the dhow, packed in like

The 're-patriation' boat at Al Mukalla

cattle, and off it went south-westwards into the night.

Next day I completed the complicated clearance procedure - fill up the application form and put the tax stamps on it, take it on a taxi ride to Khalf harbour and get it signed and stamped by the Port Captain, return to the yacht anchorage and retrieve one's passports from Omar! *Nefertiti* and *Calidris* had left earlier that morning; we left with *Sooty* just after lunch.

We had travelled only a few miles from Al Mukalla when *Sooty* radioed to say that her engine alarm had gone off and it appeared that the engine was over-heating. Both Nefertiti and ourselves offered her a tow but as *Nefertiti* was 45 miles ahead and would take time to return we went back just three miles and took her in tow. With *Nefertiti* returning at 6 knots and us, with Sooty in tow, doing about 3 knots, the closing speed was close to 9 knots. Thus it was not long before we were able to rendezvous with *Nefertiti* and hand the unfortunate *Sooty* over to them. It was a long way to Aden, where they were both heading, and the tow would be easier for the large *Nefertiti* than for *Greylag*.

After the excitement of the tow was over, we sailed on through the rest of the night and arrived off Al Gharab soon after sunrise. We had been attracted to this place by the write up in the pilot book. It described a headland with an old volcano at its seaward end and an ancient ruined town at its foot. The bay to the east of the headland looked good for anchoring. We motored in cautiously as there was a large area of shallow water over coral on the way in. Once over this we found some good sand close inshore and dropped the anchor. John worked out that the tide would fall to about 1.5 metres in that spot, leaving just enough water for us to remain afloat.

The place was completely deserted and it looked as though we would be free from the attention of the authorities. The volcano rose up from the headland, a stark edifice of black rock with only an occasional splash of dull green where some tough vegetation struggled to survive. John and I wandered round the bay to the volcano but decided not to attempt to climb to the top - a rather forbidding trip in the heat of the day. Instead we explored the ruins near its foot and extending up the slopes of the volcano for about one third of its height.

It appeared that many of the buildings had been recently excavated, the pilot book said that some Russian archeologists had undertaken the task. The ruins were all that remained of the ancient city of Qana, dating from the first century AD. The city had been over-looked by the Temple of the Moon, which we took to be the ruins further up the volcano's slopes. The buildings had been constructed from the black volcanic rock and, though roofless, sufficient had survived to allow one to walk from room to room and conjure up fantasies of the ancient life-style. I took a photo of John adopting a Roman imperial posture. Back at the boat Chee said he had seen a desert fox in the dunes near-by.

We set off for Aden next morning, intending to join our colleagues who were probably already there. For now we were on our own. Over the radio we heard reports from other boats that Aden was a dirty harbour and they had been badly oiled up while there. This did not sound much fun and as we had plenty of fuel and were sailing fast I decided to bypass Aden and press on into the Red Sea. We ran into a school of Risso's dolphin, literally thousands of them all around the boat, Many were leaping out of the water, a spectacular sight, as they are one of the bigger varieties of dolphin.

After four days we were approaching the entrance to the Red Sea. Big ships enter through the Straits of Bab el Mandeb, but coming along the Yemeni coast it is quicker to pop through the Small Strait between mainland Yemen and the island of Mayyun. I opted for the latter but soon regretted it. It was late in the day when we entered and very soon some steep seas and 30 knots of wind hit us from the stern. In our efforts to deal with this we managed to split the mainsail in two for the second time, about halfway up. We took it all down and pressed on under jib and engine. This was our introduction to the Red Sea and heralded many similar moments on that long hard struggle to Eilat. We all had to keep very quiet indeed about our intention to go to Israel. The Arab countries do not approve of boats going to Israel and so to all official enquiries we answered that we were heading for Suez. At least for now we still had a following wind but that, we knew, would not last for long.

That first night in the Red Sea passed quietly enough and by dawn we were off Khawkha. The pilot suggested we might find a place to stop there but despite several attempts we could not find a safe way in. Each time we approached, we came up against shallow coral reefs and had to turn back. In the end we gave up on Khawkha and pressed on northward through the day and the next night to Kamaran Island. We heard on the radio that *Ocean Gypsy* had run into difficulty. Despite the warnings we had all been given about the dangers of visiting the Hanish Islands - one of the disputed territories between Yemen and Eritrea - *Ocean Gypsy* had gone there. Not realising that Eritrean soldiers occupied the island at the time, she had gone in flying the Yemeni courtesy ensign! As if that were not provocation enough, Doug, the skipper, had addressed the Eritreans in Arabic! They were arrested.

At dawn on the 23rd February we were approaching Ras Isa, on our way to the southern entrance to Kamaran Bay and the small village about halfway up the eastern shore of the island. As we came closer we shuddered at the sight of large guns at intervals all along the headland. There was no sign of activity but this did little to allay our anxiety. With our eyes glued on those guns, we pressed on into the bay through the narrow pass to the south of Kamaran Island. No one fired at us.

Once into the bay we had a pleasant motor up the island coast to a small village situated at the root of an inlet from the bay. We anchored just off a dilapidated old quayside and very soon were visited by some military gentlemen from the near-by camp. They asked only to see our passports and seemed happy to agree to us staying there for a couple of days. This was good news, as it would allow us time to repair the torn mainsail.

We retrieved the ancient old Singer sewing machine from under my berth together with the roll of sailcloth I had on board precisely for this kind of emergency. It was difficult work as there was not enough room on board to spread the sail out sufficiently. But with all hands helping we managed to effect a reasonable repair - the second major repair we had done on that sail since leaving home. The first, you will remember, was at Nuie. Later John and Chee went ashore and were able to purchase a small amount of fuel and some eggs. That evening we heard that *Ocean Gypsy* had been allowed to leave the Hanish Islands and was heading up our way, perhaps to join up with us tomorrow.

Next day we pressed on northward. As expected the wind had now gone into the north, so we had to tack all the way to Banarid Island where we found a good anchorage in the lee of the island. *Ocean Gypsy* caught up with us there and anchored alongside. It was a quiet place, beautifully sheltered, and we shared it with a couple of open fishing boats. The fishermen cooked their meal on board their small boats and then appeared to doss down for the night beneath tarpaulins. It made *Greylag* seem the lap of luxury!

Next morning the two boats set off early. It was now time to try to make some real progress northwards towards Jeddah in Saudi Arabia where we hoped to refuel and stock up our food supplies. Peter Seymour had given us a letter from the Saudi High Commission in London. It was all in Arabic but we understood that it amounted to permission to call in at Jeddah even though they do not normally welcome yachts. This gave us a certain amount of confidence that we would be looked after and that would be welcome after the uncertainties of our time in Yemen.

We took a course outside the Farasan bank to a spot where our chart showed the entrance to an inshore passage. The entrance was marked 'The Pearly Gates'! This route gave us the option to go inshore behind the islands if the weather had turned nasty. In fact it stayed reasonable, although we were still hard on the wind and making only about 60 miles a day down the line. We struggled on in a rising headwind for another day and then a bit of good fortune came our way, the wind moderated and went into the west. This lasted for the daytime but then went very light and we were back on the engine. This suited me fine, we were not short of fuel and we could motor along the direct route into Jeddah.

On the radio we heard from another rally boat, *Ailsa J*, that she was having engine trouble and one of her batteries was boiling. *Ocean Gypsy*, who had now decided to come with us to Jeddah, very generously agreed to stay with *Ailsa J* in case she needed a tow. On the morning of the 1st of March we had only 90 miles to go to Jeddah, awkward timing as it meant we would arrive in the middle of the night. But the weather is so untrustworthy in the Red Sea that I decided to press on while the going was good. We could slow up for the last few miles while waiting for daylight. That is how it turned out. The weather stayed quiet and we slowed to a dawdle for most of the night. At dawn we arrived off the entrance to Jeddah; the town was ablaze with lights and there were numerous anchored vessels outside the harbour. We called up the Port Control on VHF and explained that we needed fuel and supplies. They were very professional and soon gave us clearance to enter port. As we went towards the narrow entrance channel, with serious reefs on each side, a magnificent flight of flamingos went overhead in the morning glow. They were very pretty, morale was definitely on the up. Just inside the harbour entrance, dominated by its massive control tower, we were met by a pilot boat and guided into a large basin at the southern end of the harbour where we moored up to the quayside. The port at Jeddah is huge; it probably has room to berth about 50 large ships. The basin where we ended up was about a mile long and several large container vessels were docked there.

Not long after our arrival the inevitable military gentlemen arrived. They were from the Royal Saudi Navy. The officer spoke good English and seemed impressed with the letter from the Saudi High Commission. He offered us all the help we needed but again we were not allowed to leave the harbour area. *Ailsa J* had broken one of her engine mounts and needed to get it welded together again, the Navy did the job for him for free. John was able to help him with his battery problem, there was a dead battery in the bank and this was draining the power from the other batteries.

Several port supply agents arrived and one offered us fuel at the outrageous price of $3 a litre. However, we had been advised to contact a Captain John Nippers who soon turned up and sorted things out for us. He assured us that we would probably have to pay more for the water than the fuel! Supplies were arranged with an agent, Mr Ghaze.A.Minhali, to be delivered next day and the Navy set up a small guard post with armed men to see that we did not wander from our quay. We had grown used to the omnipresent military men in this part of the world.

We spent an uncomfortable night on that quay, as the wind got up from the north and caused quite a chop. We had to deploy every fender on the boat and I was glad I had some really big ones. Mr Minhali returned in the morning with our water cans filled ($2 each!) and our laundry which was done perfectly. He then tried to up the price for fuel which Captain Nippers had assured us should cost only 50 cents a litre. The naval officer intervened and said he would arrange an alternative supplier.

Later that afternoon the wind increased further and conditions on the wall became serious. The boats were taking quite a beating in spite of the fenders, but more worrying was that it now looked impossible to get ourselves off the wall without help. The trouble was we were moored close together and unable to get a run under engine fast enough to get away from the wall against the sea. It was obvious that something would have to be done quickly or we would end up in serious difficulty. We called Port Control and explained our plight and asked for the assistance of a tug. I think they must have appreciated the problem as the tug arrived very quickly.

It was a modern vessel, clearly very powerful, and the skipper seemed a highly skilled fellow. I volunteered to go first with *Greylag* as the smallest boat. Also we had a strong centre cleat which would allow us to be pulled out sideways before moving off under our own engine. We undid all our shorelines save one at the stern which I left in the care of Barry, an Australian crew from *Ocean Gypsy*, asking him to release it immediately I gave the signal. We then threw a line to the tug from our centre cleat and the skipper immediately started to pull us away. I signalled to Barry to let go our stern line but he thought he knew better and held on, thinking this would stop us running forward and hitting *Ocean Gypsy* in front of us. This would not have happened because the tug was pulling us clear quickly and only Barry and that stern line was preventing a clean departure. In the end the tension on the stern line increased until it was hard as steel and then it snapped, at Greylag's end. Luckily it just missed Barry as it whipped across the quay with a fearsome twang. He was a lucky man, that rope had a breaking strain of several tons! Needless-to-say, as soon as the stern rope broke we were away and under our own steam. *Ocean Gypsy* went next but elected to be pulled out by the bow. The towline broke and she hit her stern against the quay and broke the starboard davit clean off. *Nefertiti* escaped unscathed, but *Ailsa J* also damaged her stern ladder against the wall. All in all the damage could have been much worse, it had been a lucky escape.

We took a brief look at a berth on the west side of the harbour; it was downwind of an ancient steamer full of goats! After that, the Port authorities gave us a goat-free berth near the other end of the basin where things were much calmer. Soon after, the fuel lorry arrived and we all refuelled at 37.5c a litre. Mind you we each had to pay a contribution towards the hire of the fuel bowser, so in the end it was not much cheaper than if we had given in to M.Minhali in the first place!

In the morning we awoke to find that the wind had moderated a bit but was still in the north. We left Jeddah at eight o'clock and made good progress for a few hours before the wind freshened yet again to 25 knots. To make matters worse the mainsail was torn again, this time it was through a stitch line and looked easier to repair. I think the prolonged exposure to UV light must have rotted the stitching in places. We put a third reef in the sail, and as the tear was lower than this, we were able to continue to use the sail. With so much windward sailing to do this was a blessing. For the rest of that day and all through the night we continued to sail tacks against the wind and into a nasty choppy sea.

Next day the wind was much the same, I was beginning to hate the Red Sea. Then yet another seam on the mainsail gave way, above the third reef, and we had to stow it altogether. We stayed on the engine for the night and thanks to a small favourable current, made steady progress directly down the line. In the morning the wind at last moderated for a short spell and then, at dusk rapidly increased to 35 knots. This was soul-destroying stuff; it was difficult to remain cheerful knowing that we might have to put up with these conditions for several more days. We had managed to repair the top tear in the mainsail by hand sewing it and so we were able to sail on our storm jib and a triple reefed main.

Relief came sooner than expected as the wind dropped off later that night. By six o'clock next morning the sea was flat calm. What a joy that was, we all recovered our sense of humour and morale improved. Our chart showed a sheltered anchorage tucked in behind a headland at Sharm Hasy. It looked like a good opportunity to have a night's rest and to mend the damage to the mainsail as well. This was significant as we were still 250 miles from the entrance to the Gulf of Aqaba when a change of course to the north-east might bring some relief from this endless windward slog. We entered the bay at Sharm Hasy only to find a coastguard post there, we were sure they would be out to see us. The bay had some substantial coral reefs and we had to look around for a while to find a suitable place to anchor. This turned out to be smack in front of the coastguard hut. Well, at least they could not accuse us of trying to hide!

As soon as we were settled the coastguard arrived in a small boat and asked us to go ashore. John and I went, leaving Chee in charge of the boat. At the coastguard post we explained that we needed to repair our sails and I showed them that letter from the High Commission and assured them that we had been well received by the Royal Saudi Navy back at Jeddah.

'Where are you going?' they asked.

'Suez', I lied.

They were clearly not sure what to do so they phoned for an officer to come and help. While we were waiting for him to arrive, they gave us drinks and some rather sickly sweet stuff - a bit like Turkish delight. They all seemed quite friendly so we did not worry too much even though we could have used the time more usefully back on *Greylag*. Meanwhile Chee definitely was worrying. We had been gone quite some while and I suppose he was beginning to think we might have been arrested.

In due course the Captain arrived. He was a friendly fellow who had once been on an exchange posting with our own Royal Navy. He asked to keep the 'letter' so that he could photocopy it before returning it in the morning. Meanwhile he was happy to agree to us staying at anchor in the bay. Overnight the wind got up yet again, but although it whistled through the rigging we were well sheltered from the sea and the anchorage remained tenable. I was very pleased to be where we were, rather than out at sea.

Next morning the Captain returned with our letter. He was in a cheerful mood and asked if we needed water or fuel. He also invited us ashore but we declined, as we needed to complete the repairs to our sail and get on our way. He told us that the other coastguards up the coast had been informed about us in case we needed further help. That was a comfort.

By lunchtime we had completed the repairs to the sail and the wind had dropped back again to about 25 knots. We decided to press on. The sea was fairly choppy outside that pleasant little bay at Sharm Hasy but conditions slowly improved through the night. By next morning we were motor-sailing down the line for the Straits of Tiran - our entrance to the Gulf of Aqaba. Conditions stayed quiet through that night and most of the next day. Then back it came again - 30 knots on the nose, 3 reefs and the storm jib! I definitely hated the Red Sea. This time it lasted only 3-4 hours before dropping away completely. We kept going on the motor despite the fact that our fuel was getting low, any chance to get out of the Red Sea was not to be missed and we could probably find fuel somewhere in the Gulf of Aqaba.

On the 12th of March, six days after leaving Sharm Hasy, and 19 days since we entered the Red Sea, we went through the Straits of Tiran and into the Gulf of Aqaba. It was my birthday and escaping from the Red Sea was the best present I could have had. Calidris had reported 8-foot standing waves in the Straits and several other boats had a rough time getting through. But for us it was virtually flat calm and we motored on towards

Eilat for 15 miles before the wind came back from the north-east. We were back sailing tacks against the wind. However it was only a moderate breeze and not too uncomfortable.

By daybreak we had only 45 miles to go. I did a quick calculation of our fuel position and found that we had just enough to motor all the way. So we did. The view to the Sinai peninsular on our left was impressive in the morning sun. Not flat desert as I expected, but cliffs along the coast and hills in the background. Over on our right was the coast of Saudi Arabia, giving way eventually to the hills of Jordan.

As we arrived at the Israeli border an armed gunboat met us and directed us to the commercial port where the formalities were completed. The Israeli officials were friendly and efficient and the attention to security was impressive. A diver was called in to inspect the bottom of *Greylag* for bombs! The formalities complete, we left the commercial port area and made our way into the brand new marina in the midst of the luxury holiday hotels. This looked like a place in which to recover from the hardships of the last few weeks. We tied up and dived into the burger shop for lunch. I was going to forget all about sailing for a while!

19 Israel - Eilat, Jerusalem and Through the Suez Canal.

We awoke to bright sunshine for our first day at Eilat. There was much to be done and I was keen to complete the work in the few days before Janet would arrive on the 20th of March. The first task was to remove the salt from the boat and especially from our sails and canvas work. Everything was caked and the canvas was stiff with it. I had not appreciated until then that one characteristic of the Red Sea is the combination of rough seas with little or no rain. At home it nearly always rains when it blows and the salt gets washed out of sails and rigging. Here the salt remained everywhere, solid white chunks in places. We followed the example of some of the other boats and filled our dinghy with fresh water and used it as a bath for the sails. The whole boat was thoroughly hosed down; even the mast had to be done as the salt encrustation extended well above the spreaders - ample testimony to what we had been through.

With the boat thoroughly valeted, a credit to my crew's efforts, I went for a short trip around the town. There were some small supermarkets close to the marina but the bigger ones downtown were cheaper. Restaurant prices looked similar to those in the UK - at least there was a Macdonald's and a pizza place near-by. I visited the travel agent and made a booking for Janet and I to go on a day trip to Petra, in Jordan, and for a weekend to Jerusalem.

I phoned Janet, she seemed in good form and was looking forward to her visit. She would be coming with our friend Eileen who was due to join *Papa Golf*. We'd booked an apartment in a local hotel which Janet and I would have for the first week and Eileen for the second. That evening we made a bad choice of restaurant, 'The Gulf' fish restaurant, the food was dreadful and the service worse. This was a pity because there were many nicer places close at hand.

Over the next few days we completed the jobs on the boat and got her refuelled. We were all enjoying Eilat, not least because it would be some time before we had to put to sea again. This was to be one of the longest stops we had made and we certainly needed a rest. We met up with a solicitor and his wife, Tony and Isobel Oberman, who had shown a keen interest in the boat and our long trip. Later we had drinks with them in the luxurious Royal Beach Hotel where they staying, as indeed they did every year. This hotel, along with several others in Eilat, belonged to David Lewis CBE, a most charming man who happened to be a member of the RAF Yacht Club. He was already giving free drinks parties to the Tradewinders as they arrived and this was but a small foretaste of the magnificent hospitality he generously extended to all of us a little later on.

In this new relaxed mood, I summoned up the energy to get my Roland electronic piano out from the back of my berth, to see if it was possible to mend it. It was a long time since I had played it and I knew that a group of eight notes had ceased to function - long-term casualties of that storm in the Coral Sea. Although it had been only slightly splashed, I suspected that some water had got into the works. The notes were still dead, so I took the back off to investigate. Few of my readers will have ever seen inside the back of an electronic piano, I can assure them it is dauntingly complicated! With my circuit tester I methodically followed the tracks of the printed circuit boards until I came across a small area where a drop of seawater had caused the copper tracks to corrode. Luckily I was able to solder a wire bridge across the broken tracks and this restored the missing notes. It still works to this day.

On the day Janet was due to arrive I moved into our holiday apartment at the Riviera Club early and stocked it up with booze and snacks. Her plane was on time and, after a little delay with the tight security system, she arrived with Eileen on the coach from the airport. How pleased I was to see her.

The next few days were spent exploring Eilat and its surroundings. We walked along the coast to an aquarium and marine observatory, where we descended to well below sea level in a tower. At the base there were large glass windows looking out into the clear sea where the coral was alive with fish of all kinds. I liked the way the fish were free to come and go as they pleased, although I suspected a bit of judicious feeding ensured they were within range for the visitors. Outside the observatory there was a fellow offering rides on a very tired looking camel. Janet bought a ticket and told the fellow to let the animal rest for her turn. There are few more genuine animal lovers than Janet.

The day for our trip to Petra arrived and we boarded a comfortable coach and headed for the Jordanian border a few miles away. There we slowly worked our way through the tight security checks - they looked long and hard at the Moroccan stamp in Janet's passport - before we were invited to board a Jordanian coach which was not nearly as comfortable as the one we had left on the other side of the border. I suppose this was good for Jordanian employment. The new coach, complete with a Jordanian guide, by-passed the town of Aqaba and started the long ascent into the hills to the north. The terrain was without vegetation, save for a few small hamlets, but there was something attractive about those wide, bare valleys among the reddish-brown hills. I remembered thinking the same thing when we were in Yemen.

Petra was carved from the rose-coloured sandstone of the Shara Mountains that divided ancient Arabia from Palestine and Egypt. Covering some 400 square miles, the ancient city of the Nabataeans was strategically situated on a pass through the mountains. The ancient caravan route from Oman passed through the Yemen to Medina, before tracking north through the mountain pass to Petra where the weary travellers could unload their camels of their precious cargo of frankincense. The journey took about 12 weeks. At its prime, in the first century BC, Petra had a population of some 30,000 inhabitants.

We left the coach at the visitor centre and our guide led us down the long Siq, a small canyon with high cliffs on each side, that led eventually to the heart of the city. The first thing that struck us was how cold it was. Although we had been given a warning by the travel agent, none of us had come adequately clothed. We chose to walk as it kept us a bit warmer, but others went on horse-back after bargaining the price with one of the seemingly hundreds of 'taxi men' plying for hire. All along the Siq we were shown the remnants of an ancient system of pipes and channels that conveyed the vital water supply to the city - one of the secrets of its success.

After perhaps a mile we came across the magnificent edifice of the 'treasury'. The buildings were carved from the solid rock faces of the 'cliffs' and we were astonished at the workmanship of those ancient stone masons. One could still see the holes where the ancient scaffolding was inserted during the original building. A little further along from the treasury we came across a cliff full of ancient tombs, and a Roman amphitheatre. We stayed at Petra for several hours but I think we managed to see only a fraction of what is there.

We returned through the hills and, after a brief visit to Aqaba which we found to be a rather grubby town with little of interest, we returned to

Eilat, once again going through the rather tedious border security.

A few days later we were off again, this time for a two-day visit to Jerusalem. The coach left Eilat early in the morning and set off northwards towards the Dead Sea. We travelled up the large valley that separates Jordan from Israel and is a geological extension of the same fault in the earth's crust that forms the Great Rift Valley in Africa. We stopped briefly at the Dead Sea to allow some of our colleagues to take to the water. Janet and I watched; it looked a bit cold even though the extraordinary buoyancy in the salty water was interesting. We passed on along the western shore of the Dead Sea, past the magnificent hill fort at Masada and Qumran, the site where the Dead Sea scrolls were found, and so to Jerusalem.

More than any other city in the world, Jerusalem has an impact on the visitor whatever his religion. I am an atheist, despite the prolonged Christian brainwashing I received at the hands of the Anglican Church through my school years. No experience in my life has ever given me any grounds to believe in a God of any kind, although I understand how such beliefs can be created by the workings of the human mind. I believe in Darwinian evolution which, for social animals such as man, includes an evolved sense of what is necessary behaviour for the preservation of the race - a sense of right and wrong, one might call it. This is at least as soundly based as any of the variety of moral codes invented by the various religions. I was born with a brain constrained to believe only in the things it senses or calculates or can deduce as likely. I have no 'faith' as such, and no religion; I have never felt the need for either.

It was Good Friday and these thoughts were in my mind that day as I entered Jerusalem, a city so pivotal to the religious beliefs of others that perhaps there, more than anywhere, one might have gained some insight into what it is that inspires them. We started at the Mount of Olives above the Garden of Gethsemane. This was a real place. It had an ambience. The old olive trees there might possibly have witnessed the events of Jesus' last day of life. Our guide then told us we could see the grave of Robert Maxwell! That broke the spell.

At Bethlehem, after we had gone through the armed checkpoint at the start of the area of Palestinian administration, we were taken to the place that 'marks the spot where Jesus was born'. But it marked the place where the Empress Helena decreed that he was born, some three hundred years after the event. In Jerusalem's Old City, we followed a procession of committed Christian pilgrims to the Stations of the Cross along the Via Dolorosa. Their unquestioning belief in the genuineness of these places was impressive, but there is not a shred of evidence that these places have any historical accuracy, they were invented for Christian pilgrims like those we saw that Good Friday. And finally to Calvary, over which the Church of the Holy Sepulchre was built. The church is real enough, but that particular Calvary was another of Empress Helena's inventions for which there is no sound historical support. As A.N.Wilson puts it in his thoughtful *Jesus, A Life* '...when the Empress Helena found out about it, she lost no time in finding the True Cross and the Crown of Thorns, and the spear with which the side of Christ was pierced. From 336 CE onwards, those who venerate the Crucified Christ have done so in the spot where Macarius found his Calvary; but Macarius was not an archeologist, and there is absolutely no reason to associate the present site in the Church of the Holy Sepulchre with the place where Jesus died.'

I will never understand this need for symbolism, or why so many of those who believe in the story of Christ are prepared to accept such demonstrably false representations of the artefacts surrounding his life and death. I felt I was in a religious theme park. All along that route the tacky manifestations of tourism, shops full of bric-a-brac, peddlers of every kind of cheap souvenir, further dispelled any sense that one was in a Holy place. I had gone there full of scepticism; I left as I had arrived.

From Jerusalem we went across country to Tel Aviv for an overnight stay in a local hotel. Along the sea front, as if to remind us that this was but a brief sojourn from a long sea voyage, we passed a marina with yachts. The sea looked horribly rough!

Next day we tracked back eastwards to the Golan Heights, with their staggering views over the Sea of Galilee. One could appreciate why the Israelis had occupied that vantagepoint from which the opposite shore could so easily be shelled. At the southern end of the Sea of Galilee we were shown the spot where Jesus is said to have been baptised. The River Jordan was little more than a shallow stream with very little flow, presumably due to the amount of water extraction from the Sea of Galilee. A shoal of catfish drifted around, waiting for any titbits that might be forthcoming from the tourists.

From Galilee we returned to the airport at Haifa and a small aircraft returned us to Eilat in a much shorter time than it would have taken by coach. I was glad we had gone on the trip, one didn't need to believe everything one was told in order to enjoy the astonishing history that surrounds the Holy Land. We felt we had gained a little insight into the difficulties of that area and now had a better perspective into which to fit the almost daily stories of trouble between the Palestinians and Israelis.

The day after our return from Jerusalem there was to be a Gala dinner at the Royal Beach Hotel and all Tradewinders, and their visitors, were invited as guests of David Lewis. No one knew what to expect and most were astonished when they arrived. The large dining area had been extensively decorated in a nautical theme. Nets and seaweed draped the walls and ceiling, 'real' mermaids languished on beds of rock. The tables had assorted shells and sprays of glass beads that took a second glance to see that they were not actually water. The dinner was superb. In a short speech at the end of dinner, David Lewis told us he was arranging a little surprise for us the next day at lunchtime. That was all he said of it, we were just to turn up at the King Solomon's Palace Hotel at 1230.

At 1230 next day we all wandered along to the King Solomon. During the morning we had noticed that the quayside in front of the hotel had been screened off, it all looked rather exciting. What we found when we got there defied belief.

'Hello Honey', said a gaudy blonde lady with a bosom for the Guinness book of records, had it been real!

Something grabbed at my ankle and I looked down.

'Gimme a shekel' said a beggar dressed in rags!

Two drunks conducted a public quarrel over an empty bottle; another spoke in endearing terms to the head of a large fish raised between his hands from a marble slab. A belly dancer advanced upon our Commodore.

The quayside had been set up as an Arab market, stall upon stall of fruit and vegetables, fish dishes of every kind, roasts carved on the spot, every imaginable kind of exotic dish seemed to be on offer. Everything was free. There were bars for beer or wine, all free! And everywhere were these marvellously talented 'actors', who were in fact members of David Lewis' hotel staff. I had never been to anything like it before; it was all done so realistically one could have been forgiven for thinking one was dreaming. David Lewis was there with his wife and joined in with the fun he had so generously provided for all of us. I look back at that party as one of the real highlights of our trip.

The next day was the last at Eilat for Janet and the *Greylag* crew. We did the last minute shopping and enjoyed a final meal out in the brasserie of the King Solomon's Palace Hotel. In the morning we waved goodbye to Janet, who was not due to depart for the airport until after we had gone, and left the marina where life had been so agreeable. We made our way to the commercial port to complete exit procedures and then set sail for Suez.

The return trip down the Gulf of Aqaba was simplicity itself, downwind all the way. By first light next day we were through the Straits of Tiran and the Enterprise Passage into the Gulf of Suez. We knew the easy conditions wouldn't last and so we were not in the least surprised when we ran back into 25-knot headwinds! But things didn't seem so bad after our good rest in Eilat.

We tacked our way through the oilfields that night, dodging the brightly-lit rigs, with progress improving as the weather moderated. By dawn we were back motoring and making rapid progress up the eastern side of the shipping lanes. There were possible stopping places on the Egyptian coast but we decided to take advantage of the calm weather and press on all the way to Suez.

We arrived there at one o'clock next morning and anchored in the waiting area, a short distance from a number of large ships anchored in the bay. *Sheet Lightning, Calidris, Saullitaire* and *Papa Golf* all arrived at more or less the same time. Not long after we arrived, a launch belonging to the 'Prince of the Red Sea' (an agent for the canal) turned up and instructed us to follow him up to the yacht harbour. Just at that moment *Sheet Lightning* got her prop fouled with a line and asked for a tow. We were happy to oblige and the two of us followed the 'Prince' to the yacht harbour where *Sheet lightning* and ourselves moored either side of *Griffyn*. As always, *Griffyn Quay* was a comfortable place to be.

Suez was not a very attractive place but the moorings were secure and we were able to get some fuel. The formalities for booking our slot through the canal were soon completed and with a spare day available, we booked ourselves on a day trip to Cairo and the pyramids at Giza. A short coach journey took us to the centre of the city where we spent some time in the museum, admiring the treasures of Tutankamun's tomb and the many other Egyptian antiquities there. Outside the museum we had to run the gauntlet of hundreds of street traders selling miniature camels and pyramids and heads of the Pharoahs - all manner of tourist souvenirs. They were extraordinarily persistent, never giving up until one growled quite fiercely! It was here, a year later, that a frightful massacre took place when some Muslim extremists opened fire on tourists.

From the city we went by coach out to the pyramids at Giza. Everyone knows what they look like, since childhood one has seen countless images of them and their famous neighbour, the Sphinx. Familiarity, however, did not detract from the colossal impact of the real structures. It was impossible to look at those massive monuments without them invoking images of the civilisation that built them and of the thousands of slaves who toiled and died in that endeavour. They are indeed awesome, not least on account of their timeless endurance. I climbed the steep tunnel that led to the centre of the biggest of the three pyramids. There was nothing there except a small chamber, perhaps 25 feet by 12. None of the glorious treasures in the Cairo Museum can be found at the Giza site, just those four magnificent stone structures standing, as they have always stood, in the natural desert surroundings where they were built. No museum exhibition could ever compete with that.

In the evening there was a Son et Lumière show. I wondered whether this modern technique would spoil the impact already created. However, it was very well done and had a most thoughtful commentary. The laser beams knifing across the desert darkness fell upon the distant pyramids, revealing them devoid of their environment, isolated against the night sky. It was a different view and impressed me in a different way, but without their desert context I felt they lost something, the darkness diminished perspective so that those colossal creations became more like photographic images. I returned to Suez with a head full of Egyptian history.

The next day the first rally boats departed on their way through the canal. Ominous reports came back of gale conditions at Port Said. *Aditi* had to turn back when she ran into the rough seas of the Great Bitter Lakes. We hoped it would be better next day. Early in the morning our pilot turned up and we were off into the canal. There are no locks on the Suez Canal, the navigation is simple and there is no difficulty keeping out of the way of the big ships that come through in convoys of perhaps a dozen. It seemed wholly unnecessary therefore to insist that every yacht had a pilot on board, ours just sat there and did nothing except urge me to put more and more revs on the engine to shorten his journey time!

It was a cold trip against a stiff northerly breeze and we had to battle quite hard against the chop in the Great Bitter lakes. By late evening we arrived at Ismalia where we were due to stop overnight at an anchorage. I gave the pilot 200 cigarettes (we had been advised that this was the standard tip) but he was not happy with these and asked for another pack of 200. I declined and he went off rather disgruntled in the pilot's launch. We turned on the boat's Eberspacher heater to warm up; it felt more like sailing at home.

Next day a new pilot turned up. Whereas the first had seemed a bit redundant, and ungrateful for the cigarettes, this fellow was a positive nuisance. We had barely got under way when he said to me

'Captain, you are my friend' - I guessed what was coming after that - 'have you got a present for me?'

'Yes, 200 cigarettes' I replied. And so it continued at the rate of one request for a present per kilometre of canal. In the end my patience with him ran out.

'If you ask me one more time,' I said 'I won't give you anything at all.'

'Have you got any money for me?' he said, pulling his trouser pockets out to show how empty they were. I ignored that one. Later he started looking around the cabin. His eyes fell on Tigger, our ship's mascot.

'My daughter would like that' he said.

We shuffled him back into the cockpit and Chee, who is a very strong fellow, made it clear that he would be physically restrained there, if the nonsense did not stop. By the time we got to Port Said we were thoroughly fed up with him. As the pilot launch arrived to relieve us of this burden, I shoved the packet of fags in his hand together with a peaked hat from Sebana Cove. He said it wasn't enough!

'Well, I'll have them back then,' I said.

He left us as disgruntled as his colleague the day before. I must say, the Egyptian pilots on the canal are a bunch of rogues and somebody should get them under control.

At Port Said the gale of the previous day had subsided. It was teatime when we got there and as conditions out at sea did not look too bad we decided to press on right away. Reports of the comforts to be found at Port Said did nothing to deter us from this decision. We set our course for Kas, in Turkey, and sailed off into the Mediterranean night.

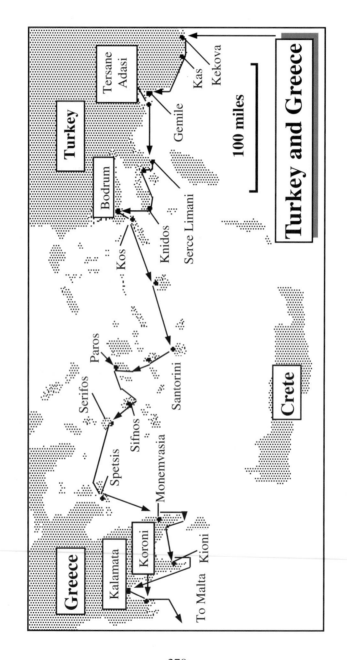

Turkey and Greece

Turkey

Tersane Adasi

Kas
Kekova

Gemile

100 miles

Bodrum

Serce Limani

Knidos

Kos

Paros

Santorini

Serifos

Sifnos

Monemvasia

Spetsis

Crete

Koroni

Kalamata

To Malta Kioni

Greece

20 Mediterranean Spring - Turkey, Greece and Malta

We had been glad to get away from the Suez Canal. Our 310-mile route would take us to the west of Cyprus and into Kas, an official port of entry to Turkey. Most of the Trade Wind fleet were heading for Crete but John was keen to see Turkey again - he had been there on a delivery trip some years before and had liked it - and I had a relative at Spetsis, one of the Greek Islands, and wanted to make a call there.

For a day and a half we made reasonable progress against a moderate headwind. Then in the afternoon of our second day the wind increased, first to 25 knots for a few hours and then up to a full gale from the north-east. This was not the Mediterranean one had heard about, although in mid-April it was still rather early to be there. We took a big wave into the cockpit that also bent one of our stanchions again. This raised again, in our minds,the spectre of that storm in the Coral Sea. I suppose one never really forgets an experience like that, and each time one subsequently meets severe conditions, one's anxiety is that much greater. The gale lasted for only a few hours and later that night the wind fell away and backed into the north-west. We started the engine and motored straight into it.

In the morning the wind started to increase yet again and by midday we had yet another full gale, this time from the west-north-west. We were just able to hold our course for Kas but progress was slow and unpleasant. We heard that several other rally boats were having a bad time getting to Crete. *Hilda* and *Ocean Gypsy* had gone to Cyprus and were safely in harbour. Doug Orchard, the owner of *Ocean Gypsy* had started his trip from Cyprus and so had completed his circumnavigation. A big party was planned. *Papa Golf* was heading for Turkey like us, but Pat's destination was Marmaris - a little further on than Kas. He too would complete his circumnavigation there. Meanwhile the two of us were struggling with the gale.

We were now only about 20 miles from Strongoli Island and Kas was just a few miles further on, 5 or 6 hours should see us in, we thought. The gale got worse however, and we studied the chart to see if there was an escape haven somewhere off the wind a little to the east of Kas. Happily there was just the place at Kekova roads, a place that Graham Watts on *Hilda* had thoroughly recommended. This was not an official port of entry but we needed to escape from that gale, preferably before darkness fell and made things still more difficult. I altered course to the east and we started making very fast progress off the wind at last.

The entrance to Kekova roads is very small and we were relieved when it showed up quite clearly on the radar. In we went over the tumbling waves, turned left and rejoiced at the marvellously sheltered conditions we found inside. I can remember to this day the bliss of that sudden transformation from the violent open ocean in a gale to almost complete calm behind those cliffs. We motored up to Sicak Bay at the western end of Kekova Roads and dropped the anchor. We could hear the wind still whistling overhead but we were comfortable and safe. We had several stiff drinks, a small meal and went to bed.

Overnight the gale subsided and we awoke to a perfect sunny morning. The sea was flat calm. All around us were rocky hills with snow-capped mountains in the distance inland. It was easy to see why this place provided such good shelter - it is almost land-locked. I would have liked to stay a day but we needed to make an official entry into Turkey, so we were soon under way. Before leaving Kekova, we motored to the east to have a look at Tersane, which had a glowing write up in our pilot book. It certainly was a very pretty place, with several interesting ruins on the beach around the tiny cove. We stayed a while and had coffee, before leaving for the short journey to Kas.

At Kas there was a good harbour and we were able to drop a stern anchor and moor ourselves bow to the quay. The town was most attractive, spread around the harbour and extending up the steep hill at the back. The cliffs rose steeply behind the town and there were ancient tombs cut into them. It looked like just the climbing job John and Chee might enjoy.

Clearing in proved time-consuming. First one went to the harbourmaster to apply for a cruising log, then over to customs to pay the fees (they were the only department with accounting facilities), to immigration for visas, back to the harbourmaster to collect the cruising permit and back again to customs for customs clearance! If only they had all been in the same part of town, but they were spread to three points of the compass.

We stayed for a couple of days at Kas, it was such a pleasant place and the restaurants were good and cheap. We especially enjoyed Smiley's.

On the 18th of April we were due to set out for Gemile. We needed to leave the harbour to empty our holding tank; the Turkish authorities are very severe on anyone caught pumping raw sewage into harbours or inshore waters. But we awoke to a stiff north-east breeze and so opted for the shorter 12-mile trip to Kalkan. We never got there. Outside the harbour we ran into a strengthening head wind and progress became tediously slow. We emptied our holding tank while we were in open water and turned back to Kas. This time we didn't go into the harbour but opted for the sheltered bay to the south. This was an attractive spot and again the cliffs were peppered with tombs. We spent a comfortable night.

By next morning the wind had gone and we motored out of South Bay and onto a course for Gemile. For a short while we got the spinnaker up in a light breeze from the east. It did not last for long before we were back motoring for the rest of the way into Gemile. The island lies close to the mainland and has very similar topography, so that it is well camouflaged. As one approaches, it is difficult to identify the way into the narrow strip of water that lies behind the island. We relied on our GPS until we were close enough to see the way in. Behind the island everything was flat calm and we anchored the boat in deep water with a line ashore for extra security.

The whole island was covered with the remains of an ancient town. No one lives there anymore but one could see that it must have once been a thriving town. It was possible to identify streets and houses, and even some drainage courses tracking down to the sea. We went ashore for dinner when the restaurateur came by in his speedboat and offered us a lift. It was simple fair - chicken and chips - served in a sort of summerhouse with two tables. At the end of the meal the owner came in with his violin and played for us. It was a stout effort but not very musical. His son drove us back to *Greylag*.

In the morning, John and Chee went ashore to climb through the ruins. Just as they disappeared over the top there was a shout from a nearby boat. I rushed up on deck to find that a breeze had come in and we had dragged our anchor. *Greylag* was perilously close to the rocky shoreline. Without my crew it was going to be a difficult job to sort her out. I quickly tied the shoreline to a fender and threw it over the side for later retrieval. Then I managed to motor in reverse to get *Greylag* alongside the other boat and tie onto her while I sorted out the anchor. This

Tersane Adasi

was retrieved without too much difficulty. I moved further up the bay and re-anchored, thinking how lucky it was that I had not also gone ashore with the others or *Greylag* would have been on those rocks. As soon as I had re-anchored, John turned up in a hurry. He had seen what had happened from the top of the hill and was quickly back on board after retrieving our shoreline and fender. Chee followed soon after and we moved the boat to a more sheltered spot at the western end of the bay.

Later that same day we moved again, this time around the headland and across the Gulf of Fethiye to a perfect anchorage in a deep inlet to the north of Tersane Adasi. This was a wonderfully protected anchorage with green hills all round and some more ruins to explore. I got my pad out and made a few quick sketches. This was the nicest place we had been in for quite some while and we sat in the cockpit with our sundowners enjoying the view and watching a flock of goats slowly making their way along the steep shoreline to a farm at the head of the inlet.

I was sad to leave Tersane Adasi next day, but time was pressing as always. Our next stop, Serce Limani, was 43 miles away across the Gulf of Marmaris. I am probably giving the impression that these stops were all carefully planned. This was not so. Most days we would set out with one

Serce Limani

or two possible venues in mind but only when we got there would we finally decide to settle or, sometimes, move on. Serce Limani turned out to be a pleasant inlet and almost as sheltered as Tersane Adasi had been. It had the added advantages of mooring buoys for visitors and a small restaurant.

Next day we planned to cross the Gulf of Symi to the harbour at Datcha, on the Datcha peninsular. The trip started well enough and we were soon around the northern end of Nimos Island and heading across the bay to Datcha. Then, quite suddenly, the wind increased ferociously from the south-east. We took all the sails off very quickly - this was a serious blow, probably around 50 knots! I soon decided that it was unwise to continue heading for Datcha. Even though it was only a few miles away, it was a lee shore and the harbour might well have been untenable in that wind. None of us had been there before so the risk seemed too high. Reluctantly I turned *Greylag* head into that blast and for more than an hour we struggled back before reaching the sheltered lee of Nimos. There we found a German boat that was also sheltering from the wind, they confirmed that the wind had touched 50 knots. The bay at Nimos was far too deep to anchor and so the two boats circled round slowly, each of us hoping the weather would moderate in time for us to find an anchorage for

Bodrum castle

the night. It did so after a couple of hours. The German boat left first and when we could see that he was coping outside the shelter of Nimos, we too left. We headed back east to get into the shelter to the north of Cape Atabol Burun and there we found an excellent anchorage at the head of an inlet just east of Point Dirsek. By the time we were settled we all felt tired and were delighted to find a restaurant there. We had a very good meal and slept soundly.

We left Dirsek early next day and quickly retrieved the ground we had lost the day before. This was a pleasant day for sailing and we decided to miss out Datcha and press on westward to Knidos. By lunchtime we were there and moored up to a slightly rickety wooden pontoon at the head of the bay. Knidos has some extensive ruins of an ancient town that covered the hill to the north of the harbour. These were most impressive and not surprisingly we found we had to pay to visit them. It was well worth the entry fee, however, and John and I spent a couple of hours exploring. There was an almost complete amphitheatre at the foot of the hill. Above that were the foundations and partially surviving pillars of several substantial civic buildings, as well as large numbers of simpler dwellings. There had been some minor attempts at restoration but mostly things lay where they had fallen.

Bodrum, our next port of call, is a very substantial town with a big harbour. It was nice to be back in touch with good facilities - showers, laundries, shops and restaurants galore. The pressure of daily moves was beginning to tell and I again felt the need to have a few hours away from my companions. They are really good with the boat but both of them are rather serious people and life could become a little dull at times. I sometimes wished we could just have a massive piss-up - hard to do with John, who I've rarely seen getting more than just slightly tiddly, and Chee who doesn't drink at all! Once the boating business is done, we don't seem to have much in common and we have little to talk about. Perhaps we've all got a bit bored with each other. In this mood, I delivered an intemperate outburst into my private diary and felt better afterwards. Diaries are a good defusing mechanism.

In the harbour at Bodrum we came across Elizabeth and Martin Svendson, who we had first met two years before in Cadiz, on our way down to Gibraltar. They had been in the Mediterranean since then. We all had dinner together. A few days later, Pat Gordon and *Papa Golf* turned up and the social side of life took a turn for the better. There was little to do on the boat now and I spent a good deal of time sketching around the town and its dramatic castle.

Bodrum was our last port in Turkey and from there it was a very short trip across the bay to Kos, our first stop in Greece. We arrived there at nine o'clock in the morning, having left Bodrum at six. Kos was another substantial town and an official port of entry. I soon completed the formalities.

We were moored next to *Andromeda*, a Westerly Discus, and soon got chatting to her new owners, Chris and Sarah Plummer. They had just purchased her at Akrotiri in Cyprus, a place I knew well from visits to the big air base there when I worked for the RAF. Interestingly they hailed from Beccles in Suffolk, near the Broads where my early sailing was done. They knew the old Ex-MTB 102 which my uncle and aunt had kept at Oulton for many years, the same who had taken us on holidays up there just after the war. The 102 is now owned by the Norfolk Sea Scouts and is quite a famous boat, having appeared in the film "The Eagle has Landed" and been a regular visitor to Portsmouth's Navy Days. It's a small world!

From Kos we set out on a 50-mile trip to Astipalia and anchored in a sheltered inlet at Vathi. There was a thunderstorm that night, but after it had passed we slept well. Next morning we left early for Santorini (or Thira as it is sometimes called). The 45-mile trip took up most of the day and we arrived around teatime. This must be one of the most dramatic landfalls in the Greek Islands. Enormously high cliffs are topped with towns and villages of white houses so that they look like white topped mountains. The whole area was created by a gigantic volcanic eruption, many times greater than Krakatoa, and which is claimed by some to have destroyed the Minoan civilisation.

We motored south in the 'crater' to a small island, Nea Kommeni, which was in fact the central plug of the volcano. We were deterred from going over to the main quay at Santorini by the sight of several large cruise ships parked there. Nea Kommeni consisted almost entirely of black volcanic boulders from which emanated a strong sulphurous odour. Anchoring was difficult because the bottom consisted of the same large black boulders, anything from 4 to 6 feet in diameter, and there was a serious chance that we would snag our anchor. We lowered it into the boulders with a tripping line attached to the far end of the anchor; this enables one to pull it up hooked end first if it becomes snagged.

We spent a peaceful night in that place despite an occasional thought that we would be blown to smithereens if the volcano erupted! Next morning a passing yacht hailed us, it turned out to be Chris and Gill Mounsey on *Pale Moon,* accompanied by John and Brenda on *Saullitaire.* Together we all moved over to Santorini and moored ourselves stern to the quay with bow lines to a large buoy.

The main town at Santorini sits along the cliff top several hundred feet above the quay. There were three ways to get to the top, on foot, by donkey or by cable car. John and Chee went first and walked up while I stayed aboard to guard the boat. A north wind had made the sea quite lumpy and uncomfortable. In the afternoon it was my turn to go ashore, I chose the easy route by cable car. Nearly all the houses were painted white and a majority of them had blue doors and windows. This created a certain amount of colour harmony, giving the town a distinctive character and style even though the houses were built higgledy-piggledy all along the cliff top and some practically into the face of it. It was an attractive place but it buzzed with tourists, 5 boatloads were delivered that day. After dinner on *Pale Moon*, we spent an uncomfortable night bobbing around on that buoy.

I went ashore first thing for a massive cooked breakfast by myself, the others couldn't be tempted. That gave me the strength to set off north against a nasty Force 6 headwind. We were hoping to get to Ios which was

278

The harbour entrance, Ios

only 19 miles away and offered the prospect of a more sheltered harbour, all three boats headed that way. It was a rough passage motoring directly into the wind and sea, but when we got there Ios provided just the shelter we had been looking for. The three boats were soon parked in the usual Mediterranean manner - sterns to the quayside and bows to anchors dropped in the harbour as we reversed into the berth. Later there were problems as a succession of large charter boats arrived, manned by slightly skilled and seriously rude German charterers, and rammed their way in between the boats already there. The final straw was when the last one, a 45-foot long, vulgar 'Tupperware' job, decided he could force his way into the 1 metre gap between us and our neighbour. The two of us hailed our objections and put a line between us to close the gap. We were treated to a hail of invective in German, but the meaning was reasonably clear. He then proceeded to pull away, taking our anchor with him! I gave him a sample of old English invective and he finally gave up and went somewhere else. We reset our anchor using our dinghy to row it out into the harbour. The rest of the evening and night were pleasantly tranquil.

I spent most of the next day painting and sketching; there was a lot of inspiring scenery. We joined up with *Pale Moon* and *Saullitaire* for dinner at a quayside Taverna. It was a meal to forget and as an aid to forgetting, we all repaired to The Talisman for some serious cheering up. That was my first experience of the local brandy 'Metaxa' and it certainly had a marked effect on one or two of my friends! That night we invented 'Metaxa Man', although my medical training suggested 'Ataxia Man' might have been more appropriate.

Next day we moved north again to Paros and eventually settled in a small cove on the west coast. There was nothing there but it was attractive and calm and we needed a good night to aid recovery from the one before at Ios. A further three miles up the coast was Paroikia, where we went next day. The old town was particularly attractive and full of artists. The streets were paved with stone slabs, the mortar joints painted white, and all the houses, a veritable rabbit warren of them, were painted in the usual colour scheme - white walls with blue windows and doors. In the sun the white walls shone out brightly while the shady sides seemed to gleam with pastel shades of blue, purple and pink. It was an inspiring place for painters and photographers alike.

It was now the 7th of May and in 15 days I had to get to Malta to meet Janet, so we planned on making daily moves to fit in as many of the islands as possible. The next one was Sifnos and we had a splendid sail there until the wind ran out behind the island. We motored for the last three miles into Ormoros Vathy. Ormoros was like a large Lulworth Cove but without the nasty swell that always seems to plague Lulworth. We found there was just enough water to allow us to moor stern to the small quayside in front of an attractive domed church. *Magic Dragon* was at anchor in the bay.

In the small village there was a shop and two Tavernas. On the beach I fell into conversation with Fritz, a German psychiatrist from East Berlin. We sat at a table in one of the tavernas and he poured me a very large glass of wine. Ormoros was his escape from a fraught previous life in the communist state and he spoke interestingly about his life and experiences in East Germany before unification. Later, I painted the picturesque church from the west side.

I was just back on board after my painting when a large charter boat approached us from the windward side. I could see at once that this looked like trouble because there would not be enough water for him at low tide and if he came alongside in that cross-wind he would not be able to get off again without running over our anchor warp which was set out to windward.

'How much water is there by the quay?' a rather pompous and

Ormoros Vathy, Sifnos

frightfully English voice called from the cockpit.

Before I could tell him, the wind had taken hold of him and he was drifting sideways fast towards us. He seemed not to appreciate the trap he would be in if he did not pull away immediately. He didn't, so he came alongside us with a bump. There was not a single fender out to cushion the bump and to cap it all, his inept crew started pushing on our stanchions to hold him off - as if they had not been bent enough already! My irritation must have been obvious; I am never one to be subtle with idiots.

'Oh dear', he said, 'I don't think we can get away without running over your anchor'

This had been obvious from the moment he came in from the windward side. He hadn't a clue how to extricate himself, although a simple line to the windward end of the quay would have held him off us while he escaped. We were about to show him how to do this when he decided for himself to put his boat in gear and drive forward over our anchor. Inevitably he snared our anchor warp around his rudder. I was furious and told him what I thought of his seamanship and general carelessness and was about to start on his ancestry, when a chance lull in the wind allowed our anchor warp to drop free below his rudder. As they went away amid a two-way slanging match I heard him say to his crew

'I don't think we want to stay here, do you?'

'That's the best decision you've made this afternoon!' I bawled back. 'Bloody charter boats', I mumbled loudly to myself.

That night the wind blew up fiercely and a German boat dragged her anchor right across the bay. They were all below decks and appeared not to realise what was happening. We yelled a warning across the water, as did Catharine on *Magic Dragon*, and finally someone appeared, but not before she had drifted right across *Magic Dragon's* anchor chain. Luckily they managed to sort out the knitting eventually by pulling the German yacht off to windward with their dinghy. After that, everyone settled down for the night. They had been lucky; if we hadn't seen them and they had missed *Magic Dragon*, the next stop would have been on the rocks!

The strong winds persisted through the next day so we stayed put in the relative comfort of the bay. I painted the church from the eastern side. A British boat *Ming* arrived and we invited Tom and Anna over for drinks before we all went to Stavrieilia's Taverna for dinner. In spite of the poor weather and excitements, we had all enjoyed our stay at Ormeros Vathy.

By the morning the weather had improved and we set sail again for Serifos. This was one of the most attractive and typical little islands we saw in the Cyclides. The houses of the 'Chora' straddled the winding road as it climbed up the high hill to the cluster of churches at the top. The old town created a 'snow-cap' of white buildings, so attractive in the late

The Church at Ormeros Vathy, Sifnos

282

afternoon when the low sun caught only one side. John and Chee walked up to the churches; it looked like hard work to me. *Ming* had come to Serifos also and we joined them again for drinks that evening.

We were off again next day, this time for the longish (50-mile) journey to Idra. It was the weekend and we found the picturesque harbour packed out with boats from Athens. We tried tying up alongside an old wooden caique but they turned us away. In the end we gave up and returned to the bay at Mandraki, about 3 miles to the east, where we found a comfortable spot to anchor. We had an excellent meal in the Taverna there.

Next day we finally made it to Spetsis and, after anchoring in the pleasant old harbour, I set out to hunt down my niece Elizabeth and her Greek husband Nikos. I had no address for them but I remembered Elizabeth saying we should just ask anyone for Nikos and they would direct us. I knew they ran a bicycle hire business so I went into the first hire shop I came across and asked if they knew Nikos. Of course they did, everyone did! I had not met Nikos before so I walked up to the young fellow mending a bike and enquired if he was Nikos. A broad smile told me he was and I introduced myself. We walked up the street to their little house to meet Elizabeth and their baby son Philipos. How surprised they all were to see us. I said I would very much like to treat them to dinner that evening and Nikos said he would arrange a place to go and call for us at six-thirty.

When the time came, they turned up at the boat in a beautiful open horse-drawn carriage. We had a wonderful ride through the town and along the coast for a couple of miles to a restaurant set among the pine trees. I love that gummy smell one gets under pine trees in the evening and the view out to sea was stunning. A Californian lady who had moved to Spetsis some years before, owned the restaurant. We had an enjoyable meal and it was great fun to hear all the details of life on that pretty island.

Elizabeth organised a party for us next evening and invited their friends along to say hello. Nikos cooked a large snapper on an open fire in the garden - it was delicious. There were two ex-pat Americans, Larry and Marco and a friend from Austria, Ursula. Also Stephanis, their landlord. It was a most interesting gathering with people of such differing backgrounds and wide experience. Stephanis gave me some photographs of how the old harbour had looked many years before.

There was now only eight days left before we had to be in Malta. We moved off next morning, heading south to Monemvasia. The old, walled

The Castle at Koroni

town on the peninsular looked attractive but we didn't have time to pay it a visit. We found a comfortable berth in the harbour and had a good night's rest. Next day we pressed on around Cape Malea and across the Gulf of Lakonia to Port Kaio. Not much of a 'port' but it was a delightful bay, well protected from most directions. The surrounding hills were dotted with houses and a large monastery dominated the northern side of the bay. At the southern end, where we anchored, there were two tavernas and in one of them we enjoyed some beautifully cooked, fresh swordfish steaks.

From Kaio we headed next day for Kalamata. There were places nearer to our route for Malta but Kalamata was an official port where we could obtain our clearance papers for Greece. On our way there we ran into a bank of fog - the first fog we had seen for two years. I felt a pang of nostalgia for the tropics, a brief yearning for the warm clear water and the white sand. Then another feeling came over me; there was something familiar here. This was more like home. Ah yes! Home was getting nearer.

At Kalamata we re-fuelled the boat and obtained our clearance papers. I phoned Janet to check that all was well and to get the details of

Valetta from Msida harbour

her flight to Malta. She told me that my son Nicholas was getting married in June, she had heard indirectly from my daughter Laurie - that's kids for you! By lunchtime next day we were on our way again south to Koroni, where we planned to stay overnight before leaving on the long trip to Malta the next day. Koroni was a stunningly attractive place and we anchored the boat right beneath the castle walls in complete shelter. This was the nicest anchorage we had found in Greece, and on our very last day.

It was the 17th of May when we set out from Koroni for Malta, a flat calm morning. We motored south to go round Venetico Island then onto 260°T - our course for Valetta harbour. Over the following 3 days we had to run the engine continuously, occasionally with the sails up as well. It was the longest calm spell of the whole trip and I was mighty glad we had topped up all our fuel tanks and cans back at Kalamata. However, it was an easy life even if a bit boring. We eventually motored into the Msida marina at Malta and settled in a good berth, although it was rather a long walk to the showers.

Msida marina, which is almost entirely devoted to pleasure boats, is in the northern arm of Valetta harbour. I found a small hotel right alongside the marina and booked a room for Janet and me for four nights,

285

she was due to arrive next day. I had been reading Nicholas Monserrat's *'The Kapilan of Malta'* and was looking forward to exploring the island a little and learning something of its stormy history.

During the day Chee had told me that he planned to leave *Greylag* at Malta and catch the ferry to Italy. His sister was touring Europe and he hoped to meet up with her. Chee had been with us ever since Thailand and had been a splendid help when we needed it most. I well understood his wish to see more of 'mainstream' Europe while he had the chance.

Janet arrived at Luqa airport and we took a taxi back to the hotel. It had been a much shorter flight than she had been used to recently, so she arrived full of energy. We wandered around the marina saying hello to everybody and then went with John and Chee to an Italian restaurant which John and I had found very good on our first evening.

For some months now, I had been considering the option of going home via the French canals. Although we would miss out on the celebrations that were planned for Gibraltar, when many of the boats would complete their circumnavigation, the canal route would avoid the long slog up the Portugese coast and across the Bay of Biscay. We would complete our own circumnavigation at the entrance to Portsmouth harbour, the first spot where we would cross our outward track. With Chee leaving, the decision was finally confirmed, as we could get to the entrance to the Rhône in easy stages with just the two of us. Janet was quite keen to do some of the canal system with us and we made a plan for her to come out to Lyons and join us soon after we had completed the long struggle up the Rhône against the flow. This, as you will see, was a fateful decision.

During the 10 days of Janet's visit we explored most of Malta. We visited the ancient city of Mdina and admired the attractive architecture there. Janet has always had a fascination for graveyards, so the ancient catacombs - those underground mazes with the stone coffins set in alcoves in the walls - were a special interest. In Valetta itself we watched the 'Malta Experience' - a film of Malta's valiant wartime struggles for which she was awarded the George Cross. We visited the Lascaris war rooms, from which much of the wartime activities in the Mediterranean were directed. We found the excellent commentary there and the realistic tableaux gave a better feel for what had happened than the film we had seen earlier. At the ancient temples at Hagar Qim, dating from 3-4000 years BC, we eavesdropped on a guided tour and learnt a little of their history, but were disappointed that there were no explanatory booklets to buy.

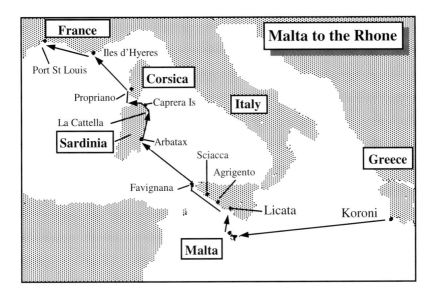

The day for Chee's departure arrived and, loaded up with more backpacks than an Arab donkey, he set off for the harbour to catch his ferry. We would miss him. Eventually it was Janet's last day also. Ominously (for John and I) the weather was becoming unsettled and for that last day it blew a gale. John treated us to dinner at the Manhattan by the marina.

The weather next day had improved and several of the rally boats departed on their way through the Balearics to Gibraltar. I took Janet out to the airport and, after some frustrating delays due to a computer breakdown at the check-in, she departed. It would be only a few weeks before I would be seeing her again at Lyons.

The next morning, the 3rd of June, John and I set out north at the start of our trek through the Mediterranean playgrounds of the rich, to Port St Louis and the Rhône. We left Msida and made our way against a northerly breeze to Gozo, passing through the South Comino Channel before going north to Dwejra Bay. We anchored there for the night, as it was comparatively sheltered. The huge rock at the entrance to the Bay is known as 'Fungus Rock' because a type of fungus is found there which has powerful medicinal properties.

The trip next day was a long one - 64 miles to Licata on the south coast of Sicily. We made an early start and the very light conditions meant

Sciacca, Sicily

that we had to motor-sail all the way. Licata was a large and well-protected harbour with a brand new sea wall. There were numerous fishing vessels occupying every available bit of quayside so we decided to anchor. But just before John dropped the hook, a fellow hailed us from the corner of the harbour and helped us tie up alongside in a space we had not spotted until then. We were visited by several 'locals' who discussed *Greylag*'s features knowledgeably (I think) but no one in authority turned up.

We left early and quietly, hoping not to be caught by the customs. Not that we had anything to hide, but we were anxious to make rapid progress while the weather lasted. We set off for Sciacca and enjoyed some fast downwind sailing for a while. Then the wind increased to an uncomfortable 20+knots and we heard on Palermo Radio that there was a gale warning for the area. We abandoned our plans for Sciacca and turned right for Empedocle Harbour. Before we got there we noticed in the distance another yacht disappearing behind a wall in the region of Agrigento and it seemed possible there was a harbour there. We approached carefully and sure enough a brand new sea wall appeared with an obvious marina behind. The sea was rough in the entrance and we shot in over the breaking waves at a rate of knots.

Inside the sea was flat but the fierce wind made mooring difficult. We tied up alongside another boat, but someone told us he would be leaving later and suggested a move to one of the pontoons further into the

288

harbour. Ordinarily this would have been an easy move but the strong cross wind made it difficult. It was one of those berthings that you line up for, hold your breath and go. Once in it was comfortable. A trio of Sicilian yotties came by and took a keen interest in *Greylag*. Alberto and Miguel were two of them, but I forget the third one's name. Neither John nor I could speak Italian but we got through after a fashion in French, with a good deal of hand signs. We shared a bottle of wine with them. Nobody charged us for the berth!

The wind had decreased by the next morning and had gone round to the north, leaving a much calmer sea in the lee of the land. We motored westward for a while but the calm didn't last and we soon found ourselves once again bashing into a nasty headwind. We could barely make three knots and it took us until three o'clock that afternoon to make the entrance to Sciacca. It was a mighty relief to get into that harbour and find a nice calm anchorage at the western end. An Australian yacht *Court Jester* was close by and we invited Robert and Joyce Denny over for drinks. They were from Brisbane. Robert told us that the local customs people did not want to be bothered with yachts! This relieved my growing anxiety at having not yet cleared into Sicily. They told us there were good shops and banks in the town above the harbour so we decided to stop for a day.

We spent a pleasant day at Sciacca replenishing our stores and refuelling. Tony and Marie from *Emily*, a small catamaran, came over for drinks. They had come down to the Med through the canals, following in reverse the same route as we had planned. They were able to give us much useful information.

For our next leg we planned to get to Favignana, an island off the western tip of Sicily. At last we had nice quiet weather and we motor-sailed all the way. We came round the eastern end of the island and thought we had only to turn left along the northern coast to run up to the harbour at Favigna. We were wrong! As we got to within a mile of the harbour a loud horn sounded from a fishing boat parked just outside. We had seen the tell-tale floats of a large tunny net offshore but assumed they would have left a passage for boats approaching the harbour inshore from the east. But they had not done so and the boat was warning us that there was no way through. They gesticulated a message which we interpreted as a request to go right round the far end of the net and come in from the west. We turned around and followed the net floats until we came to the end, which was almost two miles to the north-east. We were irritated later when we saw two motor boats come out of the harbour and run directly east inshore. *Greylag* only draws 5 feet and it looked as though we could have got through easily.

Eventually we arrived at the harbour from the west, after a detour that had taken more than an hour. The harbour was beautifully sheltered and we tied up with our bow to the quay, alongside a Dutch boat. I took an evening stroll around the little town and found it a pleasant place with most of the basic shops and several restaurants. In an inner harbour there were some really ancient wooden fishing boats, they were clearly not in use and looked as though they were being preserved as museum pieces. Their timbers were black with a mixture of old age and tar and they had large wooden capstans that might have been for controlling tunny nets.

After a peaceful night at Favignana, we left early next day for the 165-mile trip to Arbatax on the east coast of Sardinia. This was the first overnight trip John and I had made on our own and it all went smoothly. We stood 4-hour watches to allow a reasonable sleep. By mid-afternoon next day we arrived at Arbatax and were about to enter the rather unattractive commercial harbour, when we noticed a small cove just south of the harbour entrance. We went to explore and decided it was a good spot to stay for the night. In the early evening the place was swarming with bathers from the town, it was obviously a popular place to swim, but they soon disappeared and the place became peaceful.

We split the journey up the east coast of Sardinia into two legs. The first took us up to La Cattella where we found a new marina, good but expensive. We ate out in the town, and spent the rest of our Italian money on a few bottles. Next day we headed up, past the impossibly expensive Porto Cervo, where the wealthy take their gin palaces, and on to Caprera, an island off the north east coast. We found a pleasant sandy bay to anchor for the night.

Next morning we started early and motored through the Bonefacio Straits in virtually flat calm conditions. This was a relief as the place has a reputation for being nasty in bad weather. As we approached the southern coast of Corsica a fast launch marked 'Douanes Francaise' appeared from behind some large rocks where he appeared to have been hiding. They circled us once and studied us through binoculars before pushing off again. It was nice to know we looked so innocent! We rounded Cap de Zivia at the south-west of Corsica and then proceeded up the coast to Propriano. There we found another new marina and were just in time to refuel before the manager closed down for the day. The charge for the berth was 160 francs but when I passed him 2x100 notes he accepted 100 francs as he had no change. That was still quite enough - with charges like that we knew we were back in European waters. We ate out at Joey and Nadira's. We were the only customers which worried us at first but the meal was excellent - the soupe de poisson and crabe gratinière were superb, the rouget less so.

It was still calm in the morning and we motored out to Cap Muro before setting a course for the eastern end of Ile de Porquerolles in the Iles d'Hyère group. This was going to be our second overnight trip. All day the wind remained light and we motor-sailed just free on port tack. Then in the evening the wind freshened a lot and we were soon reefed down and hard on the wind. When I came on watch at midnight I put a second reef in the main. Soon after, we began to be headed again and the mainsail was doing a fair bit if flapping. I had just decided to take it down - I had postponed this too long because it meant waking John - when it split again from luff to leach - this was the third time! I called John out of bed and we took the sail down and continued on the engine, at least we had plenty of fuel.

By dawn the wind had dropped a little and we made reasonable progress. It didn't last, however and by mid-morning it was again blowing quite hard. I studied the chart and decided that we would be better off going to Ile Port du Clos which was 7 miles nearer and, more importantly, would free us 10° further off the wind and make things easier. We made it by mid-afternoon and ran into the blissful calm of Port Man, a sheltered bay on the north-east corner of the island. The bay was full of boats - it was a Sunday and these islands are within easy reach of several of the big mainland towns. We took full advantage of *Greylag*'s shallow draft and found a gap very close to the shore. After our rough trip we were both dog-tired and slept like logs after a meal of Fray-Bentos steak and kidney pies bought in Malta - delicious! I decided to leave mending the torn mainsail until we were in some quiet spot up the canals.

We awoke refreshed by a good night's sleep and also by the growing awareness that we had nearly finished with the sea for a while. That was a nice thought! We motored away from Ile Port du Clos, crossed tracks with a French submarine leaving Toulon and continued westward to Ile Maire. From there we turned north and enjoyed a spectacular view of Marseille and the Chateau d'If, famous for the story of the 'Man in the iron mask'. We were able to sail close by the Chateau and got some good photos before rounding Ile de Frouil and gaining the shelter of a small cove, Port de

L'Eoube, which we shared with a French yacht. A couple of nudists were wandering around on the rocks. The gentleman was fishing, which seemed to me to pose the same dangers to a nudist as does cooking.

The 17th of June was the occasion for our last sea journey before the canals. There was a light north-west wind so we motored directly into it, crossing the Baie du Fos, passing through the anchored oil tankers and into the Canal du Port St Louis. This canal is only a mile or so long before it opens out into a square harbour with walled quays all round. As we entered we could see, in the far left-hand corner, the large lifting bridge which allowed boats through into the lock and thence into the Rhône River. To the right was a yacht harbour and we settled in there. We had left the sea for a while; I had looked forward to this moment and savoured the prospect of the rivers and canals of France.

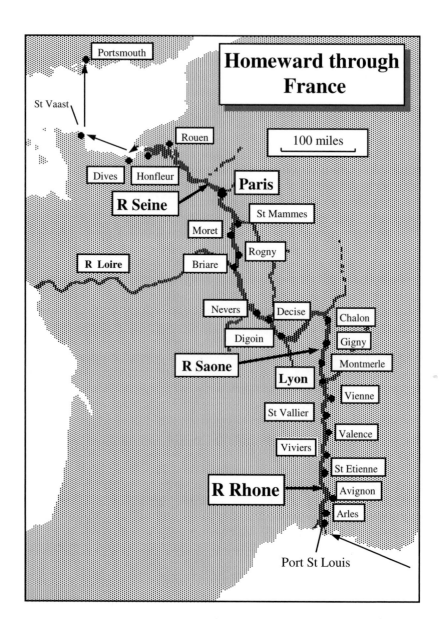

Portsmouth

St Vaast

Rouen

100 miles

Dives   Honfleur

Paris

R Seine

St Mammes

Moret

Rogny

R Loire   Briare

Nevers   Decise   Chalon

Digoin   Gigny

R Saone   Montmerle

Lyon

Vienne

St Vallier

Valence

Viviers

St Etienne

R Rhone   Avignon

Arles

Port St Louis

Homeward through France

294

21 Homeward Through the French Canals

Soon after arriving at Port St Louis, I scouted round to discover how one got the necessary permits for the canal and what one did to get the mast taken down and stowed on deck. Both were simple, the offices of VNF (Voies Nationale Fluviales, the canal authority) were right alongside the lock and just through the lock was a long established boat yard, M. Messiant, who would take our mast down whenever we turned up. Everything looked to be straightforward and with our minds set at rest we went out for dinner and back for a long and peaceful sleep.

Wednesday 18 June

The formalities were dealt with quickly and efficiently; it took thirty minutes to obtain the necessary licence from the offices of Voies Navigable de France (VNF), and to purchase some canal guides from the local chandlery. Everything was straightforward, there were none of the difficulties I had read about in going, for example, from the English canals to the River Thames or the Wey Navigation. Just one authority and one licence required to traverse the whole of the French waterway system, the licence for 6 weeks cost about £120.

We spent the rest of the morning preparing the mast for unstepping. In the calm waters of Port St Louis, we were able to remove all the shrouds and stays save for the two cap shrouds and the inner forestay - those three wires held the mast up well enough. We stowed the sails and the boom and prepared a sling for the crane to hook on to the mast for the lift. By lunchtime all was ready and we moved over to the quay by the lifting bridge to await the next lock opening which was due at 1430.

On time, the bridge opened and we were soon through the lock. Just on the river side of the lock we tied up alongside Monsieur Messiant's boat yard. I looked at the ancient old crane there and wondered when its sell-by date might have been, but it was the only one available unless we returned to the sea (perish the thought) and when I had enquired the day before, the

295

price quoted was a mere 200 francs. I popped my head round the shed door to announce our arrival to a group of yard workers sitting around a large table, playing cards. They nodded, and I glanced anxiously at the bottle of Pernod! By mid-afternoon nobody had emerged from that shed to attend to our mast, and my further enquiries were met with an assurance that they would do it in the morning! To tell the truth, I was more relieved than annoyed at the delay, drink and crane driving seemed particularly incompatible.

We got talking to Michael and Carry Hoffman on their beautiful motor boat *Van Hof.* They had come down the river and were spending a few days tied up at Messiant's yard before returning up the river. Michael was a model railway enthusiast and astonished us when he said he had one on board. You couldn't do that at sea! Later a small German yacht, a shark 24, joined us on the quay. Her skipper Frank Pohl, was heading home via the waterway system and his route was the same as ours as far as Chalon sur Saône.

We spent the evening watching a waterborne jousting match. The boats, one red and one blue, had a raised platform on the bow where the 'gladiator' stood with a long pole at the ready. The boats then approached each other from opposite directions, driven slowly by an outboard. As they closed, the poles were raised as each protagonist attempted to pole the other off his perch. They were allowed to use only one hand to control the pole. Enthusiastic, partial and noisy onlookers cheered them on. As often as not both poles would find their target on the chest of the opponent and it was then a question of who managed the hardest shove while keeping his own foothold. Sometimes it was a draw as both fell ignominiously into the water. It was great fun.

Thursday 19 June

At the crack of dawn, the crane driver arrived and within the briefest time imaginable, and with consummate skill, removed our mast and laid it neatly along the deck. As soon as we had everything stowed neatly we left the yard and motored out into the river. The journey up the Rhône was fascinating but time-consuming against the stiff current of 2-3 knots. We had heard that earlier in the year, when the melting snow on the Alps runs into the river, the current could reach 8 knots in places. That would have been impossible for *Greylag*, her maximum speed was around 7 knots. The river passed alongside the Camargue but we saw little of the famous wildlife as the banks were heavily wooded. By late afternoon we arrived at Arles. There we moored alongside a neat pontoon or *halte nautique*, the first of many such stopping places, all beautifully maintained and free. Frank on Shark joined us.

Friday 20 June

Arles is a picturesque town and an inspiration to painters, perhaps the most famous of them was Vincent Van Gogh. I enjoyed the day hunting down the various sites where Van Gogh had created some of his most memorable works. I found that the famous old Dutch bridge had been removed from its original site out of town, for preservation. They were planning to rebuild it closer to the city centre for the tourists. The 'little yellow house' in the painting was no longer there, but the buildings behind it were much as they had been. A mill he had painted was still there and one could sit beside the river and see the view he painted in 'La nuit étoilé'. The local authority had placed rather good reproductions of his paintings at each site - a novel and interesting way to allow visitors to compare Vincent's view with the present one.

Saturday 21 June

We moved on up the river to Avignon where a splendid marina allows one to moor in full view of the famous bridge. Actually it is only half a bridge these days, but attractive all the same. We were advised by some locals that the well-known song 'Sur le pont d'Avignon....' got it wrong. The dancing took place *sous* le pont. I admired the glories of the old Pope's palace; they resided in Avignon before resettlement to Rome. Popes were powerful people in those days and the admonishment not to lay up treasures on this earth was not much in evidence around that impressive palace. The next morning it rained but cleared up by lunchtime. There was a music festival in the town and I sat in the square opposite the palace doing a sketch and listening to a splendid brass band playing Wagner. The sea seemed a very long way away. I was really enjoying the river.

Monday 23 June

We left Avignon at seven o'clock and plugged against a strong current up to the first lock above the town. I was amazed that they opened the lock immediately for us, even though we were the only boat waiting. Once past Roquemaure the current decreased and we made faster progress up past the huge atomic power station near Cadolet, and on to St Etienne des Sorts where a nice pontoon had been placed to encourage visitors.

St Etienne was a sleepy little town with two shops, a café-bar, and an excellent co-operative 'caves' selling the local Côtes du Rhône. We replenished *Greylag*'s 'cellar'. In the evening we thought we would try the little café for dinner. Madame seemed pleased to see us. We soon realised

Le Pont d'Avignon

that there was no menu as such, one simply accepted whatever the 'plate du jour' was for that day. It was very good indeed and the 4 courses with coffee cost the princely sum of 70 francs each.

Tuesday 24 June

We stayed at St Etienne des Sorts as my daughter Laurie and husband Willie, who were touring France at the time, had planned to try to meet us. They arrived in due course and we toured the local vineyards. Laurie bought several cases for themselves and for us, she was particularly attracted to Domaine de Veille Fontaine - her married name is Fountain. Unfortunately they could not stop for long, as they had to be back at Macon that night.

During the day a large hotel péniche, 'Napoleon', turned up and moored alongside some stout posts just upstream of us. We had been expecting her as her Captain, Nick Borland, was our friend Eileen's son and we had made contact with him on the phone earlier. That evening we were invited aboard for drinks. Inside, the barge was truly luxurious and her passengers, wealthy Americans for the most part, showed great interest in hearing about our voyage. She was fitted out in a traditional style with no thought of the cost and she had an expert chef on board and a wine

The hill village of Viviers

cellar that would have matched the classiest of restaurants. It was one of those cruises where if you needed to know the cost, you couldn't afford to go.

Wednesday 25 June

Today we entered the serious wine country. One could read the famous names on the vineyards as we passed - Hermitage, Cote Rotie, Chateauneuf du Pape and the wine makers - Jaboulet, Guigal, Henri Bonneau. The huge engineering works undertaken during the partial canalisation of the river impressed us. At Bollène we passed through a colossal lock with a rise of 23 metres, the highest in the VNF system. To enter one ran in through an archway, the lock chamber being so high that it was unnecessary for the gates to extend the full height of the lock. There were extra gates half way along the lock chamber so that for small craft like us they used only half the lock. This speeded things up considerably. Going through was not difficult, there was little turbulence and tying up was made easy by the floating bollards, which moved up, with the water.

Above Bollène we struggled against a fierce stream through the Donzère Gorge, making barely a knot over the ground in some places. The bridges posed a particular difficulty as the narrowing between the pillars accelerated the current and we had to leave the edge of the river where the stream was less. I wondered how Frank would manage as his little boat was powered only with a small outboard. The scenery was spectacular in the gorge, rocky cliffs and hills on both sides. The newly built track for the TGV trains ran adjacent to the river in places. We were pleased to arrive at Viviers where we found a good quay to moor for the night. Frank made it all right. The town was perched on the top of a hill behind the tiny harbour - it was very sketchable.

Thursday 26 June

A long 50-kilometre leg and 3 locks took us up to Valence. There we found a modern marina with full facilities. We were able to refuel the boat, which was a relief as the struggle against the current had run us quite low.

We decided to stay put for a day at Valence and I finally summoned up the energy to mend the latest tear in our mainsail. There was a good flat area of grass by the marina which enabled us to spread the whole sail out. This made the job much easier - an important consideration, as we had to sew in a complete new panel. There was no electricity supply however and we had to use the old Singer in manual mode. A South African, Basil, very kindly helped us feed the sail through the machine. Afterwards we all went for dinner at the cafeteria in the local holiday hotel and then back to Basil's boat for drinks. An English couple, Susie and Tony, joined in - they had recognised *Greylag* from an article in Yachting Monthly.

Saturday 28 June

An uneventful day took us up to St Vallier where we found a peaceful spot to moor on a concrete wall miles from anywhere. The peace was disturbed for a short while when an enormously powerful speedboat turned up and demonstrated its capability to the full. We realised that we had chosen a bit of river where unlimited speed was allowed. It rained that evening. Next day we moved up to Vienne. The river was flowing fast through the town but we found a quiet little backwater with a nice quay and enough depth for us to get in. The 'quiet' was relative to the current in the river, but it was a noisy place as we were almost under the main A7 motorway and there was a railway alongside!

We decided to stay at Vienne for a day. It rained on and off for all of it. The town was substantial and there were some interesting Roman ruins near to our backwater. There was a superb 'Le Clerc' supermarket near-by; they even had a stock of Etienne Guigal CDR at a reasonable price.

Tuesday 1 July

We finally made it to Lyons, after 323 kilometres against the flow since our start at Port St Louis. Just before the city we departed from the Rhône River and turned left into the Saône. We found a quiet mooring in the heart of the town at Quai Marechal Joffre.

The weather, which had started to go wrong back at Vienne, was still very changeable. I hoped it would improve for Janet who was due to arrive on the 3rd. Next day I found a small hotel and booked us in for a couple of nights, and I bought canal guides for the rest of our journey from the local chandler. It rained all day - most depressing. John and I went out for moules and frites in the evening to cheer ourselves up. There was a small Dutch motor boat on the *quai* with Joannah Linden on board. She was waiting for her husband Pieter to arrive and was pleased to have company, as she was nervous about one or two shady characters who turned up on the Quai from time to time.

Thursday 3 July

It was still raining! I invested in a rather gaudy umbrella before boarding the airport bus to go to meet Janet. Her plane was on time and we were soon back in Lyons where we moved into the hotel. It was still raining so we had a stiff drink with John on *Greylag* and found a nice restaurant for a meal out.

The following morning it was still raining! Then it cleared up briefly in the afternoon, long enough to allow Janet and I to explore a little bit of Lyons. We especially liked the area around St Just, the old part of town just across the river from our mooring. We found an extraordinary wall painting there. The whole of one end of a building had been painted with a scaffolding structure with people on the various levels. By the clever use of perspective and shadowing the whole 'mural' had been made to look 3D, it was most impressive. That evening we invited John and Joannah, from the Dutch motor boat moored next to us, to join us for dinner. We offered them showers in our hotel room for starters. The offer was gratefully accepted - although we did get some rather strange looks from the lady at the desk in the hotel. I think she thought we were all going to sleep together! The meal was a Gourmand Matefaim, a local speciality, and was delicious. Platefuls of plain crêpes arrive and a dozen different dishes sit on a large rotating tray, placed in the middle of the circular table. It is a thoroughly sociable meal and much easier and more satisfying than the average fondue.

Saturday 5 July
Yes, it was still raining. But as we set off up river the weather improved and the trip became enjoyable. Here was quieter countryside, less industry and none of the huge power generation facilities of the Rhône system. The Saône itself has a gentler aspect, still a strong current but much less than in the Rhône. We made good progress and completed the 52 kilometres to Montmerle by teatime. This was a delightful small town with a good supermarket and interesting places to explore. As the weather had definitely improved we decided to stay put for a day. There was an excellent pontoon at Montmerle and we found Frank in his *Shark 24* already there, he had left Lyons the day before.

Janet and I explored the town next day. It was a beautifully kept place, everything looked clean and tidy and all along the waterfront were stone 'baskets' decked out with flowers. There were more martins' nests than human houses. We walked to the top of the hill and wandered round the little *Chapelle* built at the top. The view over the river valley was impressive. John cooked a curry for dinner which nearly exceeded the pain threshold!

Monday 7 July
We had intended to stop at Tournos, but when we got there we found the pontoon already full of boats and nobody offered to let us park alongside them. It didn't look all that comfortable anyway, so we moved on another 11 kilometres to Gigny. There we found an old disused lock that had been converted into a small harbour. The lock keeper's cottage had been turned into a facility with showers, water supplies and a small restaurant. It was a quiet spot and there was a glorious field of sunflowers alongside us. I loved the way they all turned their heads towards the sun, but I supposed that the view would be less attractive if one happened to be on the other side.

Tuesday 8 July
We pressed on to Chalon. The marina there is excellent provided one can find a berth on the inside. Outside the main pontoon, the current runs quite strongly and we saw several boats getting into difficulties as they tried to moor up. It looked like a place where one's boat could get knocked around, especially with a mast sticking out at each end.

Between the marina and the town was an island, Ile St Laurent, with several inviting little restaurants. Frank had chosen one of them and booked a table. He asked us to join him for dinner, as this was the last evening we would be with him. He would be travelling further up the

Saône, whereas we would soon be turning left into the Canal du Centre. The restaurant he had chosen specialised in *escargots* but other things were on the menu and the meal was absolutely delicious. Janet and I had smoked pork - it was very tasty.

Wednesday 9 July

We left Chalon early and soon completed the short journey to the entrance to the Canal du Centre. How small that waterway seemed after so much time in those big rivers. Once through the first lock at Chalon the canal stretches through the glorious countryside of the south-west corner of the Cote d'Or. Everything was on a smaller scale now. After the grandeur of the great southern rivers, here was a waterway more like home - albeit not quite so narrow. Around each corner we found an enchanting village or a field of sunflowers, their heads all facing the same way as usual and smiling. I am sure they smile in the sun. I have rarely seen so many herons. We would spot them up ahead and then, just as I was ready with the camera, off they would fly to settle 100 metres further on, ready to be disturbed once more. Only occasionally would a more intellectually gifted one fly back behind us for a more lasting peace!

I think it was here that I first started thinking of the future and that perhaps a canal boat could be our next adventure. After so much ocean, the sea had lost some of its attraction and the thought of sailing in the overcrowded Solent again or crossing the channel to France, which I had done more than a hundred times before, did not seem to have much appeal. I sensed that Janet was thinking along similar lines. She certainly seemed to be enjoying the canal. The peace and tranquillity, the picturesque surroundings, the lack of worry over the weather (we did not even listen to the forecasts) - somehow we both knew here was an alternative boating life. Less challenging, perhaps, but every bit as rewarding. 'Live the dream' they had said when encouraging us to sail round the world. I am glad we did so, but now we had lived that dream. Now another was taking its place, the hopes and plans of a new adventure were steadily dispelling my jaded spirits. We could sell *Greylag* and buy a canal boat instead. But we were not even home yet.

The locks in the Canal du Centre were mostly automatic. One ran into the lock chamber and when ready pulled on the blue cord (there was a red one to stop everything in an emergency). The gates then closed behind us, the paddles opened and the lock filled up. Then the gates in front opened and off we went. And through all that process one didn't have to do a thing. Even where the occasional lock was not automated, there was always someone there to operate it. John gave them a hand, in some cases with great enthusiasm - operating the locks seemed to be a common holiday job for some very attractive young lady students!

Our first night on the Canal du Centre was spent at Santenay and Joannah and Pieter joined us there. We wandered around that famous wine district but the bottles were rather expensive and we still had cases of Côtes du Rhône in *Greylag*'s stores.

Thursday 10 July

This was a hard workday, especially for John who did most of the help with the lock gates where needed. We managed 23 locks and got all the way to Montchanin where we found a good berth at the 'Connoisseur' charter company's base. This was the top of this part of the canal and next day we would be going downhill again.

We had a bit of a fright at one of the 'automatic' locks. Just as we were going in, the doors started to close. Fearing that we might be crushed, (those hydraulically driven gates looked pretty powerful) I gave *Greylag* full throttle and we shot into the lock with just a small bump from one of the gates as we went in. I was pleased we were not having any more trouble with reverse gear, as I needed full reverse power to stop before hitting the gates at the other end. For several locks after that I worried each time we entered but that was the only time the automatic system went wrong for us.

Friday 11 July

The day's journey took us downhill to Palinges, a small town famous as the original source of the Charolais breed of cattle. At the *quai* there we had our first experience of difficulty with *Greylag*'s keel. The canals are sometimes dished and quite shallow at the edges and we found each time we tried to go alongside the keel would hit bottom and prevent us getting close. Eventually we went in bow first and that enabled us to get on and off from the front of the boat although the stern stuck out rather a lot. We were hard aground and I was a little concerned about what might happen if one of the large commercial péniches came by. As they pass they push water in front of them and this causes a dip in the water, sometimes by as much as 6 inches. This would have heeled us over quite a bit, but it never happened.

Saturday 12 July

We had trouble leaving our mooring and escaped only after much pulling and shoving. Perhaps the water level had dropped a bit overnight, I wasn't sure. We stopped briefly at Paray le Monial where we were able to tie up alongside a large 'Le Clerc' supermarket. We stocked up for a long weekend as Monday would be Bastille Day and the shops would be shut.

Along this section of canal we were depressed to see large numbers of dead carp. We asked a lock keeper what had caused the trouble which we assumed was some sort of pollution. He said it was due to the high water temperatures. We pressed on through Digoin, where the Canal du Centre runs into the Canal Latéral à la Loire, and stopped for the night at Pierrefitte sur Loire. Again we had difficulty with the keel and had to moor with the stern sticking out a bit.

Next day we did another long stretch to Decize where we had planned to stop for the Bastille Day celebrations. We took a brief look at the public port alongside the canal but it was most unattractive and sited amongst industrial buildings. There was a lock which connected through to the River Loire and was the way through to the Canal de Nivernais, an alternative route through to the Seine above Paris. I had not considered this because the Nivernais was too shallow for us and even this part of the upper Loire had shallow patches. But there was a nice looking quay across the river, the Quai du Courlis, just below the bridge into Decize. We decided to give it a go and it was very nearly a disaster!

We emerged from the lock to find a narrow channel between the wall and a small green starboard buoy. I steered *Greylag* right down the middle and we went hard aground. Just behind us, a tourist boat full of passengers had emerged from the lock and was only just able to stop before hitting us. It was lucky he was there because the skipper, who probably new every hump and bump in the river, came forward and indicated that we would probably get through if we went closer to the wall. We tried this and he was right.

After that, I let the tourist boat pass us and then followed carefully in his wake. We took a brief look at the entrance to the River Aron, but a sign warned that it was only 1 metre deep so we settled for the quay below the bridge and found a comfortable berth there. After dinner, Janet and I strolled around the town and came across a concert about to start in the square. It was another brass band and we sat and listened to them for a while, but they were not as good as the one at Avignon.

Monday 14 July

Bastille Day. It was nice to have a day without moving. I had heard that delivery skippers could get a boat through the canal system in about three weeks. It must be very hard work; we were finding our 6-week schedule quite tough enough.

In the evening we all went round to the Quai de l'Office du Tourisme on the River Aron side of the town for a magnificent firework display. It was a completely professional show, complete with remote electronic ignition and very spectacular.

Tuesday 15 July

It was our wedding anniversary - our 19th. The day's trip took us back into the canal, this time without going aground on that hump. The canal still tracked alongside the Loire River, sometimes only a few hundred metres away. After five locks we came to the magnificent aqueduct across the River Allier at Le Guetin. The River Allier runs into the Loire just below the aqueduct. On the way there we passed a couple in a canoe and while we were waiting for the green light for the aqueduct, they came alongside. Their names were Wilma and Edwin and they were on holiday from Holland. They had been canoeing down the Loire and were upset because they had been capsized in some rapids and had lost their camera. We offered them a tow across the aqueduct, which they were happy to accept.

The aqueduct was 343 metres long and wide enough for one-way traffic only. Once the green light came on we set out across the valley with Wilma and Edwin in tow. At the other end we ran into the double lock that takes you down a total of 9.5 metres. We then pressed on, still towing our friends, to a splendid *halte nautique* at Cours les Barres.

Wilma and Edwin set up their tent ashore in no time flat - they were really expert campers. Then we all joined up for dinner, pooling our resources, which included a bottle of champagne for the anniversary.

Wednesday 16 July

After another strenuous day and nine more locks, we reached St Thibault where a side branch from the canal led us to a comfortable small harbour. This branch originally connected through to the Loire but the lock had fallen into disrepair, probably because of the navigational difficulties in the river which is shallow at this point. On the high hill behind St Thibault is the town of Sancerre, surrounded by acres and acres of vineyards. It was an easy decision to stay for a day's rest.

Next day Janet and I climbed the long hill up to Sancerre and looked around the town. It was clearly a popular place for tourists and there were dozens of *caves* selling the local produce. But we had bought several bottles from the harbourmaster at 43 francs, cheaper by far than those in Sancerre itself. In any case, it was a long way up that hill and I didn't fancy carting bottles as well. When it was time to return we looked for a way down through the vineyards instead of that long winding road up which we had struggled in the heat of the day. Luckily we found a footpath that led directly down the hill to St Thibault. It ran along the edge of a large vineyard and we had a good look at that year's Sancerre ripening in the sun.

Back at the boat we discovered that Joannah and Pieter had arrived. We had a Sancerre tasting and firmly decided that the harbourmaster's selection was streets ahead of that from the local supermarket. We resolved to buy some more.

Friday 18 July

This was a day of very hard work. 7 locks took us to the magnificent, 662 metre aqueduct at Briare, then 14 more along the Canal de Briare, led us downhill to the small town of Rogny.

It was during our trip along the Canal Lateral that we became increasingly aware of the amount of commercial traffic on the French canals. We came across several large péniches, barges with nearly 5m beam and 20-30m in length. On the whole they were very considerate in passing carefully, which was just as well because our 5-foot draft prevented us moving into the side in some places. Some yachts carried large signs up front with a warning of their draft in large letters. Traffic is heavy during late July when barges are used to convey the harvest to the mills.

The delightful little town of Rogny lies at a sort of waterways Clapham Junction, Two branches of the river Loing join up and flow across the canal to leave as one. Thus five waterways radiate from the centre of the town which sits at the foot of a flight of six locks. These are modern locks and the efficient 'éclusier', who manages all six of them, got us through remarkably quickly. Alongside is a flight of seven ancient ones. The seven locks of Henry IV have been preserved as a monument.

Once through the last lock we turned sharp right into one branch of the Loing and found a berth on a perfect little *halte nautique*. If one is susceptible to the charms of inland waterways then Rogny is a place to fall in love. The little village has the basic shops one needs and that 'cared for' look that one finds so often in France. There was a profusion of flower tubs, and an old wooden punt had been moored in the river and planted out with a riot of annuals, all in full bloom at that time. The attraction of that place completed my conversion to the idea of a canal boat and then, to cap it all, we met up with a famous yachting couple, Bill and Laurel Cooper, who were there in their magnificent barge *Hozannah*. Here were two people who had themselves made the conversion from ocean sailing and seemed profoundly happy with their new life. They were busy writing

A lock at Rogny

about their recent trip down the Danube, a book to follow their well-known 'Water Steps through France'.

Saturday 19 July

I remembered that yesterday marked the end of our second year on *Greylag*. All of us were so impressed with Rogny that we soon decided to stay for a day or two. We visited the ancient flight of locks. They were built entirely of blocks of stone and were directly linked, the exit gate of one being the entrance gate to the next.

Alongside our pontoon there was a curious contraption on steel wheels for which none of us could fathom out a purpose. It had a boiler and pipes all over the place, and a large wooden bowl in the centre with a lid with clamps for closing it down tightly. Janet and I discovered more of these on a walk about and realised eventually that they were stills for fermenting apples.

That evening we had dinner with the Coopers at the Auberge des Sept Écluses, alongside the bridge over the canal. After dinner we were invited back to *Hozannah*. This was the first time I had been aboard a large converted barge and I was immediately impressed with the spaciousness -

the lounge was bigger than some people have at home. Bill recounted how he had once been the navigator on the aircraft carrier *Ark Royal,* hence his liking for large steel boats! Laurel had an enviable galley with a large collection of herbs and spices. It looked a boat one could live on indefinitely, though it must have taken some manoeuvring in the narrower canals.

I spent the next day sketching some of the many inspiring scenes and objects in Rogny.

Monday 21 July

After Rogny the canal follows the course of the river Loing all the way to Moret and St Mammes where it joins the Seine. We settled for a 20-lock journey to Cepoy where we stopped for the night. I later wished we hadn't. Janet and I went for an evening walk along the canal and were severely hassled by a young Alsatian dog that appeared to be guarding one of the small canal-side cottages. We got past and continued on our way but when we returned, the dog was outside on the towpath. It was clearly not going to let us pass and stood there growling and baring its teeth. The owners were nowhere to be seen. I am not good with big dogs at the best of times and after my experience back in Curacao, when I was bitten, I was distinctly nervous of this one. We walked back a few hundred yards to where a fisherman was sitting and asked him if it was possible to walk down to the next bridge and return on the other side. He said it was difficult. Eventually we called on one of the houses and a gentleman kindly came out and controlled the dog. He seemed to know it and the dog certainly took notice of him. I was glad to get back to the boat.

Next day we moved on to Nemours, a town with lots of shops that enabled us to restock.

Wednesday 23 July

The day's trip saw us into Moret. When we got there the *halte nautique* in our guide did not exist and eventually we settled on a bit of steep bank just below the lock. At least it had a pretty view across the river to the town.

Moret was another delightful town and like Arles, of interest to painters for it was the home of Alfred Sisley, the French Impressionist born of English parents. We went in search of Sisley and were able to find many of the views he painted. How little the town seems to have changed since he painted there at the end of the nineteenth century.

Moret was probably the most picturesque town I had seen in France and we all resolved to stay another day. I persuaded Janet to accompany me in search of Alfred Sisley's grave which was on the edge of town and a fair walk away. In return she extracted a promise that I would accompany her later in search of a shower.

We found the grave in the local cemetery. He had died a miserable death from cancer of the throat and was buried beside his wife, who had died the year before, beneath a simple granite rock brought from the Forest of Fontainbleau by his friends Monet and Renoir. It always saddens me to see the tragic lives so many famous painters endured; Sisley was no exception. A few weeks after his death, a sale of the 27 paintings in his studio totalled 112,320 francs. Yet these paintings had been on sale for 100 francs each during his lifetime and had not found a single buyer.

Ever the pragmatic one, Janet had discovered that an easy way to get a shower was to visit the local swimming pool. Off we went to the one at Moret, paid the entry money and disappeared to our respective changing rooms. I emerged by the pool only to be confronted by a stern young lady shaking her head.

'Pardon', she said, 'zees are not permitted'.

Her gaze fell on my thoroughly decent, if utterly tasteless, Bermuda shorts. I had acquired them in Antigua the year before.

'Shorts are not permitted', she said in her heavily accented English.

For a moment I wondered whether I should take them off, but in the end I gracefully retreated through the showers, which was of course why we had gone there in the first place! Enquiries on the way out revealed that this was a national rule imposed to prevent people entering the pool with cigarettes in their pocket.

'Eet is ze same in ze ole of France' said the girl at the cash desk as she refused to refund my entry fee!

Well, at least we had got our showers. It rained that night and sleep was disturbed by a wretched bull-frog in a nearby reed bed.

Friday 25 July

It was only a mile or so down to the Seine at St Mammes but it was a depressing mile. The banks of that last stretch of the Loing River were obliterated with old péniches moored bow to stern and several deep. Some were occupied as houseboats; others were just slowly rotting away. We saw many more such places on the Seine, they are such an eyesore and what a pity that there is not some simple way to get rid of the old barges at the end of their commercial lives.

We ran into the Seine 36 days after leaving Port St Louis. After the canal, the river was impressively grand - wide and slow and with surprising amounts of commercial traffic. The large locks were easier than those in the canal. For our first night we stopped at a tiny little marina at Saintry. Our peace was disturbed by the delivery of a small powerboat which proceeded on a demonstration for her new owners. Several runs at speed, up and down the river, left us bobbing around in the wash. These were followed by repeated practice moorings in the marina, carried out with spectacular ineptitude.

It had rained on and off all day and set in hard in the evening, so we abandoned plans to eat out and cooked our dinner on board. The night was mostly calm except for the wash of occasional péniches - they kept going all night. I resolved to find a mooring off the main river next time.

Saturday 26 July

This was the day we arrived in Paris. Surprisingly there is a good marina right in the heart of the city, a stone's throw from Notre-Dame Cathedral. We stayed a day and visited the Musee d'Orsay for most of it. The museum has been created from an old railway station and is quite spectacular. I enjoyed their fine collection of impressionist paintings.

We studied the one-way system for controlling boats through that central part of the city. The tourist boats ran continuously anti-clockwise around Notre-Dame but private boats were controlled by a system of traffic lights that allowed movements in one direction for 15 minutes, followed by a gap and then 15 minutes for movements in the other direction. It did not look too difficult but we would see next day.

Monday 28 July

We left the marina at 0745 in order to be out by the traffic lights in good time for the green light at 0835. It was punctual and off we went on that spectacular trip through the famous landmarks of central Paris. We passed Notre-dame on our left, just a few metres away, then through all those famous bridges and down past the Eiffel tower. There was a large illuminated screen on the tower giving the precise time to the new millenium. After that came a long stretch through the industrial area, past the Renault factory and the tower blocks of St Cloud. At Argenteuil I tried to visualise Monet's famous painting of the bridge. It was a wooden one in his day but I thought the modern replacement had something of the same style about it.

How different this was from the Rhône. Now we were going downstream and the kilometres melted away quickly. We were soon past St Denis, Chatou, Port Marly, Conflans-Ste-Honorine. Then, approaching the lock at Andresy after 72 kilometres, we came up behind a large sand barge that was waiting for the lock. By now it was late in the day and on

Notre-Dame Cathedral

the Right Bank we could see the entrance to a quiet backwater. It looked a good place to stop and would be away from the wash of the péniches passing through at night. We found a perfect *halte nautique* in the backwater. Janet shared an ice cream with a small tomcat that was sleeping in a dinghy. It had been a long day and we all slept well.

Tuesday 29 July

We started early, intending to get to Poussy. However, by lunchtime we had reached Limay and decided to go into the backwater (Bras de Limay) there for lunch. When we got down to the village the place was so stunningly attractive that we decided to stop for another day. Another halte nautique gave us a berth to ourselves, with a wonderful view back upstream to the old bridge. It was a miniature version of the famous one at Avignon and similarly was only about half a bridge. It was perfect for sketching. We were surrounded with ducks and downstream there were several old barges - these ones were attractively maintained.

That evening we were sat in the cockpit for sundowners when I spotted a small rat on the bank. Now Janet cannot resist anything with fur or feathers and she immediately put some of the pizza left over from lunch in some scallop shells and positioned them along the bank opposite. We waited for only a few minutes before they re-appeared, several of them this time. We watched them have their evening meal, then we had ours.

Wednesday 30 July

We moved on quickly to Vernon. We had always intended to stop there, as it was the nearest place to Giverny - where Monet's famous house and the garden with its lily pools may be visited. Again we were able to get away from the main river to a pontoon at the Vernon Sailing Club.

Next day Janet and I went off to Giverny and I thoroughly enjoyed seeing the house and gardens which, unlike Janet, I had not visited before. John went off on a massive hike through the countryside. Later I did some sketches of the beautiful old mill house that is right alongside the club.

Friday 1 August

It was hard to believe but this was the day when we would reach the last lock on the Seine. This was at Poses and again there was a very pretty backwater with a few spots to moor. We walked along to the barrage alongside the lock and I was surprised to find a fish ladder there, with a viewing room from which one could see the salmon travelling upstream. That is what the notice said, but unfortunately it was closed that day.

Near where we had parked we found a small artist's studio with an exhibition of works for sale. The artist, Michéle Rattel, showed us around and we were very impressed with her work - mostly river scenes and very painterly. We would have bought one if she had been able to accept a card.

Saturday 2 August

Next morning we were quickly through the lock and sped off downstream to Rouen. We were there by midday, moored on the pontoons at the Port de Plaisance. We were now back in tidal water and the stream ran quite hard for the middle part of each tide. For the first time since our arrival in France two customs officers visited us! They were very informal and showed great interest in *Greylag* and the voyage we had so nearly completed. One of them was a keen racer and asked our advice on a good sailmaker in the south of England where he was going soon.

Janet and I visited the famous cathedral, another place with strong echos of Claude Monet - this was the cathedral he painted in different weather conditions in one of his famous series paintings. At the supermarket we bought some live crabs and prawns. Janet went for a walk while I cooked the crabs and assembled a splendid Plateau de Fruits de Mer for our evening meal.

Next day we stayed at Rouen as it was Sunday and there was no possibility to get the mast put up again until Monday. It was a nice lazy day for wandering around. We spent a little time in search of Joan of Arc and found a very modern church with a memorial outside in the place where she was burnt at the stake. There was a small museum with a number of realistic tableaux to illustrate her sad history.

Monday 4 August

We made an early start, as this was the day I hoped to get the mast up again. We were soon under the last low bridge and went past the major port area before turning left into the Darse des Docks, an old and largely disused harbour basin where the Lozai boatyard is situated. We tied up to a rather grubby set of floating pontoons by a crane which if anything looked more shaky than the one at M.Messiant's. I wandered over to the yard office; there was bad news. The crane was out of action. I pondered for a while, trying to remember if there was a facility at Le Havre for erecting masts. Then the fellow in the office said he could hire a mobile crane for us but it would be expensive.

'How expensive?' I asked, '800 Francs.'

Normally it would have been 300. Nevertheless I accepted the offer and he phoned for the crane; it would be there at about 1300. We used the waiting time to get the mast out onto the pontoons and prepared it for hoisting.

At about 1215 we had a big shock. Suddenly the metal pontoons started shaking around, clanking together and straining at their mooring lines. It was all quite unnerving until I realised what was happening. The Seine is one of those rivers where a tidal bore travels upstream at the head of the incoming tide - similar to the Severn bore at home. We had read that this occurred only around spring tides and, as we were only half way between neaps and springs, we had not been expecting one. The water level rose 3 or 4 feet in a period of about 15 minutes before everything settled down again. I went cold at the thought of what might have happened if we had been in the middle of stepping the mast when it arrived!

The crane came along at 1330. The driver was very skilled and by 1350 our mast was up. We spent another two hours getting the rest of the rigging sorted out and re-fixing the boom and sails. It was a real pleasure to see *Greylag* back in sea-going shape. The evening passed slowly as there was not much to do in that place. We felt we should stay reasonably alert until gone midnight in case another bore arrived with the next tide. It didn't.

Tuesday 5 August

As soon as it was light enough to see, we moved out of the basin and off down river. We had calculated that we could make it to Honfleur if we got a shift on. The tide was favourable (ebbing) until about 1100 by which time we had done about 77 kilometres and were at Vieux-port. In that mad dash downstream we passed a couple of steamers on their way up to Rouen. Then we slowed up as the tide turned foul, but it was only 2-3 knots, so we continued to make progress albeit much slower than before.

Approaching Honfleur we ran into driving rain and visibility became very poor. We navigated from post to post on the starboard side of the channel and eventually made it to Honfleur and through the new lock to the outer harbour. We had to wait more than two hours in the outer harbour before the bridge opened to let us into the picturesque inner harbour. Not that it was all that picturesque in the rain. We tied up to a Westerly yacht; we were the 4th boat out from the quay - not unusual for Honfleur. As I had been there many times in the past, I considered that I had now sailed round the world. It wasn't in the same voyage of course, but we celebrated all the same. The trip through France had taken 47 days, going at a fair

Traditional boats at Honfleur

pace but with plenty of days off without moving. Now we were back in the sea.

We spent a couple of days at Honfleur and were visited by my brother Michael and sister-in-law Ellie. They arrived by car so we were able to drive around the pretty Normandy countryside for an afternoon. When the time came for them to leave, they took Janet with them. She would be at Portsmouth on the 16th of August to welcome us home.

22 Homecoming

We left Honfleur on August the 9th in thick fog. It was a tricky time finding our way by radar from post to post until we were clear of the estuary and could turn to port and head for our destination - Port Guillaume le Conquérant at Dives. We arrived there early and had to wait for the tide before we could enter the splendid new marina. In the evening we walked along the coast to Houlgate, a dull bucket-and-spade sort of place. Both of us had that slight sadness one feels when a long voyage is nearly over. We had arranged with our club, the Portsmouth Offshore Group of the Civil Service Sailing Association, that we would try to arrive at midday on the 16th. They were keen to lay on a big welcoming party, as we would be the first club boat to have sailed around the world.

Next day there was thick fog again as we left Dives and travelled across Seine Bay to St Vaast La Hougue, on the north-east coast of the Cherbourg peninsular. This had always been a favourite destination of mine, as indeed it is for many yachtsmen, and it was a pleasure to sail into that familiar harbour. As soon as we were berthed we paid a call on Peter and Gizela Payne, old friends who have lived on their boat *Nikki* at St Vaast for a number of years. They were surprised to see us and full of questions about our experiences.

We spent the next day cleaning up old *Greylag*. We de-stained and polished the hull and brightwork and generally spruced her up until she looked better than she had for a long while. I wanted to arrive back looking ship-shape and not in the shambolic water-worn state I'd seen some circumnavigators on their return.

The day after, we set out for home. It was foggy at sea until we were right across the shipping lanes, when it cleared and we had a fair trip back to Bembridge Ledge. During those last few miles the wind piped up and we had a hard sail in towards St Helen's Fort before deciding to put into Bembridge for the night. The tiny harbour was full to the brim as usual but

317

I always enjoy the place. Once the tide recedes and the outer harbour dries, the little marina is always peaceful.

We left Bembridge in the morning and motored round to Priory Bay where I planned to dry out and scrub the bottom of the boat. We parked on the beach and as soon as the tide had gone out, we set about the task. Considering the boat had not been scrubbed since Thailand, she was not as fouled as I had expected, I think some of the growth had been killed by the freshwater in the canals. Anyway, we cleaned her up thoroughly.

When the tide returned but before the boat was properly afloat, (my usual impatience), I used the engine rather vigorously to try to get her off the beach. Eventually she came off in a rush and as soon as she was more or less over her anchor I put her into reverse. Nothing happened! The gear appeared to be engaging and I got John to check below that it was. John thought that the gearbox may have gone but I had another thought.

'I think we've lost the propeller' I said.

I am not sure why I had that conviction, perhaps it was just the feel of the boat, but when I got in the water to look I found I was right. The prop had disappeared completely. I could hardly believe it, '*28,000 miles around the world*', I said, '*and now, seven miles from home, we loose the prop*'. We swam around for a bit trying to spot it on the bottom but the water was too murky and the sun was getting low. We decided to stay another night and dry out again in the morning to look for the prop at low tide. Meanwhile a kind fellow offered us a tow out to deeper water to anchor for the night. He lent me his mobile to phone Janet with the joyful news. She thought I was joking at first!

In the morning we sailed on the tiny breeze back inshore and anchored as near as I could judge to the point where we had lost the prop. As soon as the tide had gone down to about 2 feet of water we commenced the search. I started a competition among the holidaymakers there and offered a bottle of wine to anyone who found it. At low tide we still hadn't succeeded and I fitted the spare folding propeller so that we would be controllable again. Then, when I had almost given up hope, a shout went up from along the beach. John had found the cone that (normally) holds the prop on to the shaft. Then a few minutes later, a fellow called Chris found the propeller. He got the bottle of wine - I was delighted.

When the tide returned we set off for Langstone harbour and the Southsea marina, as this was a place from which we could pretty well guarantee our arrival at Portsmouth on time for the welcome party. Halfway across we ran into a thick bank of fog and had a difficult time finding our way into Langstone in about 50 metres visibility. We passed close to a small coaster on her way out to sea. Thank heaven for the radar.

The next morning, Saturday August 16 1997, we set out for the official homecoming. Before we left, we hoisted a string of flags in our fore-triangle. They were the courtesy ensigns of the 32 countries we had visited on our voyage. First we called just east of South Parade Pier to wave to my elderly aunt who lives in one of the flats there. The self-same aunt, now 95 years old, who had taken us on holiday on the Broads, and hired the dinghy on which I first tried sailing fifty years before. She was expecting us and waved a Union Jack.

John's daughter Kate arrived in *Elite*, the boat John shared with two colleagues. They escorted us back to the harbour entrance at Portsmouth and as we drew close we found yachts arriving from all directions to greet us. They waved and blew their horns and fell in behind us to form a neat V of boats with ourselves in the van. As we motored into the harbour and crossed the line marking the start of our circumnavigation, a round of three cheers went up from the flotilla. I had a terrible lump in my throat, it was a truly emotional moment. Even John, rarely one to reveal his feelings easily, had a tear in his eye as he caught sight of his wife Connie on the pontoon. He had not seen her for two years.

The club had turned out in force and many of our relatives and friends had come down to Portsmouth to welcome us home. There was a terrific party that got off to a tremendous start thanks to lashings of bubbly provided by Hugh Brody, one of John's co-owners.

Later that afternoon, when all had gone quiet, I looked at *Greylag* as she lay at her berth in the evening sunshine. She had looked after us well through all those good and bad times of the voyage. Yet somehow I knew this was the end of our relationship. Perhaps for me it was the challenge that had counted; I would not claim any great love for the open ocean. I had grown weary with the sea and a new adventure was on the horizon. A more peaceful adventure, less testing perhaps but one for which my enthusiasm had grown during those six weeks on the French canals. We would buy a canal boat. The circumnavigation had been a voyage of discovery - of the world, of other people and of myself. Yes, especially of myself. Was I pleased to have done it? Certainly. Would I sail around the world again? I didn't think so. It was a goal achieved, and now others beckoned.

Glossary of Nautical Terms

(See also the sail and accomodation plan, page 21)

Anchor rode. The chain or rope attached to the anchor.

Beam. The maximum width of the boat. Also the side of the boat.

Crosstrack error. Deviation from the straight line course to a waypoint.

Delta anchor. A popular anchor design, especially convenient for mounting permanently on the bow of the boat.

Double-headed rig. A balanced arrangement for sailing downwind with a headsail deployed on each side of the boat and held out with poles.

Draft. The depth of the boat below the water surface.

Drifter. A large, lightweight headsail used in very light winds.

Fortress anchor. A light alloy anchor.

Furler. A device on the bow of the boat that enables the headsail to be rolled up.

Genoa or Genny. The largest of the headsail*s*, usually overlaps the mainsail.

GPS. The Global Positioning System. An electronic navigation system that calculates a boats latitude and longitude from satellite signals. It is accurate to within a few metres. It also gives the boats speed over the ground.

Halyard. A piece of rope used to hoist sails.

Quarter. The corner of the boat at the stern.

Reach. A fast point of sailing with the wind over the side of the boat.

Sheet. A piece of rope used to control a sail. *Sheeting in* refers to pulling the sails in tight against the wind. *Easing sheets* is the opposite.

Sight. The angle of the sun or other heavenly body above the horizon as measured with a sextant

Spinnaker. A large, lightweight, balloon sail used for downwind sailing.

SSB. Single Sideband Radio operating on high frequency and capable of transmission over many hundreds of miles.

Tacking. The technique used to get to windward by sailing at approximately 45 degrees to the wind. A boat is said to be on port tack when the wind is coming from the port side and starboard tack when it comes from the starboard side.

Waypoint. A position or destination entered as latitude and longitude into the GPS. The instrument then gives the distance and bearing of the waypoint from the boat's position.

List of Yachts in the Trade Winds Rally

Name	Owners	Length(ft)
Aditi of Hamble	Frank and Beryl Hole	35
Ailsa J	Stuart Laycock	38
Alb	John and Carol Forsyth	40
Alstromeria	Dave Sutherland	34
Arabian Sands	David Macmillan	53
Baker Street	David and Barbara Wardle	55
Best Respects	Tom and Pat Smith	41
Brandy Cove	Clive and Sally Roberts	42
Calidris Alba	John and Inga Chapman	41
Chinatown	John and Jill Sudbury	55
Freeaz	Mike Van Gent and Tracy	37
Excess Line	Jean and Valentine Thierry	46
Enarkay	Tom and Lucille Parker	55
Gallivanter III	Mike Cuthbert	54
Gambatte Go	Taka and Kiki Fujinaga	45
Gaviota	Roy Newey	38
Greylag	Dick and Janet Allan	33
Griffyn	John and Ruth Roberts	46
Hilda	Graham and Mary Watts	36
Jonathan III	Paolo Grassi	45
Luck of Argent	Ted Weekes	46
Lucky Seven	Geoff Fielden and Linda	48
Magic Dragon	Stephen and Catharine Thomas	55
Malmac	Malcolm McLaren	44
Miss Molly	David and Linda Hughes	55
Nefertiti	David Buckpitt	62
Ocean Gypsy	Doug and Laura Orchard	42
Ocean Venture	Ken Murray and Heather	60
Oyster Haven	Michael Clear	53
Pale Moon	Chris and Gill Mounsey	43
Papa Golf	Pat Gordon	37
Paper Moon	John and Jan Hunt	55
Saullitaire of Wight	John and Brenda Cheeseman	42
Sheet Lightning	Chris and Fiona Tonge	33
Simon Dee	Adrian Robertson	38
Sooty	David Phillips and Jill Gilpin	34
Taos Brett IV	Brian Gehleken	50
Vandal	John Wormald	38
Wizzardry	Simon & Frederica Kirkpatrick	55
Yaba Daba Doo	Peter Hopkinson	43